Love in the Afterlife

Love in the Afterlife

Underground Religion at the Movies

Richard Striner

FAIRLEIGH DICKINSON UNIVERSITY PRESS
Madison • Teaneck

Published by Fairleigh Dickinson University Press
Copublished by The Rowman & Littlefield Publishing Group, Inc.
4501 Forbes Boulevard, Suite 200, Lanham, Maryland 20706
www.rowman.com

Unit A, Whitacre Mews, 26-34 Stannary Street, London SE11 4AB

British Library Cataloguing in Publication Information Available

Library of Congress Cataloging-in-Publication Data

Names: Striner, Richard, 1950- author.
Title: Love in the afterlife : underground religion at the movies / Richard Striner.
Description: Madison : Fairleigh Dickinson University Press, New Jersey [2016] | Includes biblio-
    graphical references and index.
Identifiers: LCCN 2016007376 (print) | LCCN 2016015157 (ebook) | ISBN 9781611478846 (cloth :
    alk. paper) | ISBN 9781611478853 (Electronic)
Subjects: LCSH: Supernatural in motion pictures. | Love in motion pictures. | Religion in motion
    pictures.
Classification: LCC PN1995.9.S8 L68 2016 (print) | LCC PN1995.9.S8 (ebook) | DDC 791.43/67--
    dc23 LC record available at https://lccn.loc.gov/2016007376

Printed in the United States of America

To Bill Shepard and Stephen Simon, with gratitude for their help

Contents

Preface

Love, death, and the afterlife comprise a cinematic trinity: "spooky romances" at the movies are a cultural tradition of very long standing. But when I first began to take an interest in films of this type, a study of them had not been written. So I decided to do it myself. The result was my book *Supernatural Romance in Film* (2011), a probe that examined a number of individual films in sequential order. So far as I knew, my book was the first study of the subject.

It was a highly preliminary foray.

I had noticed these particular films—and the pattern that they presented—in a casual way for many years. Over time I began to appreciate the magnitude of what they meant.

Others had been studying a number of important and related cinematic issues: the depiction of ghosts in cinema, for instance, and the ways in which the afterlife as such has been depicted (or else hinted at) by various film makers. Interesting articles about these subjects had been written as early as the 1970s, and the scholarly analysis continues.[1]

But it was *love* in the afterlife that interested me—at least as it figured in cinema—since this particular theme has been haunting the Western mind for thousands of years and haunts it still. The polarity of "Eros and Thanatos" (to use the Freudian formulation) stretches all the way back to the ancient Egyptians and Greeks as a literary motif.

Since the publication of my book *Supernatural Romance in Film*, my research has continued. And the more that I study and analyze this subject, the more powerfully it emerges as a cinematic and cultural tradition. This book is a more extended and analytical study of the films that I call supernatural romances: it looks at them through their patterns of historical development. My new research has revealed that this genre began much earlier than I had suspected—as early as 1921. My research has also included an analysis of films that were unobtainable for viewing until very recently. The 1930 film *Outward Bound*, for example, was only digitized at the Library of Congress in 2014—at my request.

My aim is to make this volume definitive, though further analysis by others will naturally occur, and especially so as more films of this type are produced.

Among the most interesting features of this cinematic tradition is its quality as underground religion: as a channel for presenting a range of theological heterodoxies, as well as some related philosophical and scientific issues of cosmology that overlap inevitably with religious issues. What attracted me to these films in the first place are qualities that many thoughtful people might find attractive: they offer commentary—and extremely entertaining commentary at that—on issues that cut to the heart of the human condition. They occupy an interesting place in intellectual and literary history, since they serve up formulations that date to classical antiquity and contain salutes to (or reprises of) classic works in Western (and in some cases Eastern) literature. And they serve as illustrations of the way in which serious intellectual content can, if capably handled, be rendered as mass entertainment. In short, these movies may not "have it all," but they have quite a lot. They occupy an extremely interesting place in the history of cinema.

The task of establishing the boundaries of this cinematic tradition, however, can be vexatious. For example, a number of interesting "afterlife" films from recent decades—films such as *Resurrection* (1980), *Poltergeist* (1982), and *Flatliners* (1990)—do not conform to my love-death-afterlife pattern since the theme of love and death is not their principal focus.[2] Some, like *Poltergeist*, should perhaps be classified as simply "ghost stories," "horror films," and so forth.

So: should my love-death-afterlife films be regarded as a subset of a larger genre containing the related subject matter of ghosts, the afterlife, and theological issues that pertain to eschatology? Questions such as these have bedeviled the scholarship of cinema studies for years, since there are different kinds of films that resist tidy classification into hierarchic sets that can be stacked up like "Chinese boxes," one within another.

This book will seek to demonstrate that "genre" as a classificatory (and analytical) category in film studies possesses both strengths and weaknesses. *Love in the Afterlife* will show that a great many significant films are (in generic terms) *hybrids*, a fact that should be more generally understood, appreciated, and emphasized by scholars.

The term "genre" is the subject of debate within cinema studies. Indeed, the study of a great many things can lead to debates about classification. Such is the issue of "genre" in the study of film, and such is the issue of "style" in the study of architecture. Many more examples from the arts and humanities could be given.

Certain kinds of films—westerns, for instance—possess a similarity of content that seems to lend itself readily to the genre label, but even films such as these can present some very interesting problems. Film noir movies are frequently crime films, but some crime films (or at least detective films) have been comedy-of-manners productions, like the *Thin Man* series.[3] Many musicals contain plots that relate to screwball comedy (or romantic comedy). Generic hybrids are legion in the history of film, and this constitutes a particularly interesting and worthwhile topic for study.

The literature on the subject of genre is considerable.[4] And the scholars who have entered into this particular discourse have—predictably enough—fallen short of an overall consensus. After roughly a generation's worth of debate on the subject, Richard Maltby wrote in the 1990s that "genre criticism usually identifies up to eight genres in Hollywood feature film production." He continued as follows:

> The Western, the comedy, the musical, and the war movie are four uncontested categories. Different critics will then argue the relative independent merits of . . . the thriller and the crime or gangster movie, and list the horror movie and science fiction as either one or two additional genres. Each of these genres is usually seen as stable enough to possess a history of its own.[5]

But almost any one of these categories could easily overlap with one or more of the others, as for instance when a western is played for laughs (thus fusing western and comedy, as in the 1994 film *Maverick*), or when a western that is played for laughs is also a musical production (as in the case of the 1945 MGM film *The Harvey Girls*)—and so on.

One can easily drive one's self to distraction by obsessing about these issues instead of taking them in stride. Academicians in media studies have offered many theoretical constructs that become exercises in sharp-focus myopia. We have been told (alternatively) that we should concentrate on iconographical approaches to genre or semantic approaches to genre or syntactic approaches, or to use the methods of structuralism or post-structuralism in studying genre.

My approach is different: to study the *pattern* of love, death, and the afterlife—as it figures in these particular films—in as humanistic a manner as possible. I seek to place these movies in a large historical, cultural, and intellectual perspective. I also prefer to write for lay readers everywhere, in addition to a specialized readership. What is most important to me is the *films* and what they seem to mean. Formal theory, as such, can be helpful, but not when it gets in the way of independent critical analysis. And I will not allow that to happen.

It matters little to me whether scholars of film choose to call the love-death-afterlife tradition that I have discerned in these movies a "genre." Yet a label is in order, since many of the films that I regard as exemplars of "supernatural romance" were once placed in the vague catch-all category of "fantasy" film. But all "fantasy" films do not explore the theme of love and death.

So what should the love-death-afterlife movies be called?

Many other genre labels might have first seemed inscrutable or arbitrary when the terms were introduced: "screwball comedy" and "film noir" were hardly perfect tags for the films to which they referred. But once the terms were in use, they stuck, and over time they became canonical. So I will stick to the term that I employed in the earlier book, supernatural romance, since it seems to me as good a term as any—except for one caveat.[6]

The term is also widely used nowadays to refer to the "vampire romances," as the teens often call them, productions (some made for television) that derive from modern gothic fiction. Once upon a time, such films were subsumed in the catch-all category of "horror films." An able recent study of the recent vampire romances is Victoria Nelson's *Gothicka: Vampire Heroes, Human Gods, and the New Supernatural* (2012).

The point is that the vampire romances overlap with the love-death-afterlife movies. And yet the latter films partake of themes with far greater scope than gothic fiction (and the folktales upon which it draws). Something larger and far more significant was being explored in films such as *Death Takes a Holiday* (1934), *The Ghost and Mrs. Muir* (1947), and *Portrait of Jennie* (1948). The love-death-afterlife theme has its sources in antiquity and pertains to philosophic and theological subjects of vast dimensions.

So for purposes of convenience, I will use the term "gothic supernatural romance" for the vampire romances and reserve the more encompassing term "supernatural romance" for the love-death-afterlife scheme in its fullest development. These preliminary terms will hold good for the purpose of this study. Do these movies constitute a genre?

Let's call it anything that makes good sense to us—genre, pattern, tradition, or any other term-of-art that we prefer. But in the meantime, let's by all means get busy with the presentation and analysis.

One more thing: for those who wish to delve deeper, additional background material on individual films is furnished in the footnotes. Moreover, theological issues are explored in these notes—along with corollary issues from the worlds of philosophy and physics that relate to the films.

NOTES

1. See Peter L. Valenti, "The Film *Blanc*: Suggestions for a Variety of Fantasy," *Journal of Popular Film*, 4, no. 4 (1978), 294–303; and Andrew Sarris, "The Afterlife, Hollywood Style," *American Film*, 4, no. 6 (April, 1979), 25. Valenti's "scenario" for the films that he called "blanc" was comprised in a list of four attributes: "1. a mortal's death or lapse into dream; 2. subsequent acquaintance with a kindly representative of the world beyond, most commonly known as Heaven; 3. a budding love affair; 4. ultimate transcendence of mortality to escape the spiritual world and return to the mortal world." For more recent studies whose subject matter overlaps the themes of this book, see Lee Kovacs, *The Haunted Screen: Ghosts in Literature and Film* (Jefferson, NC: McFarland, 1999); Tom Ruffles, *Ghost Images: Cinema of the Afterlife* (Jefferson, NC: McFarland, 2004); Alec Worley, *Empires of the Imagination: A Critical Survey of Fantasy Cinema from Georges Méliès to* The Lord of the Rings (Jefferson, NC: McFarland, 2005), 98–99; Clive Marsh, *Theology Goes to the Movies: An Introduction to Critical Christian Thinking* (London and New York: Routledge, 2007); Christopher Deacy and Gaye Ortiz, *Theology and Film: Challenging the Sacred/Secular Divide* (Malden, MA: Blackwell, 2008); Christopher Deacy, *Screening the Afterlife: Theology, Eschatology and Film* (London and New York: Routledge, 2012); and Lyn and Tom Davis Genelli, *Death at the Movies:*

Hollywood's Guide to the Hereafter (Wheaton, IL: Quest Books, 2013). Other contemporaneous work in this field includes the contribution of film blogger Richard Scheib. See http://moria.co.nz/fantasy/ghost-and-mrs-muir-1947.htm.

2. The issue is even more complex, since in their studies of "afterlife movies" both Christopher Deacy and Lyn and Tom Davis Genelli cover issues of eschatology that are different from the concept of an "afterlife" *as such*. They explore the perennial idea that "the kingdom of God" might well be understood as an eternal state that pertains not only to the hypothetical future of the soul after death or to the hypothetical future of the cosmos after the Apocalypse, but also to an earthly condition in which the "kingdom of God" may be said to be with us at every single instant—"heaven on earth." Hence Deacy includes coverage of films such as *Working Girl* (1988) and the *Shawshank Redemption* (1994) whose context is quite mundane but could be said to epitomize the theme of "realized eschatology." And the Genellis include in their study of "transit" as depicted in film not only stories of passage into the hereafter but also the stories of films such as *Casablanca* and *The Wizard of Oz* that might be said to encompass tales of spiritual enlightenment that constitute alternative forms of "transit."

3. It is interesting that Dashiell Hammett, the author of *The Thin Man* (1933), was also one of the originators of the literary genre of "hard-boiled detective fiction" via the novels and stories that he wrote in the 1920s. Hammett's influence, together with that of Raymond Chandler, would play a key role in the development of film noir. The comic elements in *The Thin Man*—so distinctive in comparison to Hammett's previous work—represented an interesting departure in his fiction. Perhaps he was inspired by Dorothy L. Sayers, whose Lord Peter Wimsey novels in the 1920s established a superb prototype for the fusion of comedy and "who-dunnit" plots.

4. For a mix of views on the subject of genre classification in film, see Steven Neale, *Genre* (London: British Film Institute, 1980); Steven Neale, *Genre and Hollywood* (London: Routledge, 2000); Thomas Schatz, *Hollywood Genres: Formulas, Filmmaking, and the Studio System* (New York: Random House, 1981); Barry Keith Grant, ed., *Film Genre Reader* (Austin: University of Texas Press, 1986), especially the essays "Genre" by Andrew Tudor, "Genre Film: A Classical Experience" by Thomas Sobchack, and "A Semantic/Syntactic Approach to Film Genre" by Rick Altman.

5. Richard Maltby, *Hollywood Cinema* (Malden, MA: Blackwell Publishing, 1995), 2003 edition, 85.

6. The use of the term "romance" is much older than the cluster of literary (and intellectual) movements that constituted "Romanticism" in the eighteenth and nineteenth centuries. The term romance derived from the Middle Ages and it referred to the tales of court poets, minstrels, and troubadours. Medieval romances were derived from the literary culture of courtly love and some forms of the genre, such as the "Romance of the Rose," became extremely stylized. Some literary commentators have identified a series of Shakespearian plays as "romances" distinct from the comedies and tragedies—plays, for example, like *The Tempest* and *The Winter's Tale*, which were tales of miraculous reconciliation. As poet and Shakespeare scholar Mark Van Doren once wrote, "the form of the romance" permitted Shakespeare to "create such a universe as men might like to end their days believing in." In light of the all-compensatory nature of the afterlife in many of the films included in this study, the term romance in the sense that Van Doren invoked it seems highly appropriate. See Mark Van Doren, *Shakespeare* (New York: Henry Holt, 1939), Doubleday Anchor edition, 254.

ONE

Philosophic and Literary Sources

Films about love, death, and the afterlife have been produced for years. These films represent a cinematic tradition—a tradition that has not been sufficiently studied. It is time for "supernatural romance" to be recognized in cinema studies and to take its place as an established cinematic category.

The theme of *life* and death is fundamental: people wonder if death is *the end*. But the *love*-and-death formula cries out for exploration: the association of themes is more complex.

The love–death duality was central to Freudian theory, and the influence of Sigmund Freud was vast when the genre of supernatural romance began to take shape. Freud wrote of a primeval tension between the force he called "Eros" and the counterforce he called the "death instinct." He spoke of "the eternal struggle between the trends of love and death."[1] Later Freudians matched his invocation of "Eros" (a Greek proto-deity) with the mythological counterpart, Thanatos.[2] The significance of this pattern will be explored at greater length momentarily.

But the invocation by Freud of mythology from the archaic Greeks is a clue that leads straight to the ancient sources of the love–death duality.[3] Supernatural romance at the movies is part of a tradition—a tradition in religion and philosophy and literature—that spans centuries, and some of the films in question display an explicit recognition of this fact.

The place to begin is with the ancient Egyptians, whose myth of Isis and Osiris was perhaps the source of the love–death motif in the West. The god Osiris was murdered, but his consort Isis resurrected him: through the love of Isis, Osiris rose to be the lord of the underworld and Isis was thenceforth the universal force that could overcome the power of death. The cult of Isis and Osiris, for the ancient Egyptians, was apparent-

1

ly a central rite of passage in the soul's quest for immortality.[4] Isis was the queen of love and death.

The archaic Greeks—so influenced by the Egyptians, as Herodotus noted—applied this theme in a number of interrelated myths. The myth of Orpheus and Euridice was perhaps the most poignant. In this particular tale, the quest of a lover to resurrect a loved one ends tragically.

In the classical period of ancient Greece, the love-death-afterlife theme was developed in a range of optimistic and pessimistic variations. Two plays by Euripides reveal this range of polarity. In *Alcestis*, a loving wife (the title character) offers herself at the suggestion of Apollo as a substitute for her husband, who was destined to die. But at the play's conclusion, Herakles decides to intervene. He descends to the underworld, rescues Alcestis, and reunites the couple. Love has triumphed over death, since the loved ones are together again *among the living*. In *Suppliants*, a mourning wife, Evadne, leaps onto the funeral pyre of her husband, vowing to stay with him, to be united with him, even in death—through surrender. This motif would recur in medieval romances and in Renaissance tragedies. The lovers stay united in a way—a consolation, but only if one believes in the afterlife. If not, then the ending is tragic.

The legend of Tristan and Isolde is a medieval version of the theme. *Romeo and Juliet* (the most famous version of a tale that had been circulating for at least a hundred years) is one of innumerable examples in Renaissance drama.

Richard Wagner's *Tristan und Isolde* brought the medieval story to the stage in a manner that dovetailed with gothic fiction as a stimulus for love–death stories in the mid- to late-nineteenth century. Eros and Thanatos intertwined in a particularly sinister fashion in Bram Stoker's *Dracula*, thus launching a gothic variation that would ramify on screen from the movies *Dracula* (1931) and *The Mummy* (1932)—which explicitly invoked the myth of Isis—to recent "vampire romances" such as *Twilight* (2008–2012). In Edgar Allen Poe's *Ligeia*, a supernatural possession results from a deathless love. In Emily Brontë's *Wuthering Heights*, the demented Heathcliff yearns for reunion with his dead love, Catherine Earnshaw, and finds it at last in the grave. And in 1891, an influential novel, *Peter Ibbetson* by George du Maurier, established a love-death-afterlife plot template that would be repeated countless times on stage and screen decades afterward.

Contemporaneous with these developments was the emergence of "spiritualism," the occult art of extrasensory perception—the attempt to commune with "the other side" via séance. This movement developed from the claims of such "mediums" as Andrew Jackson Davis and the Fox sisters in the 1840s all the way to the publication in 1926 of Arthur Conan Doyle's *History of Spiritualism*.[5] Supernatural romances would use this theme, both in comic variations such as Noël Coward's *Blithe Spirit* (1941/1945) and in suspense productions such as Kenneth Branagh's *Dead*

Again (1991), which used the theme of reincarnation (and retrogressive hypnosis to a past life) as a séance-surrogate. Centuries' worth of occult and mystical lore fed into the work of the Theosophical Society, which was founded in 1875 (in New York City) by Helena Patrovna Blavatsky, Henry Steel Olcott, and William Quan Judge. The heterodox teachings of "theosophy" can be traced in many of the supernatural romances on screen.

Contemporaneous with the nineteenth-century developments of gothic fiction and spiritualism was the emergence in philosophy of a trend that would deeply influence the doctrines of Sigmund Freud. Metaphysical speculation among philosophers as to the hypothetical realities that might exist behind the appearance of things—from Plato's assertion that unchanging Forms or Ideas underlie our temporal reality to the insistence of Immanuel Kant that "noumena," "things in the themselves," lie behind the appearances or "phenomena" that our minds perceive—led to the "continental school" of European philosophy, a school whose practitioners sometimes sought to identify the *fundamental* "thing in itself."[6]

The result was a succession of (mostly) atheistic cosmologies, from Arthur Schopenhauer's dictum that "will" is the primal and completely unexplainable "thing in itself" to Friedrich Nietzsche's doctrine of the "will to power" to Henri Bergson's conception of a cosmic "élan vital" to Freud's derivative offering: "Eros" as the basic "life force"—the force of universal creation, generation, and cohesion—with the libido serving as its spearhead within the human psyche. Against this life force Freud theorized the existence of a counterforce, the death-instinct, locked in a dialectical and eternal struggle with Eros.[7]

Love and death.

The work of Freud was hugely influential in the early to mid-twentieth century. It was contemporaneous with the emergence of love-death-afterlife films. And Freud's formulations—as much philosophic and literary as they were nominally medical—can be aligned with the oracular pronouncements of others such as D. H. Lawrence, who was deeply interested in psychoanalytic theory regarding "Eros."[8] As with Eros, so with Thanatos: the struggle between them that Freud discerned was transmuted in the minds of others to the love–death *synthesis* of the kind that was featured by Wagner in the *liebestod* of *Tristan und Isolde*. Consider the rhetoric of Thomas Mann in his short story "Tristan" (1902): "To him who has looked upon the night of death and known its secret sweets, to him day never can be aught but vain, nor can he know a longing save for night, eternal, real, in which he is made one with love."[9]

The films to be presented in this book are exotic fare. They present for us ideas that have been haunting reflective people for thousands of years. The fact that such movies have a simultaneous appeal as entertainment adds to—rather than detracts from—their fascination.

In short, they are eminently worthy of the detailed examination to follow.

NOTES

1. Sigmund Freud, *Civilization and Its Discontents* (1930), James Strachey, trans. (New York: W.W. Norton, 1961), 96, 106.
2. The proto-deities Eros and Thanatos were presented by Hesiod in his *Theogony*, written in the eighth century BC. See Hesiod, *Theogony and Works and Days*, M. I. West, trans. (New York: Oxford University Press, 1988), 6, 9.
3. Freud's invocation of archaic Greek terms derives from the huge "Greek revival" of the nineteenth century, a cultural movement in which Nietzsche's *Birth of Tragedy* (1872) played a key role. Freud made his borrowed use of the ancient term Eros explicit when he wrote that he invoked "the Eros of the poets and philosophers which holds all living things together." See Sigmund Freud, *Beyond the Pleasure Principle* [1920], James Strachey, trans. (New York: W.W. Norton, 1961), 60–61.
4. Ancient Greco-Roman authorities, notably Plutarch, passed along the essentials of the myth. The cult of Isis eventually extended throughout the Mediterranean world, and the Isis cult in Rome was significant enough to influence the plot of *The Golden Ass*, by Apuleius. See Apuleius, *The Golden Ass*, Jack Lindsay, trans. (Bloomington: Indiana University Press, 1960), 237–38. See also Homer W. Smith, *Man and His Gods* (Boston: Little, Brown, 1953), 34–44.
5. See Andrew McCann, *Popular Literature, Authorship and the Occult in Late Victorian Britain* (New York: Cambridge University Press, 2014); Elana Gomel, "Spirits in the Material World: Spiritualism and Identity in the Fin de Siècle," *Victorian Literature and Culture*, 35.1 (2007), 191; Marlene Tromp, "Spirited Sexuality: Sex, Marriage, and Victorian Spiritualism," *Victorian Literature and Culture*, 31.1 (2003), 70; Diana Basham, *The Trial of Woman: Feminism and the Occult Sciences in Victorian Literature and Society* (London and New York: Macmillan, 1992); and Alex Owen, *The Darkened Room: Women, Power, and Spiritualism in Late Nineteenth-Century England* (London: Virago Press, 1989).
6. Plato's doctrine of Forms was presented in most of his dialogues, but the most famous passages occur in the *Republic*, books III, V–VII, and IX–X. Kant's doctrine of noumena was introduced in the "Transcendental Analytic" section of the *Critique of Pure Reason* (1781) and developed further in the "Transcendental Dialectic" section under the heading "The Antinomy of Pure Reason." In Kant's *Critique of Practical Reason* (1788), the doctrine of noumena was presented with greater insistence, even to the point of dogmatism, as the basis for ethics, including the "categorical imperative."
7. Schopenhauer's doctrine of "will" was presented in *The World as Will and Representation*, first published in 1819 and reissued in an expanded second edition in 1844. Nietzsche's doctrine of the "will to power" developed in the late 1870s and emerged full-blown in his near-hallucinatory book *Thus Spake Zarathustra* (1883–1885). For a sympathetic account, see Walter Kaufmann, *Nietzsche: Philosopher, Psychologist, Anti-Christ* (Princeton, NJ: Princeton University Press, 1950), third edition, 1968, Vintage books, 178–207. Bergson's doctrine of *élan vital* was introduced in *Creative Evolution* (1907). Freud's doctrine of Eros was introduced in *Beyond the Pleasure Principle* (1920).
8. Lawrence, in his 1919 foreword to *Women in Love* proclaimed, "Let us hesitate no longer to announce that the sensual passions and mysteries are equally sacred with the spiritual mysteries and passions. . . . The creative, spontaneous soul sends forth its promptings of desire and aspiration in us." These ideas may be traced to the oracular doctrines of William Blake and many others; indeed, they have scriptural provenance in the Song of Solomon and other passages in the Old and New Testaments.
9. Thomas Mann, *Death in Venice and Seven Other Stories*, H. T. Lowe-Porter, trans. (New York: Alfred A. Knopf, 1950), Vintage edition, 345.

TWO

The Cultural Milieu after World War I and the Seminal Plays

The carnage of World War I dwarfed anything that people could remember, even elderly veterans of the American Civil War. The Civil War killed approximately 600,000; the "Great War" that lasted from 1914 to 1918 killed 16 million with an additional 20 million wounded. Historian John Keegan has observed that in his own English village the war "brought heartbreak on a scale never known since the settlement was established by the Anglo-Saxons."[1] He adds that the British male population between ages nineteen and twenty-two shrank by "one in three. Little wonder that the post-war world spoke of a 'lost generation.'"[2]

Several dramas that appeared on stage during World War I or its aftermath led to supernatural romances on screen, and the plays were all meditations on mortality. Tales of love, death, and the afterlife can serve many different emotional functions, but one of the most fundamental in the 1910s and 1920s was to help the grieving cope with all the death.

PETER IBBETSON AND SMILIN' THROUGH

The 1891 novel *Peter Ibbetson* by George du Maurier told the story of an ill-fated couple who find their bond through a spiritual process that continues after death.

This story was adapted for the stage by John Raphael and it appeared on Broadway in 1917. John and Lionel Barrymore, Constance Collier, and Laura Hope Crews starred, and the production was so successful it prompted a film adaptation, a 1921 silent film called *Forever*. This movie, produced by Lasky-Famous Players and distributed by Paramount, appears to be the first supernatural romance on screen, but the print has

5

(alas) been lost for a long time.[3] The producers had hoped to get the Barrymore brothers, along with their sister Ethel, into the movie, but the plans did not come to fruition. Instead, the film—which was directed by George Fitzmaurice—starred Wallace Reid and Elsie Ferguson.

Peter Ibbetson was then turned into an opera, which was first performed in 1931. The music was by Deems Taylor and the libretto was a collaboration between Taylor and Constance Collier (who had also appeared in the 1917 play). This opera was also quite successful, running for four seasons at the Metropolitan and featuring singers Edward Johnson and Lucrezia Bori.

Paramount then produced a sound-film version of *Peter Ibbetson*, starring Gary Cooper and Anne Harding. A number of changes were made to the original story. In this version, the title character, Peter Ibbetson, falls in love with a married noblewoman, Mary, the Duchess of Towers, who—he later realizes—is in fact his childhood playmate and sweetheart, whom he hasn't seen in years. Mary's jealous husband pulls a gun on Peter, who quickly turns the tables and kills the Duke of Towers after shoving Mary to safety. Wrongly convicted of the duke's murder, Peter languishes in prison. But he and Mary can communicate through telepathy, a mystical foreshadowing of their ultimate destiny, for they will be reunited forever in the afterlife.

Released in 1935, the film was directed by Henry Hathaway and, though scorned by a number of critics, it won some immediate praise and then developed something of a cult following down the years. Andre Sennwald wrote in the *New York Times* that Hathaway had rendered the story "with astonishing success. With his directness . . . he skillfully escapes all the lush pitfalls of the plot and gives it a tenderness that is always gallant instead of merely soft. The photoplay, though it scarcely is a dramatic thunderbolt, possesses a luminous beauty and a sensitive charm that make it attractive and moving."[4]

The telepathic scenes vary from hallucinatory to super-realist, with Peter and Mary shown revisiting some childhood locales, communing in mountain eyries, and conversing in Peter's dungeon as shafts of light play around them. After Mary predeceases Peter, her voice from the afterlife is heard as golden rays of light flow downward.

The theme of a star-struck couple who find consolation in the afterlife would be the basis for countless supernatural romances on screen—as the chapters to follow will show. This simplest version of the love-death-afterlife trinity in cinema drew not only from *Peter Ibbetson* in its successive incarnations but also from a play that premiered in 1919—a play that supplied the basis for no less than three different film versions of the story: *Smilin' Through*. This play was the work of Jane Cowl and Jane Murfin. It opened on Broadway at the Broadhurst Theater on December 30, 1919, and ran for 175 performances.

The play told the story of a nobleman named John Carteret, who loves a girl named Moonyeen Clare. She was killed on their wedding day by an ex-suitor named Jeremy Wayne. Moonyeen communes with John from the afterlife, and the two of them are finally reunited after John's death. In the meantime, Moonyeen's niece Kathleen is adopted by Sir John when her parents die at sea. As she grows up, she falls in love with none other than Kenneth Wayne, who is the son of the very same man who had killed Moonyeen. John interferes with this incipient romance, and then Kenneth goes off to fight in World War I. Sir John is reconciled to the romance when Kenneth returns wounded. John blesses the marriage just before his own death, after which he is of course reunited with his own lost love, Moonyeen.

Smilin' Through was made into a silent film in 1922 by First National Pictures. Then Hollywood produced two more successive versions of the play, the first in 1932 and the second in 1941. Both of these films were made by MGM. The 1932 version, directed by Sidney Franklin (who also directed the silent version), starred Norma Shearer as both Moonyeen and Kathleen, Leslie Howard as Sir John Carteret, and Fredric March as both Kenneth and Jeremy Wayne. The love-death-afterlife theme is presented *immediately*, for the movie begins with John Carteret at Moonyeen's grave. Her ghost appears to him with words of comfort that we gather he has heard many times: be patient, she says, for they will be together in the afterlife by and by.

This film was nominated for an Academy Award as best picture, and for good reason since the direction and performances were generally excellent; indeed, Shearer was highly charismatic. The 1942 technicolor remake, directed by Frank Borzage, starred Jeanette MacDonald, Brian Aherne, Gene Raymond, and Ian Hunter.

These two plays—*Peter Ibbetson* and *Smilin' Through*—may be viewed as the sources of supernatural romance on screen. But three other plays appearing after World War I applied the love-death-afterlife trinity in ways that were much more inventive. These plays—*Outward Bound* by Sutton Vane (1923), *La Morte in Vacanza* (*Death Takes a Holiday*) by Alberto Casella (1924/1929), and *Berkeley Square* by John Balderston (1925/1929)—were adapted for the screen within a decade after their premier on stage; *Outward Bound* was filmed by Warner Brothers/Vitaphone and released in 1930, *Berkeley Square* was adapted by Fox Films and released in 1933, and *Death Takes a Holiday* was released by Paramount in 1934.

OUTWARD BOUND

Outward Bound can be linked to World War I indirectly, since the author served on the western front, enduring shell shock. After being taken out of action by this incapacitation, the playwright (and actor) Sutton Vane returned to entertain the troops.

Anyone serving on the front during World War I was "in the land of the dead" psychologically, since the troops all knew that attacks against machine-gun emplacements protected by barbed wire could be regarded as suicide missions by anyone who analyzed the odds. The psychology of being "recalled to the living" after dwelling "in the land of the dead" was fundamental to the mood of this playwright, at least when his orders removed him from harm. It seems natural enough that the hero and heroine of *Outward Bound*, after seeking a love that survives after death, are recalled to the living.

Outward Bound takes place on an ocean liner, a vessel that travels through fog. There is no captain and no crew—just an elderly steward named Scrubby who serves drinks and answers the passengers' questions. As the play opens, the passengers seem to be contented enough, notwithstanding the fact that some of them are hard to get along with. But they gradually realize that none of them has any idea where they are going or why. At last one of them, a man named Tom Prior, starts to understand that they are all dead. Scrubby confirms it.

They are headed for the afterlife, which contains both heaven and hell; an "examiner" will come on board at the end of the voyage and determine their fates. Among the passengers is a young and quiet couple named Henry and Ann, who have a secret: they are suicides. They had an extramarital romance and the persecution that they had to endure made them choose to end it all so they could be together—untroubled and united—in eternity.

They are: except as suicides they cannot go to heaven or to hell; they are "half-ways." And so is Scrubby. Their fate is to travel with him aboard the spectral ocean liner for eternity as it makes its endless rounds. He explains it:

Scrubby: "It happens to all half-ways like—like we are."

Ann: "But what are we, Scrubby? We—we are half-ways?"

Scrubby: "We're the people who ought to have had more courage."

Ann: "For what?"

Scrubby: "To face life."

But then Henry suddenly hears the sound of glass breaking, and the sound of a dog barking. It turns out that their dog intervened in their suicide pact; when they turned on the gas in their London flat, the dog knew that something was amiss, so he crashed himself through a window, letting in the air.

Thus Henry and Ann are recalled to the land of the living.

The play opened in London on September 17, 1923, at the Everyman Theater. Diana Hamilton played Ann, William Stack played Henry, and Frederick Cooper was Prior. The British reviews were positive. The *Daily Telegraph* called it "a play of quite outstanding interest—a magnificent idea." The reviewer for *Punch* wrote that "nobody ought to miss this. . . . Hats off to Mr. Sutton Vane."[5]

On Christmas Eve, the play premiered in the United States—at the Apollo Theatre in Atlantic City, New Jersey. This time Leslie Howard played Henry, Margallo Gilmore played Ann, and Alfred Lunt played Prior.[6]

The play was a success in the United States as well. Howard recorded the following impressions in his diary: "Monday, 7th January: 'Dinner with Alfred Lunt. Opening of Outward Bound at Ritz Theatre. Much heart-pounding and jumping of nerves. Get through pretty well. Audience reduced to jelly.'" Two days later he wrote, "success of play seems assured. Both houses packed and apparently thrilled."[7] John Cobbin of the *New York Times* wrote that *Outward Bound* "caught the attention of a New York audience . . . stirring it to very considerable depths of human pity and mortal terror."[8]

The film version of *Outward Bound* was produced by Warner Brothers/ Vitaphone and released in 1930. Robert Milton, who served as stage director for the American performance of the play, was recruited to direct the film and Leslie Howard again played a leading role, but this time a different one—he played Prior, the one who intuits that he and all the others are dead. Helen Chandler was cast as Ann and Douglas Fairbanks, Jr. played Henry. The screenplay by J. Grubb Alexander adhered closely to Sutton Vane's script.

After the opening credits, the film contains a long foreword that testifies to the impact of the play; with due allowances, the text does not come across as hyperbole. It called Sutton Vane's creation "one of the most important stage plays of this generation," one that "launched a new era in playwriting." The play "presented for the first time to the peoples of the world an entirely new and different imaginative conception of life, death, and the hereafter."

The film version of *Outward Bound* is a subtle production; the aesthetics are understated, the eerie mood is sustained without appreciable effort, the special effects—the ocean liner in motion, for instance—are achieved through some simple but highly effective animation, and several performances are outstanding, especially Howard as Prior and Chandler as Ann; the latter performance creates a superb and sweetly ethereal effect.

And the reviewers loved it. Some excerpts from Mordaunt Hall's review in the *New York Times*:

Figure 2.1.   Leslie Howard, in the 1930 film *Outward Bound*, played one of the passengers aboard a spectral ocean liner who realizes that he and all the others on board are deceased and headed . . . "outward." Courtesy of Photofest.

Barely a whispered word escaped the lips of the spectators last night in the Hollywood Theatre as they watched a most impressive Vitaphone version of Sutton Vane's play, "Outward Bound." . . . It was a memorable evening in more ways than one, for aside from having the temerity to produce the shell-shocked soldier-actor's stirring work dealing with a ship aboard which all the passengers, except two known as "Halfways," are dead, the Warner Brothers offered their film without the

Figure 2.2.   Douglas Fairbanks, Jr. and Helen Chandler played Henry and Ann in *Outward Bound*, **spirits who remain in a state of limbo due to their suicide pact. At right is "Scrubby," played by Alec Francis, the steward on the ocean liner of the dead. Courtesy of Photofest.**

usual pomp and fanfare. . . . It is, in fact, a picture in which everybody shines, a picture that, like the play, sends one away from it deeply moved.[9]

Variety called the film "a laboratory experiment for the rest of the film world to ponder and learn."[10] Reviewer William Haskell in the *Albany Evening News* wrote that its religious theme "is developed in a way that is both pathetic and rarely beautiful. All the scenes are photographed in a misty atmosphere to accent the ethereality of the story, and the actors' faces all seem to express the Eternal Puzzle."[11]

In 1924, as *Outward Bound* continued its successful run on the American stage, the next of the prototypical plays was created in Italy: Alberto Casella's *La Morte in Vacanza*. And in 1925, yet another play, *Berkeley Square*, was written by John Balderston.

Casella's play premiered in Florence, and was successful.[12] Balderston's play was performed in London to mixed reviews in 1925, when the playwright, who was also a journalist, was covering the excavation of Tutankhamen's tomb in Egypt. Neither one of these plays would achieve its full potential until the end of the decade, when both became successes in New York. The rights were then purchased by Hollywood studios and the films were made a few years later.

The American success of *Berkeley Square* came first, but only by a month.

BERKELEY SQUARE

Balderston based the play *Berkeley Square* upon an unfinished novel by Henry James: *The Sense of the Past*, which was published posthumously in 1917. Balderston's play followed James's plotline closely. The play tells the story of a man in modern London who becomes obsessed with the life of an ancestor and dreams of changing places with him—of being teleported to the 1780s. The miracle occurs, and then the hero falls deeply in love with a woman from the eighteenth century. Though he loses her when he is wafted back to the present, he knows that they will meet again in eternity.

Leslie Howard, who played such a prominent role in the success of *Outward Bound*, would play an even larger role in the success of *Berkeley Square*. He recalled in his memoirs (written in the third person) that the play would "change [his] career . . . pronouncedly" when Alexander Woolcott called his attention to it in 1927.[13]

The producer Jed Harris owned the rights. Howard, who was also busily producing plays, talked his partner Gilbert Miller into purchasing the rights because the play was "nagging at his mind." Howard "managed, while he was at Harris's office, to get his hands on a copy of *Berkeley Square*. He read it and found that the play was burning holes in his brain. He cabled Miller about it—and, to his complete surprise, Gilbert replied: 'Dear Partner, have bought *Berkeley Square*. Good luck—but don't blame me.'"

Howard produced the play in London, with himself in the lead role. The production, which opened on March 6, 1929, did reasonably well (it got mixed reviews), but when Howard brought the play to Broadway, where it opened on November 4, 1929, it ran for 229 performances. Critic Heywood Broun wrote that "*Berkeley Square* is easily the finest play now to be seen in New York . . . and, among other things, the play contains the finest acting performance of the season, which is given by Leslie Howard."[14]

Richard Watts, Jr. of the *Herald-Tribune* wrote that "amid all the justified enthusiasm for the adult intellectual qualities and the fascinating metaphysical conception of time that distinguish *Berkeley Square* and make it the most important play of the season, there has been too little said for the work's enormously moving emotional values."[15] And the *London Times*'s reviewer wrote that "there is magic in this play, enough to set it apart from all the common traffic of the theatre, and to send dreams scudding in the wake of dreams. Therefore, first of all, let us welcome and rejoice in it, for magic is very rare."[16]

The 1933 film version was produced by Fox Films; the director, Frank Lloyd, had won acclaim for his *Cavalcade*. Producer Jesse Lasky—one of the founders of Paramount Pictures and a major figure in Hollywood—made the obvious decision to recruit Leslie Howard to reprise the lead role. Ernest Palmer was the cinematographer and the music for the film was composed by Louis de Francesco. Balderston and Sonya Levien produced the screenplay.

The film opens with a glimpse of a stagecoach rattling along an English road in the eighteenth century. In the coach is one Peter Standish (played by Howard), an American who has come to visit England to see some relatives in 1784.

Then the scene shifts to London in the 1930s. A descendant of Standish (also played by Howard) is living in the house of his ancestors on Berkeley Square. He is engaged to be married, but he keeps procrastinating, to the consternation of his fiancée. Something odd has been happening since he moved into the family home, which still contains most of its eighteenth-century furnishings. He is becoming obsessed with the life of his ancestor and namesake. The two men were look-alikes: an old painting on the wall reveals this. He becomes a shut-in, poring over surviving letters and records, including his namesake's voluminous diary, which he reads by candle-light.

He confides to a friend that a weird inspiration has occurred to him: if he could somehow change places with his ancestor, he could pass for the old Peter Standish, since he knows the man inside and out. But there is more: he has the overpowering conviction that this *will* happen—and soon. Most uncanny of all, he relates that a philosophic (or religious) revelation has been given to him:

> Suppose you are in a boat, sailing down a winding stream. You watch the banks as they pass you. You went by a grove of maple trees, upstream. But you can't see them now, so you saw them in the *past*, didn't you? You're watching a field of clover now, it's before your eyes, at this moment, in the *present*! But you don't know yet what's around the bend in the stream ahead of you, there may be wonderful things, but you can't see them until you get around the bend, in the *future*, can you? . . . Now remember, you're in the boat. But I'm up in the sky above you, in a plane. I'm looking down on it all, I can see *all at once* the trees you saw upstream, the field of clover that you see now, and what's waiting for you, around the bend ahead! All at once! So the past, present and future of the man in the boat are all one, to the man in the plane. Doesn't that show how all Time must really be one? Real Time with a capital T is nothing but an idea in the mind of God.

He is convinced that the past is still back there, *alive*, and will always be back there, eternally.

Just after this conversation, Peter is returning to his home in a drenching storm when he hears, amid the hubbub of modern London, the sound of horses' hooves. He walks up the steps to his house, and he opens the door.

He finds himself in eighteenth-century attire. The miracle has happened.

But the experience goes wrong. Peter commits all sorts of faux-pas that give him away: his expressions and his gestures and his habits are "out of place," and his eighteenth-century relatives sense that something weird is occurring. The situation worsens as he says things (inadvertently) that intimate a foreknowledge of events that have not yet happened. By the time the film's central crisis has developed, his relatives regard him as a diabolical changeling who has stolen away the soul of the real Peter Standish.

And he has also fallen deeply in love with a cousin named Helen Pettigrew (played by Heather Angel).

In the course of many plot complications, Helen gradually discerns the truth: Peter Standish is a man from the future. As she stares into his eyes, she can somehow read his pictorial thoughts: she sees visions of steam locomotives, airplanes, soldiers on the front during World War I, and skyscrapers. "There's never been a kiss like this since the world began," says Peter as the two of them embrace.

Peter notices an ancient and curious artifact that he recognizes from the furnishings that were still within the house in his own day and age: a small sculpture in the form of an Egyptian ankh (or "crux ansata"). Helen tells him that her father had found this object on an expedition in Egypt. This symbol, which Peter knows somehow to denote "the eternal," manifests itself as the charm that brought about the miracle.

But the miracle ends. A storm begins to blow outside. Peter hears the sound of motors and he knows that the far-off London of the 1930s is seconds away. He tells Helen he will never marry. She consoles him:

> Love will give me strength. Don't be too sad about a girl who's been dead so long. As I grow old, your youth will seem to me eternal youth, for you will come, young as I see you now, to my grave in St. Mark's Churchyard. To you, that will be tomorrow. And yet, 'twill be generations after I am dead. I'll ask for a stone with the letters cut deep, so they won't wear away.

As the film concludes, Peter sits within the house after visiting the grave of Helen. Her epitaph: "Here lies, in the confident hope of the blessed resurrection, Helen Pettigrew . . . who departed this life June the fifteenth, 1787, aged twenty-three years." He knows at this point that the two of them will meet again . . . in God's time.

The film, released on September 13, 1933, was a critical success. Mordaunt Hall of the *New York Times* wrote that "in the matter of poetic

Figure 2.3. In the 1933 film *Berkeley Square*, Leslie Howard and Heather Angel played lovers from different centuries who meet through time travel. They will part, but they both have faith that they will meet again in "God's time." Courtesy of Photofest.

charm, nothing quite like it has emerged from Hollywood. It is an example of delicacy and restraint, a picture filled with gentle humor and appealing pathos. It is in a class by itself. . . . Mr. Howard revels in the role. He has done excellent work in other films, but it is doubtful whether he has ever given so impressive and imaginative a performance."[17]

Howard was nominated for the Academy Award as Best Actor for his work in *Berkeley Square*. On December 4, 1934, a radio version of the play and film was performed by Howard and Helen Chandler (both of whom had played leading roles in the screen version of *Outward Bound*) for *Lux Radio Theater*.

The cinematography and the general aesthetics of *Outward Bound* and *Berkeley Square* were similar: both were understated, subtle, delicate films that developed the quiet sort of power that can hit both critics and audiences hard.

DEATH TAKES A HOLIDAY

Casella's *La Morte in Vacanza* was translated into English by Walter Ferris and brought to Broadway under the title *Death Takes a Holiday*. It opened on December 26, 1929, at the Ethel Barrymore Theatre, which means that its run in New York was concurrent for a time with the American success of *Berkeley Square*. The American impact of these two plays was simultaneous. *Death Takes a Holiday* was produced by Lee Shubert and directed by Lawrence Marston.[18]

The play tells the story of an Italian nobleman, Duke Lambert, who is entertaining guests at his mountain villa. His son Corrado is courting a lovely young woman named Grazia.

A shadowy form has been manifesting itself around the villa, and then, very late, while Lambert is sitting alone, the shadow materializes into a figure that is all too familiar in Western iconography: Death personified, the Grim Reaper.

Death reveals that he intends to assume a mortal shape for three days to experience life, to know why people fear him, to know . . . what he has missed. In the course of his three-day "holiday," Death and Grazia . . . fall in love. Death, who has taken the form of a recently deceased nobleman named Prince Sirki—Death borrows the body to become incarnate—feels the ecstasy and agony of carnal desire: Thanatos at last encounters Eros. He can tell now why people fear him since the sensuousness of this life is so compelling. Grazia, who is clearly a mystic or medium, responds. She has already sensed that there are beauties out there "beyond," and now she knows that this supernatural being is both her destined love and her guide to the beyond. She becomes his queen as he takes her away and the curtain falls.

Many critics liked it. The *New York Mirror* said it "merits superlatives—received with roaring, enthusiastic applause." The *New York American* called it "thrilling." The *Philadelphia Inquirer* praised the "audacious theme . . . that holds one taut."[19] The cast included James Dale as Lambert, Rose Hobart as Grazia, and Philip Merivale as Death.[20]

Paramount purchased the rights to the play in 1930. At first they planned to call the film *Strange Holiday* and the role of Death would have been played by William Powell.[21] But the film took several years to produce and the plans changed. The screenplay by Maxwell Anderson and Gladys Lehman used much of the Ferris script from 1929. Mitchell Leisen was chosen as director, and the following cast was selected: Frederic March as Death/Sirki, Evelyn Venable as Grazia, Sir Guy Standing as Lambert.

The film begins with a credit sequence that introduces the cast: the camera sweeps among them in panoramic sequence from left to right. They are enjoying themselves at a flower festival in a village. Then Grazia is introduced—by herself, in church. Her character is established at the outset: different and mystical.

The revelers return to Duke Lambert's villa in two swift cars, racing along mountain curves. Grazia tells her fiancée Corrado that she senses a shadow following them. "Let's lose it," she says—"let's go fast enough to reach the illimitable."

After a brush with death on the road—one of the cars collides with a horse cart—the shaken travelers attempt to relax with drinks and music at the villa.

Corrado urges Grazia to commit to a definite wedding date, but she procrastinates. The situation is comparable to *Berkeley Square*: the protagonist keeps putting off marriage because of an intuition of "something else"—something uncanny that is destined. "There's a kind of happiness that I want to find first," she says; "There's something out there that I must find." She goes off by herself in the garden. But then she screams as she feels the mysterious shadow drawing nearer.

All retire to bed. Lambert sits alone and then a shrouded figure approaches. Death introduces himself: "I am not of your world. I am—how shall I describe it—a sort of vagabond of space. I am the point of contact between eternity and time." He is death. And he explains his intention to visit the duke and his guests for three days in the form of Prince Sirki.

Amusing plot developments keep the action moving. Lambert and his guests read newspaper stories of miraculous escapes all over the world by people who should have been killed—in car crashes and other disasters—but instead walked away unscathed. Death is on a holiday. But only Lambert knows the identity of "Prince Sirki." And he has promised to keep it a secret.

Several of the women compete for the favors of the guest, and when one makes a determined attempt to seduce him, Death finds himself tempted. But he decides to reveal himself: "I *will* you to know who I am," he declares, and as she stares into his eyes the film uses a point-of-view shot to show what she sees. She does not see a death mask, and yet the face of Sirki is disturbingly gaunt, and then—"no, I want to live," she screams, flinching away.

Corrado strides up and inquires what might be the matter. Death's holiday is coming to an end, and so "Sirki" starts to give himself away: "I came among you to warm my hands at your fires," he says. "Your poor, pitiful fires that flicker out in the night. Well, let them all go out! . . . If only I can save one spark for the eternal cold."

Grazia encounters him again in the garden, but her earlier fear is now gone. They dance, but this is no *danse macabre*. The script becomes lyrical. He tells her that her name is like music; "it has overtones that go singing on and on. . . . They are full of grace and light." "When you speak like that," she replies, "I hear music too. Great sweeping chords."

She tells him that his eyes are like "the worlds I visit in sleep" and that beneath his words is "a sound I've heard in dreams." Their passion increases, so they start to reveal their love. When he tells her he has to return to his "distant kingdom," she asks him to take her.

Lambert by now has revealed the identity of Sirki. As Death and Grazia commune, the fear of the others—especially the fear for her safety—increases. Sirki comes out of the garden, and they beg him to spare her. "You know nothing of the meaning of death," he says; "to go with me now—*in love*—would be triumph, not death as it is known to you." They insist that he tell her who he is, so she can make a fair choice. He ponders the matter and begins to experience doubt, ambivalence, and guilt.

Midnight approaches, the hour when the "holiday" must end. Grazia emerges from the garden. Sirki has decided to release her, so he says that she must stay with her loved ones. She refuses. Nothing he can say will make a difference. She has found her love.

A clock strikes midnight, and Sirki becomes shrouded Death. "Goodbye, my friends," he says. "Remember there is only a moment of shadow between your life and mine. And when I call, come bravely through that shadow. And you will find me only your familiar friend. Goodbye, Grazia. Now you see me as I am."

But her face is glowing. "I've always seen you like that," she declares; "you haven't changed." And Death is stunned: You have seen me . . . like this?"

Grazia: "Yes, always."

Death: "Then there *is* a love which casts out fear! Love *is* greater than illusion! And as strong as death."

He wraps his cloak around her and they both dissolve in radiance. The film ends.

The performances in the screen version of *Death Takes a Holiday* were effective. Fredric March played Death in the form of Prince Sirki with a combination of wonderment and lordly arrogance. He wore a uniform (with a monocle) and throughout the film he spoke with a light foreign accent. Evelyn Venable gave a fine performance as Grazia, giving warmth to the role, quite essential for her mysticism to be plausible; without it, her character would only seem deranged. [22]

Leisen's direction was also effective. He developed an optical illusion with mirrors in order to make the figure of shrouded Death look translucent. The shroud itself was composed of multilayered black and charcoal-colored chiffon. [23]

The film was a success. Richard Watts, Jr. of the *New York Herald Tribune* called it "an interesting, frequently striking and occasionally beautiful dramatic fantasy."[24] The *Chicago Daily Tribune*'s critic wrote that "Fredric March's inspirational performance will prevent my thinking of him as Fredric March for a long time to come. The man is completely submerged in probably the greatest role he has ever played."[25] The *Baltimore Sun* observed that March was "careful to underplay rather than emphasize the fantastic note."[26]

A TRADITION—OR A GENRE—IS BORN

Outward Bound, Berkeley Square, and *Death Takes a Holiday* exerted force between 1930 and 1934 and they advanced the development of supernatural romance as a Hollywood tradition that would have ramifications through the rest of the twentieth century and beyond. The tradition developed even greater momentum in World War II, when mass grieving again cried out for a cinematic response.

The 1944 remake of *Outward Bound*—another Warner Brothers creation entitled *Between Two Worlds*—was significant, though the casting was less effective than the original, and *Outward Bound* continued to project its influence. The British film *A Matter of Life and Death* (1946) told the story of a loving couple who return to the living after proving their devotion to each other through a love-*in*-death experience. The lesson that is learned by Henry and Ann in their interlude as "half-ways" can also be compared to the lesson that is learned by George Bailey in Frank Capra's classic *It's a Wonderful Life* (1946). In a realm between life and death—George wishes he had never been born, so the heavenly powers place him in a parallel half-way world with no identity—he learns the value of what he had attempted to forsake through suicide. And the devotion of a couple in the afterlife after one of them commits suicide figures in the plot of *What Dreams May Come* (1998).

Berkeley Square would be influential through its plot—essentially the template that would be used for *Somewhere in Time* (1980)—and the historical locus of its time-travel imagery (the eighteenth century in Britain), which was possibly a factor in the genesis of Alan Jay Lerner's *Brigadoon*. One can also see the influence of *Berkeley Square* in the television series *Outlander* (2014–2015), which is based upon a series of novels (1991–2014) by Diana Gabaldon. In this story, a nurse gets swept from 1945 into the Scotland of 1743, where romance awaits her.

The correspondences between the plot trajectories of *Somewhere in Time* and *Berkeley Square* are striking. In both cases the protagonist is wafted into the past, where he meets the great love of his life, and then loses her when he is wrenched back to the future. In both cases, the romantic consolation is (or will be) found in the afterlife. In both cases, a symbolic plot device symbolizes "the eternal" and serves as a physical talisman that effectuates the dark magic: the ancient Egyptian ankh in *Berkeley Square* corresponds to a mysterious watch in *Somewhere in Time*.

In *Brigadoon*, as in *Berkeley Square*, the protagonist delays getting married because of a mystical sense that tells him something else is in store. Then he finds his way into an eighteenth-century British (in this case Scottish) environment, where he meets the great love of his life, but then he loses her (at least for a time), when he returns to his own milieu.

Death Takes a Holiday inspired many supernatural romances that would personify death. The Grim Reaper appears as "Mr. Brink" in *On Borrowed Time* (1939) and in *Here Comes Mr. Jordan* (1941) he is the top bureaucrat in a celestial hierarchy, a theme that is reprised with modifications in *A Matter of Life and Death*. In 1998, *Death Takes a Holiday* was revived in a remake entitled *Meet Joe Black*.

But the plot permutations of supernatural romance are almost endless, and the films that were produced from the 1920s to the present show the almost infinite potentialities of the love-death-afterlife theme.

NOTES

1. John Keegan, *The First World War* (New York: Alfred A. Knopf, 1999), 4.

2. Keegan, *The First World War*, 423.

3. For coverage of this film, see John T. Soister, *American Silent Horror, Science Fiction, and Fantasy Feature Films, 1913–1929* (Jefferson, NC: McFarland, 2012), 214–15.

4. Andre Sennwald, review of *Peter Ibbetson*, *New York Times*, accessible via http://movies.nytimes.com/movie/review?res=9A0CE4D61F3DE53ABC4053DFB767838E629EDE.

5. Sutton Vane, *Outward Bound* (London: Chatto & Windus, 1926), 145.

6. Sutton Vane, *Outward Bound* (New York: Liveright Publishing Corporation, 1924), 13.

7. Leslie Howard, *Trivial Fond Records*, Ronald Howard, ed. (London: William Kimber, 1982), 41.

8. John Cobbin, "Outward Bound," *New York Times*, January 8, 1924, cited in http://www.tcm.com/tcmdb/title/363/Outward-Bound/articles.html.

9. Mordaunt Hall, "The Screen: Away from the World," *New York Times*, September 18, 1930, accessed via http://www.nytimes.com/movie/review?res=940DE2DD1038E433A2575BC1A96F9C946194D6CF.

10. Review, "Outward Bound," *Variety*, December 31, 1929, accessed via https://variety.com/1929/film/reviews/outward-bound-1200410297/.

11. William H. Haskell, Review "Outward Bound," *Albany Evening News*, April 16, 1931, accessed via http://inafferrabileleslie.wordpress.com/films/outward-bound-1930/.

12. http://www.nytimes.com/movies/person/316502/Alberto-Casella.

13. Leslie Howard, *Trivial Fond Records*, 107–8.

14. Leslie Howard, *Trivial Fond Records*, 109.

15. "Berkeley Square, Publicity through Your Local Papers," appendix to John L. Balderston, *Berkeley Square: A Play in Three Acts* (New York: Samuel French, Inc., 1931), 124–25.

16. "Berkeley Square, Publicity through Your Local Papers," 125.

17. Mordaunt Hall, "Leslie Howard and Heather Angel in the Pictorial Version of 'Berkeley Square,'" *New York Times*, September 14, 1933. Accessed via http://www.nytimes.com/movie/review?res=9B07E6DC1631E333A25757C1A96F9C946294D6CF.

18. Walter Ferris, *Death Takes a Holiday: A Comedy in Three Acts* (New York: Samuel French, Inc., 1928), 1.

19. Ferris, *Death Takes a Holiday*, 153–54.

20. Ferris, *Death Takes a Holiday*, 1.

21. Patricia King Hanson and Alan Gevinson, eds., *The American Film Institute Catalog of Motion Pictures Produced in the United States* (Berkeley: University of California Press, 1993), Feature films, 1931–1940, Film Entries A–L, 481.

22. One problem that resulted from the casting of the twenty-one-year-old Venable was that her father, a college professor, insisted that no kissing scenes should be included. March, who thought that this stipulation in Venable's contract was ridiculous, tried to get it changed. He asked his co-star, "What would your father say if he saw me sitting here with you on this luxurious divan, midst music, low lights and sundry, if I *didn't* kiss you?" But Venable's father wouldn't budge, and the love scenes were still effective. Deborah C. Peterson, *Fredric March: Craftsman First, Star Second* (Westport, CT: Greenwood Press, 1996), 78.

23. Peterson, *Fredric March*, 77–78.

24. Cited in Lawrence J. Quirk, *The Films of Fredric March* (New York: Citadel Press, 1971), 110.

25. Cited in Peterson, *Fredric March*, 78.

26. Cited in Peterson, *Fredric March*, 78.

THREE

The "Mythical Method" as Applied to the Plot Templates of Supernatural Romance

In the early years of its development, supernatural romance was influenced by a fad among the literary modernists for using plots from ancient myths, medieval romances and legends, and folktales as templates for avant-garde fiction. When applied to film, this method linked the cinematic genre of supernatural romance directly to the ancient sources of the love-death-afterlife trinity.

The early examples of what T. S. Eliot called the "mythical method" in fiction appeared in the first decade of the twentieth century. By the 1920s, the method was all the rage among the avant garde. The literary fad of giving legends and myths the ineffable power to compel their own reenactment can be seen in the short stories *Tristan* (1902) and *Blood of the Walsungs* (1905) by Thomas Mann, in the central plot conceit of James Joyce's *Ulysses* (1918–1922), where a day in the life of three characters in Dublin is the structure of the Odyssey compressed into a day, and in *Mourning Becomes Electra* (1931), where Eugene O'Neill transported the Oresteia of Aeschylus into Civil War America.

Of course the reuse of ancient myths (especially on stage) was nothing new. This particular practice can traced to the Renaissance; the dramas of Racine in the seventeenth century provide a convenient illustration of the practice in the early modern era. And this dramatic convention related to broader trends in classical revival.

The depiction of scenes from Greco-Roman mythology in European art became commonplace from the Renaissance onward, as did the revivals of classicism in architecture.[1] The trend affected poetry as well: in the early eighteenth century, Alexander Pope translated Homer into English iambic pentameter and in the early nineteenth century, John Keats, Percy Bysshe Shelley, and others produced verse fantasies that were based upon Greco-Roman themes. Examples of ongoing classical influence could be piled up indefinitely.

But the classical revival that led to what Eliot called the mythical method gathered special force through a sequence of events in the late nineteenth century. The huge "Greek revival" that affected so many different arts was given intellectual impetus in philosophy and drama by Friedrich Nietzsche's essay *The Birth of Tragedy* (1872) in which the author (writing both as a philologist and as an acolyte of Arthur Schopenhauer) hailed Richard Wagner as "the modern Aeschylus." Wagner's use of the Nibelungenlied (augmented by elements of Norse myth drawn from the two Icelandic Eddas) as the basis for his Ring-cycle operas seemed to Nietzsche and others a revival in modern times of an ancient precedent— it seemed comparable to the use of *archaic* Greek myths as the basis for the later Greek *classical* dramas by Aeschylus, Sophocles, and Euripides.

In addition to the influence of Wagner's three *Ring* operas, there can be little doubt that his rendition—his *direct* rendition—of the tragedy of Tristan and Isolde in his opera prompted Mann to use the theme *indirectly* by embedding the structure of its plot within a short story set in modern times. Joyce's use of Homer's *Odyssey* as a comparable structure or framework made the technique a sensation among literary sophisticates. In a review of *Ulysses*, T. S. Eliot wrote that "in using the myth, in manipulating a continuous parallel between contemporaneity and antiquity, Mr. Joyce is pursuing a method which others must pursue after him. They will not be imitators, any more than the scientist who uses the discoveries of an Einstein. . . . Instead of the narrative method, we may now use the mythical method." [2]

Outward Bound was created in the midst of this literary fad. To be sure, the fact must be acknowledged right away that the choice of an ocean liner as a vessel for the dead can be linked to some obvious memories among Sutton Vane and his contemporaries—memories of the fatalities of submarine warfare. The most famous of the ocean liners to be sunk during World War I, the *Lusitania*, haunted the imagination of the Western world with great force because the liner went down only three years after the *Titanic*.

And yet the vision of souls crossing *water* to the afterlife has an obvious antecedent in the Greco-Roman myths about Hades, which the souls of the dead approached by crossing a river—alternatively the Styx or the Acheron. Once the souls were ferried across the water by the boatman Charon, they were judged by one of several other spirits: Minos, Aeacus, or Rhadamanthus. [3] (A single "examiner" in Sutton Vane's play served the same function, and Charon the boatman is embodied in the steward, "Scrubby"). The imagery of crossing a very different river—the Jordan—

is a commonplace in popular culture as a metaphor for the process of "passing" into the afterlife.

As with *Outward Bound*, so with *Death Takes a Holiday*: both partook of the mythical method. Alberto Casella's *Morte in Vacanza* was a clear reiteration in 1924 of the myth of Hades and Persephone—and so, of course, were the derivative English-language versions of *Death Takes a Holiday*. The 1934 film was therefore one of the earliest (though by no means the very earliest) uses of the "mythical method" in supernatural romance on screen.

The Roman poet Ovid told the tale of how Venus bade Cupid to incite the desire of Pluto (i.e., the Greek Hades) for the woman Proserpina (i.e., the Greek Persephone); here is a nineteenth-century public domain translation by Henry T. Riley:

> He opened his quiver, and, by the direction of his mother, set apart one out of his thousand arrows. . . . And he bent the flexible horn, by pressing his knee against it, and struck Pluto in the breast with the barbed arrow.

The lord of death approached the lake where Proserpina played; then

> while Proserpina is amusing herself, and is plucking either violets or white lilies . . . and is striving to outdo *her companions* of the same age in gathering, almost at the same instant she is beheld, beloved, and seized by Pluto; in such great haste is love. [4]

Casella, of course, changed the myth by eliminating the element of rape (or abduction). Casella's heroine Grazia falls sincerely in love with Death, though the upshot remains the same: the mortal woman becomes Death's consort, thus (through apotheosis) rising in essence to the stature of goddess in this transmutation. Consequently, Ovid's theme of "metamorphosis" was also retained in the modern version of the tale.

Both *Outward Bound* and *La Morte in Vacanza* used the mythical method in the manner of Mann and Joyce: *indirectly*, as a presence in the work that defines the structure of the plot.[5] There are no references to the River Styx in *Outward Bound*, nor is there a single reference to Hades and Persephone in *Death Takes a Holiday*. A different use of the mythical method can be seen in the work of John Balderston (the author of *Berkeley Square*) when he was recruited by Universal Pictures to help produce the screenplay for *The Mummy* (1932). Balderston invoked some ancient myths directly, though he changed and adapted their content for his own purposes.

Producer Carl Laemmle, Jr. conceived the idea of creating a "horror" film that would exploit the still-sensational story of the excavation of Tutankhamen's tomb (from which a vogue for Egyptology spread outward into many areas including Art Deco design). Laemmle gave the idea to screen writers Nina Wilcox Putnam and Richard Schayer, who

Figure 3.1. Like Persephone in the ancient Greek myth, Grazia, played in the 1934 Paramount version of *Death Takes a Holiday* by the young Evelyn Venable, will become the consort of Death himself—shown here as the shrouded Grim Reaper—after he becomes incarnate for a while in a role played by Fredric March. Courtesy of Photofest.

changed it in fundamental ways. But when Laemmle turned their preliminary screenplay over to Balderston, the playwright decided to reinstate Laemmle's original Egyptian scheme. Balderston after all had a penchant for Egyptology, since as a journalist he had covered the excavation of Tutankhamen's tomb. And the Egyptian *crux ansata* played a key symbolic role in *Berkeley Square*.[6]

The resulting "horror film" could be regarded as a gothic supernatural romance as well, since love, death, and the afterlife define the plot. And the film made use of the mythical method indirectly through its use of the Isis and Osiris myth.

The film tells the story of an ancient Egyptian priest, Imhotep (played by Boris Karloff), who attempts to use the spell of Isis—inscribed in this story on an ancient papyrus sheet called the "Scroll of Thoth"—to resurrect his dead love, a princess named Anck-es-en-Amon. Alas, he is caught in the act, which is held by the pharaoh and the high priests (and also, apparently, by the goddess Isis herself, as the film's conclusion reveals) to be sacrilege, since it violates the normal protocols through which the soul enters the afterlife.

And so Imhotep, as punishment, is buried alive as a mummy: he is covered with bandages under which he smothers to death. The Scroll of Thoth is buried with him.

When some British archaeologists unearth the tomb of Imhotep in 1921, the mummy and the Scroll of Thoth fall into the hands of an archaeologist's apprentice, who, as he recites in whispered tones the hieroglyphics from the scroll, reanimates the mummy of Imhotep. Imhotep escapes into modern-day Egypt where he searches for his lost love, the princess.

Reincarnation is now introduced into the plot. And the appearance of this theme in a film making use of the Isis myth shows the possible influence of Helena Petrovna Blavatksy, an occultist whose book *Isis Unveiled* (1877) included reincarnation in its "theosophical" mixture of occult doctrines. The issue of whether the ancient Egyptians believed in reincarnation has long been disputed.

The soul of the princess, after many transmigrations, inhabits (as an alter ego) the mind of a modern-day woman named Helen Grosvenor (played by Zita Johann). Unfortunately for Imhotep, Helen is in love with someone else.

And so, in order to achieve his particular version of love-and-death triumph, Imhotep decides he has to kill Helen Grosvenor (hence the film's horror element), reanimate her body, which he knows somehow (the film's plot is conveniently vague about this) will contain the living soul of the princess, and then bid farewell to the soul of Helen, which will presumably flit away to other incarnations. As is so often the case with pulp fiction, we have to suspend our critical analysis in order to enjoy the action, that is, we must abandon any effort to make the reincarnation theme consistent or to understand why the princess will stay within the corpse of Helen as Imhotep presumes instead of slipping away (like the soul of Helen) to some other incarnation.

Regardless, Balderston made his script effective as stagey histrionics; after summoning Helen, Imhotep hypnotizes her and tells her that "my love has lasted longer than the temples of our gods. No man ever suffered as I suffered for you. But the rest you may not know. Not until you are about to pass through the night of terror and triumph."

At the film's conclusion, Imhotep is just about to do the deed—he is about to kill Helen in a Cairo museum that is full of ancient Egyptian artifacts—and the mind of Helen seems possessed by the soul of Anck-es-en-Amon. She says to him, "No man has ever suffered for woman as you suffered for me," and he reassures her: "You shall rest from life, like the setting sun in the west, but you shall dawn anew in the east, as the first rays of Amon-Ra dispel the shadows."[7]

But Helen's lover (and others) burst in upon them, and the shock for some reason makes the princess conclude—the film leaves this point quite murky as well—that their love is in danger of becoming blasphemy, so Helen (possessed by the princess) climbs away from the altar where Imhotep has placed her, kneels down before a statue of Isis, and prays to the goddess in the following incantation:

> Oh Isis, holy maiden, I was thy consecrated vestal. I broke my vows . . . . save me now . . . teach me the ancient summons, the holy spells I have forgotten, I call upon thee as of old!

After these words from the "ancient summons," the statue of the goddess *comes to life*. The stone arm, which is holding a *crux ansata*, reaches out, and then, in a cinematic miracle of understated special effects—a flash of light, fast cutting and splicing, and a sequence of time-lapse photography—the impression is conveyed that the goddess transfixes Imhotep and shrivels his flesh to the bone. The film ends with a crumbling skeleton, a glimpse of the Scroll of Thoth on fire, and the sight of Helen coming back to consciousness . . . coming back to life.

Laemmle tapped Karl Freund, already famed internationally as a cinematographer, to direct *The Mummy*, and the choice was excellent. The picture was his directorial debut. The sets were designed by Willy Pogany and the music was composed by James Dietrich. The film was released in December 1932 and it was a box office success. It quickly became a horror classic in the formative years of that genre.[8]

The Mummy is one more example of an early supernatural romance—a *gothic* supernatural romance, or in cinematic terms a horror hybrid—that was in aesthetic terms an unqualified masterpiece. In the opinion of critic Pauline Kael,

> the lighting is so masterly and the moods are so effectively sustained that the picture gives one prickly sensations. . . . It's silly but it's also disturbingly beautiful. No other horror film has ever achieved so many effects by lighting; this inexpensively made film has a languorous, poetic feeling, and the eroticism that lives on under Karloff's wrinkled parchment skin is like a bad dream of undying love.[9]

Surely the sublimity of supernatural romance gave this horror film its special feeling.

The mythical method was at work in another supernatural romance from the 1930s, a film that will be considered at greater length in a subsequent chapter: the 1939 MGM film *On Borrowed Time*, which was based upon a 1937 novel by Lawrence Edward Watkin and the derivative 1938 play by Paul Osborn. *On Borrowed Time*, like *The Mummy*, uses classical themes in an offhand manner, in a fashion that is merely associative—or allusive, or in this case perhaps just a matter of coincidence. Nonetheless, the film is worthy of note since the issue at the center of its plot is a theme of ancient provenance.

Put briefly, this film is a fable in which an old man—making use of a magic wish that he receives in return for a good deed—finds a way to trap personified Death in the limbs of an apple tree. This feature of the plot is like the Irish folk tale of "drunk Jack" who traps the devil in a tree by carving a cross in the trunk.[10] But when *Death* is the one who gets trapped, the plot moves in a direction that was used for merely *comic* effect in *Death Takes a Holiday*: no one can die while the Reaper is out of commission. But the effect here is anything but comic. When other characters learn the uncanny truth (a doctor, for instance, who discovers that none of his mortally ill patients can die), they try to talk the old man into letting Death go, because he and countless others will confront a life of misery: their bodies will diminish and sicken without any hope for release from the agony.

As a plot situation, this is comparable to the myth of the Cumaean Sybil, as told in the *Metamorphoses* of Ovid and mentioned in passing within the *Satyricon* of Petronius. In return for her carnal favors, Apollo grants the Sybil the gift of prophecy and also the gift of immortality. But the Sybil never thinks to ask for the corollary favor of eternal youth.[11] In the *Satyricon*, one of the characters remarks that he had once seen "the Sybil at Cumae dangling in a bottle, and when some children asked her in Greek, 'What do you want, Sybil?' she used to answer, 'I want to die.'"[12] T. S. Eliot used that passage as his epigraph for *The Waste Land*.

Back to the movie. Realizing the truth, the old man releases Death, and in return he is promptly wafted into the Elysian Fields where he hears the voice of his deceased wife calling out to him.

Several other supernatural romances used the mythical method in subsequent decades. One classic love-and-death movie must also rank as a classic in the use of the method: *The Red Shoes* (1948). Granted, this love-and-death film does not involve the afterlife at all, though the presence of sinister magic in the story—hence the supernatural—is suggested. But since the film was made by Michael Powell and Emeric Pressburger, who a few years earlier produced an explicit love-death-afterlife film (*A Matter of Life and Death*), it seems appropriate to associate *Red Shoes* with the other films in this study. Regardless, *Red Shoes* employs the plot template of its namesake fairytale by Hans Christian Andersen on two levels.

It is the story of a ballerina (played by Moira Shearer) who is playing the lead in a new ballet that is based upon the Andersen fairytale. She is torn between her love for the man who composed the ballet's score (played by Marius Goring) and the impresario (played by Anton Walbrook) who will tolerate no romantic entanglements that might distract his performers and reduce (he thinks) the libidinous ardor that they bring to their artistic careers. She must make an all-or-nothing choice, he insists: she may allow herself to fall in love or else she must decide to stay focused and become the greatest dancer of the age.

At the film's conclusion, the heroine is conflicted. At the moment of crisis, she decides to go ahead with the performance, and then—in a brilliant sequence of close-ups and point-of-view shots—she looks down at her feet in red shoes and grasps the terrible truth: she is *in* the Andersen tale. She is trapped in a free-floating template of evil that repeats itself over time. She *has become* the girl who puts on a pair of diabolically enchanted red slippers, only to discover (1) that she can never take them off, and (2) that they will never let her stop dancing. So they dance her to death, and the character in the film dies a horrible death as well.[13]

Should a film such as this be related to the love-death-afterlife tradition? The point is arguable. But this love–death tale without question relates to the issues under study and it certainly exemplifies the mythical method—exemplifies the method to perfection. In his study of James Joyce's *Ulysses*, Stuart Gilbert (who met Joyce in Paris and talked with him at length) wrote that he was often asked the following question: "Did Joyce believe in theosophy, magic and so forth?"[14] The reason was simple: when readers grasped the fact that the template of *Ulysses* was the Odyssey rendered in the course of a single day in Dublin, they associated this fact with some hints from the text that the transmission of this archetypal plot was akin to reincarnation: the overall situation repeats itself in serial "incarnations" (like the Andersen fairytale). Consider the following hint in a conversation between two characters in *Ulysses*, Leopold and Molly Bloom. Molly has been reading a book in which she finds a word she doesn't understand. She asks her husband the meaning of "met him pike hoses," and he gently corrects her:

> "Metempsychosis?"
> "Yes. Who's he when he's at home?"
> "Metempsychosis," he said, frowning. "It's Greek: from the Greek. That means the transmigration of souls."[15]

This subliminal suggestion must be understood for what it was: a literary trick for creating in the mind of a reader the sense that a plot (as an *archetype*) can somehow travel through time by a supernatural process, forcing people to *act it out*. The concept of "archetypes" that subsist in the "collective unconscious" of humanity was a key to the psychological theories of Carl Jung. And Joyce made use of this idea in his final book *Finnegans Wake* (1939), which presents in a "dream language" the nocturnal circulation of archetypes that repeat themselves within the human mind in eternal recurrence. This idea became the basis for a play by Thornton Wilder: *The Skin Of Our Teeth* (1942).

Of course the theme of reincarnation could be understood in a simpler way: with Leopold Bloom as the reborn Odysseus himself. But in the case of characters from myth who may or may not have existed in real life—

and with characters from fiction like the girl in the Andersen fairytale who obviously never existed—the use of the plot structure as the entity that gets "reborn" is in fact much simpler.

The mythical method can also be shown to have played an important role in a film that is famous for reasons that appear to have nothing to do with supernatural romance: the Alfred Hitchcock classic, *Vertigo* (1958).

This iconic film is widely regarded as a masterwork to be understood on its own unique terms within the patterns of the Hitchcock oeuvre and also (at least to some extent) as an emanation of the film noir movement: a tale of a detective who is drawn into a vortex of murder and deceit that lays bare the possibilities of evil.

It is the story of a detective named Scotty Ferguson (played by James Stewart) who is hired by an old acquaintance to tail his wife Madeleine (played by Kim Novak), who according to the husband is possessed by the soul of "someone dead." This "someone" appears to be the ghost of the wife's great-grandmother, Carlotta, who killed herself a hundred years earlier. The husband fears that his wife, in the grip of this insane possession, may do the same thing. In the course of keeping track of this woman, the detective falls head over heels in love with her, but he loses her when she plunges to her death from a tower.

But it's a sham, for this is really a murder plot. The woman, an imposter who is dressed up to look like the real-life Madeleine, does not really jump: the whole thing has been a trick to convince the detective that the wife went crazy and killed herself. The truth is very different: the wife has been strangled and her husband throws her body from the tower. Then he and the imposter sneak away.

In any case, the detective sinks into a deep and clinical depression as he mourns his lost love. And then—in a chance occurrence, he encounters a woman who, if only her hair and her makeup and clothing could be altered, would pass for the living embodiment of Madeleine. At this point Scotty himself becomes possessed—by erotic agony (and ecstasy). He woos this woman and he dresses her up like a doll so she will look like Madeleine.

The moment when he succeeds is a magnificent resurrection scene, and Bernard Herrmann's score uses themes from the "liebestod" music of *Tristan und Isolde* for their maximum erotic effect.

This woman is of course the imposter, and her name is Judy Barton. And it turns out that Scotty's ardent love has been reciprocated by Judy in full: we learn that in the course of the plot she fell deeply in love with Scotty, but she found herself unable to withdraw from the murder pact in time. Now she hopes that Scotty will fall in love with her all over again— "for herself."

But he loves her as Madeleine, of course. And then she makes a fatal slip that gives the whole thing away. And so, Scotty, deeply angered, takes her back to the scene of the crime, and as they struggle and argue at the top of the tower, she slips and suddenly falls—in reality this time—to her death. That is the story of *Vertigo* as millions of moviegoers know it. But look at it for just a moment in a very different way: before the plot is revealed, this appears to be a gothic supernatural romance, a tale of love and death with a twist that intrudes from the afterlife, the possession of "Madeleine." Now look at what happens to Scotty: he thinks he has lost the great love of his life, and then he finds a way to . . . "raise her from the dead." And then he loses her . . . a second time.

This is nothing other than the myth of Orpheus and Euridice.

Orpheus, a gifted musician, was beside himself when his wife Euridice died. He descended to the underworld and charmed both Hades and Persephone into giving Euridice back, with this single proviso: he must not look behind him as he takes her. Here, in Riley's prose translation, is the text that was composed by Ovid:

> The ascending path is mounted in deep silence, steep, dark, and enveloped in deepening gloom. And *now* they were not far from the verge of the upper earth. He, enamoured, fearing lest she should flag, and impatient to behold her, turned his eyes; and immediately she sank back again. She, hapless one! both stretching out her arms, and struggling to be grasped, and to grasp him, caught nothing but the fleeting air. . . . No otherwise was Orpheus amazed at this twofold death of his wife; sorrow of mind and tears were his sustenance.[16]

Is the parallel here between the myth and Hitchcock's *Vertigo* coincidence? No, this was not a coincidence. *Vertigo* was based upon the novel *D'Entre les Morts* by Pierre Boileau and Thomas Narcejac. The first writer whom Hitchcock commissioned to produce a screenplay was Maxwell Anderson, who co-wrote the screenplay for *Death Takes a Holiday*. And in Anderson's screenplay, the detective carries a cigarette lighter with a simple inscription . . . "Eurydice."[17]

The myth of Orpheus and Euridice applies to one more cinematic supernatural romance, this one released a generation later in 1998: *What Dreams May Come*, starring Robin Williams and Annabella Sciorra. This film, to be considered at length in a subsequent chapter and appendix, is set largely in the afterlife. The gist of the connection is this: in the afterlife, a husband decides to rescue the soul of his wife, who has gone to hell as a suicide.

And he succeeds.

NOTES

1. Of course the application of ancient philosophic and literary legacies to latter-day doctrines and productions had been ongoing in Western thought. The actual connection between pagan religious ideas, Neo-Platonist philosophy, and other pagan influences with the formation of Christianity itself is well-known, and many themes from classical antiquity were carried directly forward through modification into the

Middle Ages. The rediscovery of Aristotelian philosophy in the thirteenth century and its assimilation into orthodox Christian theology by Thomas Aquinas and others is a good example of the conscious reapplication of ancient themes in Western culture, and so is the comparison of Roman politics and pagan civic ethics with latter-day Christian norms by writers such as Petrarch and Machiavelli. The rendering of Old Testament themes in the format of classical epic by John Milton is an example of ancient modes being renovated and conflated through revival. The ongoing seventeenth- and eight-eenth-century literary debate about the merits of the "ancients" versus the "mod-erns"—the issue, for example, of whether Shakespeare was a greater dramatist than the Greek tragedians and the question of whether his tragedies fell short by compari-son since they did not observe the "rules" set forth in Aristotle's *Poetics*, a debate that led to commentaries by John Dryden and Samuel Johnson—shows the ongoing cultu-ral connections between classical antiquity and modern intellectual life.

2. T. S. Eliot, "*Ulysses*, Order, and Myth," in *Selected Prose of T. S. Eliot*, Frank Kermode, ed. (New York: Harcourt Brace Jovanovich, and Farrar, Straus and Giroux, 1975), 177–78.

3. As was frequently the case, this mythology was engrafted later into Christian traditions: Minos appears in Dante's *Inferno*, and the Sistine Chapel ceiling mural of the Last Judgment by Michelangelo includes both Charon the boatman and Minos.

4. Ovid, *The Metamorphoses*, Book V, Henry T. Riley, trans. (London: George Bell & Sons, 1893), public domain, accessible via http://www.gutenberg.org/files/21765/21765-h/files/Met_IV-VII.html#bookV.

5. In an early draft of *Ulysses*, Joyce inserted episode titles that would guide the reader to their counterparts in Homer's Odyssey. But he decided to abandon this method as too "easy on the reader" for avant-garde fiction; consequently, readers of the book had to ferret out this pattern for themselves until the publication of *James Joyce's Ulysses* by Stuart Gilbert in 1930. Joyce allowed his readers only one clue: the title itself, *Ulysses*.

6. See Michael Brunas, John Brunas, and Tom Weaver, *Universal Horrors: The Stu-dio's Classic Films, 1931–1946* (Jefferson, NC: McFarland, 1990), 48–59; and Mark A. Vieira, *Hollywood Horror: From Gothic to Cosmic* (New York: Harry N. Abrams, 2003), 55–58.

7. Additional lines of great interest that were cut during production from the Balderston screenplay include the following. In a scene at the Cairo museum, Imhotep encounters Helen, who is admiring some jewels in the Anck-es-en-Amon collection. "I watched you admiring her jewels," he says. "Her *ka* may live today, in a body as beautiful as hers was in Old Egypt." Additional dialogue was cut from a scene in which Helen is possessed by the soul of the princess. Helen: "Are we in the kingdom of Set? Are we both dead?" Imhotep: "We *were* dead, we are alive again." John L. Balderston, *The Mummy* screenplay, quoted in Brunas, Brunas, and Weaver, *Universal Horrors*, 54, 55.

8. Published accounts of the production of *The Mummy* reveal that this project was fast-paced and arduous. Beginning in September 1932, the picture was shot in seven weeks and Freund drove his cast very hard. Zita Johann, the leading lady, recalled the experience with bitterness. The work was particularly hard on Boris Karloff, whose make-up, conceived by Jack Pierce, took eight hours to apply and then shooting would commence and continue all day. Sets were designed by Willy Pogany and studio shots were supplemented by location shots in the Mojave Desert. These scenes were inter-spliced by location shots in Egypt. The music was composed by James Dietrich. See Brunas, Brunas, and Weaver, *Universal Horrors*, 48–59; and Vieira, *Hollywood Horror*, 55–58.

9. Pauline Kael, *5001 Nights at the Movies* (New York: Henry Holt, 1991), 501.

10. I am indebted to my student Nathaniel Ford for calling my attention to this tale.

11. Ovid, *The Metamorphoses*, Book XIV.

12. Petronius, *The Satyricon*, J. P. Sullivan, trans. (London and New York: Viking Penguin, 1965), 1986 edition, 67. A written introduction that follows the opening cred-

its of the film claims the story was inspired by Chaucer, but this connection was in fact less significant as provenance. But for what it is worth, here it is: the "Pardoner's Tale" in the *Canterbury Tales* concerns some drunks who vow to track down Death and kill him. They have heard that he resides under an oak tree, but they never find him. Instead, they wind up killing each other.

13. On *The Red Shoes*, see Mark Connelly, *The Red Shoes* (London: I.B. Tauris, 2005); and Scott Salwolke, *The Films of Michael Powell and the Archers* (Lanham, MD: Scarecrow Press, 1997). In 1934, Alexander Korda decided to make a film about Nijinsky and the Ballet Russe; he intended the film to be a vehicle for Merle Oberon. Emeric Pressburger worked out a preliminary treatment for Korda in 1937, but then Korda delayed the project for a number of reasons. During World War II, Pressburger and his new partner Michael Powell negotiated with Korda to buy the rights to the project and they finally succeeded in 1946. They also got financial backing from J. Arthur Rank. The film that resulted was so avant garde in Rank's opinion that he worried about its prospects and released it in Great Britain with little fanfare on September 6, 1948. The film got good reviews—Dilys Powell called it "an extreme pleasure"—but much greater success awaited it in the United States, where it became a highbrow sensation. Bosley Crowther told readers of the *New York Times* that "this is a film you must see." Over the years *The Red Shoes* has become a cult classic and an impressive literature on the film has been produced. Connelly has proclaimed that the film "expanded the boundaries of cinematic invention and created unforgettable images that have left a lasting legacy on cinema." Connelly, *Red Shoes*, 3. As usual, however, disparaging critics are not hard to find, and Pauline Kael declared decades later that the film was "blubbery and self-conscious. . . . It affects some people *passionately*, and it's undeniably some kind of classic. Written, produced, and directed by Michael Powell and Emeric Pressburger, master purveyors of high kitsch." Kael, *5001 Nights at the Movies*, 621. This latter comment in relation to the range of critical views about the movie—some regarded it as avant garde while others have derided it as the opposite, kitsch (albeit "high kitsch")—is a commentary on the cultural politics of avant-gardism among the literary and artistic intelligentsia. Many forms of romance, including supernatural romance, have been dead on arrival with certain types of self-advertised sophisticates due to the issue of "sentimentalism." And "the sentimental," as such, at least among some people, is in its nature a symptom of intellectual (if not mental) weakness. Supernatural romances in the 1990s proved especially vulnerable to such high disdain. The cultural politics concerning these issues reaches back at least as far as mid-nineteenth-century attacks on "kitsch" (denoting vulgarity) by German art critics and the related invocation of the term (and concept) of "philistinism" in England by Thomas Carlyle and Matthew Arnold as a means of attacking anti-intellectualism—and also as a ploy of one-up-manship. This polemical tradition advanced steadily in intellectual culture with the publication in 1915 of Van Wyck Brooks's essay "America's Coming of Age." This essay introduced the terms "highbrow" and "lowbrow" to the culture wars. "Middlebrow" was added to the terminology a decade or so later by Virginia Woolf and then developed further by Dwight MacDonald in his 1960 essay "Masscult and Mid-Cult." Susan Sontag's "Notes on Camp" (1964) advanced the tradition even further. Related to this trend was the very long artistic tradition of glorifying (directly or indirectly) the absurd as a criterion of sophistication. This tradition became an important component of modernism, though it also has to be noted that a countertendency of rationalism was present as well. Le Corbusier's architectural polemics in the 1920s exemplified both tendencies. So did Dadaism, whose participants (at least some of the time) declared that they were deliberately using absurdity to expose the deeper absurdity of social arrangements that masqueraded as rational. The chapter on "Embracing the Absurd" in Jacques Barzun's *From Dawn to Decadence* (2000) is an illuminating example of the vast literature on these subjects.

14. Stuart Gilbert, *James Joyce's Ulysses* (New York: Random House, 1930), 1958 Vintage edition, viii.

15. James Joyce, *Ulysses* (1918) (New York: Vintage, 1961), 64.

16. Ovid, *The Metamorphoses*, Book X, public domain, accessible via http://www. gutenberg.org/files/26073/26073-h/Met_VIII-XI.html#bookX_fableI.

17. Dan Auiler, *Vertigo: The Making of a Hitchcock Classic* (New York: St. Martin's Press, 1998), 33–34. For commentary on the proposition that "*Vertigo* is devoted to the dream of re-animating the dead," see Robert Baird, "*Vertigo*: Love, Desire, and the Grave," http://imagesjournal.com/issue02/features/vertport.htm. Anderson's screenplay (produced in 1956) proved unsatisfactory in some respects, and so Hitchcock recruited playwright Alec Coppel to produce a second one. This too proved less than satisfactory, so Hitchcock brought in third playwright, Samuel Taylor, to revise the existing script.

FOUR

Berkeley Square and the Philosophic Problem of Time

Berkeley Square was an extremely important supernatural romance, not only because of its influence on subsequent productions — *Brigadoon* (both the play and the film), *Portrait of Jennie*, and *Somewhere in Time* — but also for its treatment of a metaphysical issue that is important in and of itself: the problem of time. In *Death Takes a Holiday*, personified Death introduces himself as "the point of contact between eternity and time." But what is "eternity?"

And what is time?

Eternity could be defined as an unending sequence of duration. It could also be construed as "timelessness" — atemporality — a realm in which no such thing as "before and after" exists. We, who have been born into a world of *becoming*, cannot *experience* a state of "timelessness," though we can articulate the concept as an abstraction. Whether this abstraction in any way corresponds with a state that is metaphysically "real" is a tantalizing question.

In *Berkeley Square*, Peter Standish says that "real Time with a capital T is nothing but an idea in the mind of God." This is the conclusion of a longer observation by simile: time as we experience it, says Standish, is like a stream. We are floating down this stream in a boat, and the things that we see on the banks of the stream pass along in a sequence of past, present, and future. But to a man in an airplane looking down on the stream, this sequence can be seen as "all one." He can see it "all at once."

This is an apt distillation of a venerable doctrine of metaphysical theology, one that can be traced all the way to St. Augustine, who wrote that God is "outside time in eternity."[1] St. Thomas Aquinas reached the same conclusion centuries later. God, he wrote, "stands on the summit of eternity where everything exists together, looking down in a single simple glance on the whole course of time."[2]

But St. Augustine, who wrote with such assurance in regard to "eternity," confessed that he was mystified when he contemplated the nature of time as process and thing:

> What is time? I know well enough what it is, provided that nobody asks me; but if I am asked and try to explain it, I am baffled. . . . How can . . . the past and future, *be,* when the past is no longer and the future is not yet? If the future and the past do exist, I want to know where they are. . . . We measure time while it is passing. . . . But while we are measuring it, where is it coming from, what is it passing through, and where is it going? It can only be coming from the future, passing through the present, and going into the past. In other words, it is coming out of what does not yet exist, passing through what has no duration, and moving into what no longer exists. . . . My mind is burning to solve this intricate puzzle. O Lord my God, good Father, it is a problem at once so familiar and mysterious. . . . Through Christ I beseech you, do not keep it hidden away but make it clear to me.[3]

Among the pre-Socratic philosophers, the time problem framed the famous dispute between Heraclitus—who argued that change and becoming were the essence of reality—and Parmenides, who insisted that the ontic pattern of "becoming" conceals an underlying unity of "being," wherefore "becoming" is illusion.[4] This dispute has extended itself into modern times, with Friedrich Nietzsche, for example, defending Heraclitus, and Martin Heidegger showing at least an affinity for Parmenides.

Immanuel Kant, in his *Critique of Pure Reason*, tried to argue that time is an inner mental state: "Time is nothing but a form of inner sense," he wrote; as to "objects as they may be in themselves, then time is nothing."[5] This position was taken up more emphatically by Arthur Schopenhauer, who insisted that time is an illusion.

Other philosophers—and scientists—treated time as a macro-cosmic force, as our own commonsense might lead us to believe. But there is nothing commonsensical about the malleability of time as Albert Einstein explained it in his theories of relativity. His theory of special relativity (1905) argued that space and time were mutable structures whose nature depends upon one's state of motion. His theory of general relativity (1915) argued that time can curve or warp in response to other forces.

As Sigmund Freud was an iconic figure in the early twentieth century, so was Einstein, whose influence prompted many to reexamine their commonsense notions of time. And several theories of time developed by early twentieth-century philosophers correlate with the presentation of time in such supernatural romances as *Brigadoon, Portrait of Jennie,* and *Somewhere in Time.* They correlate because they treat the concept and the manifestations of time as *malleable.*

Berkeley Square was roughly contemporaneous with the appearance (in German) of Heidegger's philosophic classic *Sein und Zeit* (*Being and Time*), which was published in 1927. In this difficult and paradoxical work, the philosopher struggles to define the nature of "being," and his exploration flows predictably toward the nature (and mystery) of time.

Heidegger wrote about the "ordinary understanding" of time, which consists of "a flowing stream of 'nows.'"[6] Heidegger called this experience the phenomenon of "within-timeness." He acknowledged its genuineness, within limits, as an ontological truth. But he also argued that this "ordinary" experience of time is derivative from a larger and more mysterious "primordial temporality."

This temporality, he theorized, is more flexible than our conventional experience of time permits us to understand clearly. But its nature may be grasped through paradox. Past, present, and future are modal "ecstases," or outward projections, of temporality, which can manifest itself in different "horizons." It bears noting that "horizon" for Heidegger denoted a situation where a thing is half-revealed and half-hidden.

As Heidegger neared the completion of his volume, the time problem loomed ever larger to him as the key to the mystery of being. "Does time itself manifest itself as the horizon of Being," he asked in the final sentence of the book.[7]

But *Sein und Zeit* is a truncated work—an uncompleted study—for its author never crossed the next horizon. He had planned another section of the book that would develop the relationship between Being and primordial time. Yet he had reached the outer limit of his own conceptual powers. So he simply . . . stopped.

Contemporaneous with both *Berkeley Square* and *Sein und Zeit* was a metaphysical treatise by Alfred North Whitehead, *Process and Reality*, published in 1929. Like Heidegger, Whitehead treated time as a genuine cosmic force and he viewed it as malleable. And he also generated paradoxes. As Heidegger had written that "temporality" could "temporalize different ways of itself," Whitehead wrote that "physical time" was not the sole channel for development. He argued that "creative advance" in the cosmos is not just "serial advance." "Genetic passage from phase to phase is not in physical time," he wrote; "Physical time expresses some features of the growth, but not the growth of the features. . . . Each phase of the process presupposes the entire quantum."[8]

In 1927, an Irish engineer named John William Dunne published *An Experiment with Time*.[9] This book theorized that past, present, and future relate to each other in a manner very different from the simple arrow of time that we experience.[10] Like Baldsteron's Peter Standish—like St. Thomas Aquinas—he saw them present "all at once." The psychic power of mind, he believed, could access other temporality (he claimed to have experienced precognition). He also developed a doctrine called "serialism" suggesting that the same events are always present in other channels of temporality. He wrote that time has multiple dimensions that "cross" each other to infinity. A brief quotation from his popular account *Nothing Dies* (1940) provides a sample of his doctrine:

> What *has been* in time 1 must remain unchanged, though present, throughout the eternity of time 2. Nothing which has been passed by the time 1 "now-mark" dies in real time. A rose which has bloomed once blooms forever.[11] (original emphasis)

Among those influenced by Dunne was the novelist and playwright J. B. Priestley. In a series of "time plays," such as *Time and the Conways* (1937), he inserted into his dramas the doctrine that the past, the present, and the future are co-present. Another Priestley "time play," *I Have Been Here Before*, explores the relationship between precognition and déjà vu.

The doctrines of Dunne were contemporaneous with—and can be correlated with—a mystical cult that was created by a Russo-Greek-Armenian, George Ivanovich Gurdjieff (1866–1949). This cult, which drew upon a number of ideas from the "hermetic" tradition, developed an international influence that became quite significant by the 1920s.[12] Gurdjieff and his followers called their doctrines "the Work," and these doctrines unfolded in different ways in the books of different disciples. One of these disciples, Peter D. Ouspensky (1878–1947), a Russian writer, developed a theory of three-dimensional time and a new variation on a very old philosophic idea: "eternal recurrence."[13] The doctrines of Ouspensky were comparable in some respects to those of Dunne, except that in Dunne's system the dimensions of time (and space) were *infinite*.[14]

Enough: having set the conceptual stage in this manner, we will now examine some flexible treatments of time in supernatural romance.

Alan Jay Lerner, in collaboration with composer Frederick Lowe, created the musical play *Brigadoon* in the middle of the 1940s. After opening on March 13, 1947, it ran for 581 performances at the Ziegfeld Theatre on Broadway. *Brigadoon* tells the story of an American, Tommy Albright, who goes hunting in the Scottish highlands with his buddy Jeff Douglas. The men get lost, and then they encounter a town that is not on any of their maps, the town of Brigadoon. Tommy, who has been postponing his marriage, experiences love at first sight when he encounters a beauty named Fiona Campbell.

But there is a problem. The town of Brigadoon is enchanted. Tommy and Jeff have noticed that the town's inhabitants are dressed in eighteenth-century attire, and then they learn the reason: Brigadoon is in fact an eighteenth-century town that is floating through time and space. It appears only once, and for just one day, every hundred years. Then it vanishes, and its inhabitants sleep in some half-way holding pattern, in a different channel of time that exists "between the mist and the stars," between heaven and us, and every morning, when they all wake up, it is a hundred years later.

Tommy is in love with Fiona, but he has to make up his mind and do it quickly: will he stay in Brigadoon, which will vanish at nightfall, to be with this exquisite woman, thus giving up his life, his family, and his friends in the twentieth century? Or will he walk away from the town and, after watching it vanish, live in agony?

Though the afterlife is not present in this story, Brigadoon is in many ways a surrogate for heaven, or at least a vivid foretaste of heaven, where, in order to experience bliss, you must give up your earthly connections.[15]

Tommy walks away from the town: the whole thing has happened too fast. He goes back to New York and lives in agony. But his agony prompts him to return to the Scottish highlands, where he broods one night upon the emptiness of the valley that contained Brigadoon. And then, through a miracle, the town of Brigadoon reappears in the mist, and its inhabitants awaken (for once in the middle of the night). Fiona has been lost to Tommy, just as lost as if she had been dead. But love (once again) conquers death (or a surrogate for death), and both Fiona and the town are resurrected, if only for a moment, so that Tommy can enter and join them.

The Broadway production starred David Brooks as Tommy and Marion Bell as Fiona. The choreography was by Agnes de Mille.[16] Critics liked the play; Ward Morehouse wrote in the *New York Sun* that *Brigadoon* was "a stunning show" with "whimsy, beguiling music, exciting dancing . . . by far the best musical play the season has produced."[17]

Critic George Jean Nathan suggested that Lerner was inspired by a German story by Friedrich Gerstäcker, a tale about the town of Germelshausen that is cursed and will appear only one day every hundred years.[18] Lerner protested that the resemblance between the two stories was coincidence.[19]

Regardless, it seems likely that Lerner was also influenced, perhaps unconsciously, by *Berkeley Square*. In both cases a protagonist is wafted into an eighteenth-century setting where he meets the great love of his life and then loses her when he returns to his own time and place. Of course there were differences. In Lerner's version, the story has a definite happy ending: we see the couple reunited, instead of contenting ourselves with the happy presumption that all will be resolved in the afterlife. And in Lerner's version, the time-travel feature of *Berkeley Square* is changed: in this case the past *comes to us* because a part of it is lifted out of its preexisting time channel and placed in a different concurrent channel—a channel that interpenetrates our own sequence of "within-timeness" once a century.[20]

The film version of *Brigadoon* was produced by MGM, and the studio chiefs were determined at the outset that Gene Kelly would play Tommy Albright. Cyd Charisse was cast as Fiona. But when Louis B. Mayer retired in 1951, his successor, Dore Schary, instituted a frugality regime at

MGM. This meant that location shooting in Scotland was rejected; all the colorful highland scenes would be created as sets on the MGM lot. Ansco Color was used, along with the wide-screen dimensions of CinemaScope. The director was Vincente Minnelli.

When the film was released on September 8, 1954, it got mixed reviews. Some critics complained (justifiably) that some memorable dance numbers had been cut. And the aesthetics of the sets (created by Cedric Gibbons and Preston Ames) and the CinemaScope format (the cinematographer was Joseph Ruttenberg) were sometimes criticized. Kelly, who had scouted scenes for location shooting in Scotland, was disappointed, complaining that "it could have been magical, and in the old days, it would have been." [21] Kelly biographer Clive Hirshhorn has written that "Schary's decision to confine *Brigadoon* to a sound stage was, unfortunately, a bad one." [22] Pauline Kael opined later on that "CinemaScope . . . for dance in studio settings was disastrous." [23] Others have been more charitable; Michael Dunne has argued that "the CinemaScope camera encourages the kind of across-the-screen dancing best suited to Kelly's style." [24]

Assessment of the film on aesthetic grounds must remain a matter of taste, but one dance number—"Heather on the Hill"—exemplifies "across-the-screen dancing" magnificently, and its subtle eroticism blends with an interplay of lyrics and sets, as when a line in the song about the clouds "holding still" is compared to the threatening weather held at bay beyond the line of mountains in the distance.

Before leaving *Brigadoon*, it would be useful to examine its explicitly religious component. The miracle of Brigadoon was commanded by God, at the behest of the town's Presbyterian minister. In the course of the story, we (along with Tommy) learn that a roving band of highland witches had made the minister of the kirk, Mr. Forsythe, fear for the safety of his flock. Mr. Lundie, the Brigadoon schoolmaster, tells Tommy exactly what Forsythe decided to do:

> Then one day he came to me and told me that he had decided to ask God for a miracle. And on an early Wednesday morning, right after midnight, he went out to a hill beyond Brigadoon and made his prayer to God. And there in the hush of a sleeping world he asked God that night to make Brigadoon and all the people in it vanish into the highland mist—vanish—but not for always. They would return, just as they were, for one day every hundred years. The people would lead their customary lives; but every day when they awoke it would be a hundred years later. And when we awoke next day—it *was* a hundred years later.

Mr. Forsythe must have seen his town vanish, but he had to stay behind. Divine blessings, after all—read the Old Testament—must often be procured by a sacrifice, and Mr. Forsythe's sacrifice was to lose his

church and congregation. The sacrifice also encompasses the people of
the town: if any of them dares to leave, the enchantment will be broken
for all and Brigadoon will "disappear forever." And that is why Fiona
cannot consider the possibility of leaving Brigadoon with Tommy Albright.

But Forsythe's prayer made provision for people in the future who
might wander into the town and fall in love: they can stay if they love
someone enough to "give up everything," explains Mr. Lundie.

The film *Portrait of Jennie* employs the same device of concurrent and
interpenetrating time channels. But the device is more startling this time
and the film involves the afterlife directly.

Portrait of Jennie was based upon a 1940 novel of the same name by
Robert Nathan. Producer David O. Selznick bought the rights in 1944 and
he commissioned a screenplay that was written by Peter Berneis and Paul
Osborn, who had previously turned the story of novelist Lawrence Edward Watkin into the stage version of *On Borrowed Time*. This screenplay
would be revised in the course of shooting, not least of all because Selznick took a strong interest in the picture.

Selznick tapped William Dieterle as director. Joseph August was cinematographer and the music by Dimitri Tiomkin included Debussy
themes and a short but memorable composition by Bernard Herrmann.
Shooting began in December 1946 and the film was released on Christmas Day 1948.

The film tells the story of an artist, Eben Adams (played by Joseph
Cotten), who is desperately trying to pay the rent and put food on the
table in Depression-era New York. One day, in the wintertime at dusk, he
meets a quaint and charming girl named Jennie Appleton (played by
Jennifer Jones) in Central Park. She regales him with childish chatter. But
she seems to be living in the past; she says that her parents are acrobats at
a vaudeville theater that was torn down years ago. She thinks that the
Kaiser is "king of Germany." She sings a song, *Where I Come From, Nobody
Knows*. She says that she hopes her new acquaintance Eben Adams will
wait for her as she strives to grow up quickly so they can be together.
Then she darts down a lane and is gone.

Eben talks to some people who worked in the old vaudeville theater
and they remember Jennie. They reveal that her parents were killed years
earlier when they fell from the tightrope.

The gist of the plot is quite simple: Jennie shows up (when Eben least
expects it) in successive appearances and each time Eben encounters her
she is older and more beautiful. She thanks him for waiting as she tries to
grow up fast. In one of her appearances (Eben encounters her again in
Central Park), she is weeping because she says her parents have *just been
killed*. She says an aunt is going to send her away to a convent school—
and Eben visits her there. The incipient romance emerges full-blown:

they are in love. She says she will marry him when she returns from a summer vacation with the aunt.

The truth: Jennie is a ghost. When she fails to return, Eben visits the convent school and he learns from one of the nuns (played by none other than Lillian Gish) that Jennie died years ago: she was killed in a tidal wave near a lighthouse, the Land's End Light, in New England. The nun says that in her very last letter Jennie poured out her fear that she would never find love in this life.

Adams notices the fact that the anniversary of Jennie's death is a few days off. So he takes a train to New England, rents a boat, sails out to the Land's End Light—and sure enough, a huge storm shapes up, Jennie makes an appearance in a sailboat, the two of them meet upon the rocky island where the Land's End Light (abandoned) awaits them, and Jennie gets swept away (*again*) by the tidal wave, but before she goes she tells Eben they will be together in eternity.

This film makes a vivid and self-conscious statement of the time problem. At the very beginning of the movie, a spoken prologue contains this statement: "Since time began, man has looked into the awesome reaches

Figure 4.1. Joseph Cotten and Jennifer Jones played star-crossed lovers in *Portrait of Jennie*, a 1948 film about an artist named Eben Adams who falls in love with a girl named Jennie Appleton, the incarnate apparition of a woman who died years before. Courtesy of Photofest.

of infinity, and asked the eternal question: What is time? What is life? What is death? . . . Science tells us that nothing ever dies but only changes, that time itself does not pass but curves around us, and that the past and the future are together at our side forever." The allusions not only to Einstein and his theory of general relativity ("time curves") but also to Dunne and his doctrines are absolutely clear, right down to a salute to one of Dunne's book titles: *Nothing Dies*.

All through the film this theme is manipulated for effect. At the convent school, Jennie says, "How beautiful the world is, Eben. The sun goes down in the same lovely sky, just as it did yesterday and will tomorrow." Eben: "When is tomorrow, Jennie?" Jennie: "Does it matter? It's always. This was tomorrow once."

In the death scene at the lighthouse, she says that "time made an error" that the two of them have finally corrected. They are together— however briefly—in this world, as they were destined to be. And they will be together in eternity. "We're just beginning," she says, "it's all right, whatever happens, we'll have all eternity together. There is no life, my darling, until you have loved and been loved, and then there is no death." Then she says, "from world's end to world's end" there is only one love for us.

Figure 4.2. An aerial image of New York City which, in an early scene from *Portrait of Jennie*, appears as part of a supernal background to a spoken prologue exploring metaphysical mysteries. Courtesy of Photofest.

So: Jennie was deprived of Eben's love—a love that she was destined to have—before she died. She says that "time made an error" somehow (an important doctrine, to be considered later in the book). To correct it, the spirit of Jennie, from a "holding pattern," is projected back into the world. She comes in episodes, so that she and Eben get a tantalizing sample of what might have been. And their situation will all be straightened out in the afterlife, where everything is put right forever.

Eben Adams exists in a conventional sequence of temporality. But this sequence is altered when a different temporal process *interpenetrates* it. This occurs every time the spirit of Jennie comes back. She is something of a time traveler: she brings with her the template of the life she already had. And then she gets to live it over again (episodically), but this time something is different: Eben is with her, as he should have been the first time.

This film is a controversial item among the critics. It was not a commercial success, and some have complained that the movie was a mess, not least of all because Selznick was having an affair with Jennifer Jones at the time (he later married her after his divorce from Irene Mayer Selznick) and because of this relationship he kept interfering in production in a manner that infuriated everyone. Selznick biographer David Thomson proclaimed that Selznick was "not the film's ideal maker" and that *Portrait of Jennie* is "a confused movie . . . pretentious and foolish."[25]

Here again, the subjective nature of criticism is laid bare by the opinions of those who have reached the opposite conclusion. In his comparative study of ghosts in literature and film, Lee Kovacs has written that "*Portrait of Jennie* is a work that translated beautifully from novel to film."[26] Many scenes are exquisite, especially the wintertime encounters in Central Park, and the shift in the hurricane scenes from black-and-white to a green tinting is startling—in the very best sense. The sped-up view of the inverted storm clouds descending conveys monstrousness in a way that is nothing short of brilliant.

Joseph August was nominated for a (posthumous) academy award for his cinematography, and the score (in effect a collaboration between Tiomkin and Herrmann, the two most accomplished film score composers at the time) is extremely effective.

Before we leave *Portrait of Jennie*, we should consider its religious implication. The scenes at the convent school are developed with great delicacy and care. Jennie says she feels peaceful—and that she understands her situation much better—in this quiet and meditative place. Eben soliloquizes: as the wind blows and as the sea flows, God knows the truth about their fate.

The film *Somewhere in Time* shows the very clear influence of *Berkeley Square*. The film was inspired by a 1975 novel by Richard Matheson, *Bid Time Return*, and the novel makes an explicit reference to *Berkeley Square* and its theme.[27] *Bid Time Return* tells the story of a man who (significantly) has a terminal illness. This man, Richard Collier, visits a historic hotel where he sees a photograph of an actress from the 1890s that obsesses him. Using "psychic projection"—an idea that was directly inspired by the writings of Priestley according to the novel—he projects himself into her time dimension and they fall in love.[28] But then he loses her when he is wrenched back into his previous channel of time.

Producer Stephen Deutsch came across the book and approached Matheson in 1976. It took them three years to sell the project to Universal, but they did. Jeannot Szwarc directed the resulting film, and Matheson wrote the screenplay. The music was composed by John Barry, who employed a theme from Rachmaninoff. The film was released in 1980 as *Somewhere in Time*. Deutsch, who changed his name later to Stephen Simon (for reasons to be explained in a subsequent chapter and appendix), was destined to collaborate on another supernatural romance with Matheson in the 1980s and 1990s: *What Dreams May Come*.[29]

Somewhere in Time begins in the early 1970s at a Midwestern college. The scene is the opening night of a play written by a gifted student, Richard Collier (played by Christopher Reeve). During the reception, an elderly woman approaches Collier and hands him a beautiful silver pocket watch. "Come back to me," she whispers.

The action fast-forwards several years to show Collier an accomplished playwright in Chicago. But he is at loose ends for some reason. He takes a break and drives north in a sports car to revisit his old college haunts. On the way, he sees a sign for the Grand Hotel, an illustrious and historic hotel near the college that he always meant to explore, but never did. (The hotel that was used in the film was the 1887 Grand Hotel on Mackinac Island in Michigan). He decides to stay there.

Killing time before dinner, he wanders into a room with museum displays. Then . . . he has a mystical experience—a psychic experience—he feels an ineffable "force" reaching out to him, and pivots to behold . . . a picture of a woman from the early twentieth century, a portrait on the wall. And we can tell right away: this is the most angelic face he has ever seen.

He is obsessed—he tosses and turns that night in consternation. This woman is the love of his life, but he never ever met her and she probably died long ago.

He investigates, and ascertains that the woman was Elise McKenna (played by Jane Seymour), an actress who had visited the hotel in 1912. He immerses himself in old books and periodicals at the local library. In a journal he encounters an article about McKenna. There is a picture of her that was taken just before she died. The picture shows the elderly woman who gave him the watch.

Through a complicated sequence of events, he learns (from a former philosophy professor at his college) about the theory that "psychic projection" might propel his consciousness into another time channel. It is

Figure 4.3. Richard Collier, played by Christopher Reeve in the 1980 film *Somewhere in Time*, falls in love with a picture of the long-deceased Elise McKenna, played by Jane Seymour. Profoundly influenced by *Berkeley Square*, this film presents yet another poignant time travel romance that gets resolved in the end, after death, in the cloudy middle distance of the afterlife. Courtesy of Photofest.

just a theory, but the key is to hypnotize himself into believing it. So he buys a turn-of-the-century suit, puts 1912 money in his pocket, strips his room of anything that could remind him of the times in which he has been living, and gives it a try. It doesn't work.

But then, browsing in the museum display room, he sees old guest registers, and it suddenly dawns on him that he should find the ones from 1912. He does . . . and there, on one of the signature lines, is his signature. So his mind can now relax in a spell of confidence and certitude. He conducts the experiment again, and it works. He is in 1912 at the Grand Hotel and he meets and woos Elise McKenna, who adores him.

But the miracle ends, as it did in *Berkeley Square*. After making love, they are sitting on the floor in their pajamas, laughing and joking in a mood of sweet contentment. She asks what time it is, and he hands her the silver pocket watch. She jokes some more and she tells him that she needs to buy him a brand new suit since the one he has been wearing is ten years out of date. He laughs and tells her what a great suit it is, with so many pockets, all sorts of pockets, including a coin pocket out of which he pulls a coin . . . from 1979.

As the camera pulls backward, we see what he sees in a point of view shot: the room swiftly diminishes into darkness as the wormhole sucks him back to "the future," which is to say back to his earlier dimension. The face of Elise, showing fear and horrid shock, diminishes as well.

He wakes up shattered, and, finding himself unable to return to 1912, he just sits in his hotel room, determined to end it all. He starves himself to death. And then . . . the camera takes our gaze toward the ceiling, where an "out of body" experience lifts the consciousness of Richard to a cloudy nexus, where Elise is waiting for him.[30]

The critics panned this film; Vincent Canby of the *New York Times* wrote that it deserved a prize as the "big screen romance with the highest giggle content," that it "did for time-travel what the Hindenburg did for dirigibles."[31] But the film developed a cult following as it made the rounds of cable television in the 1980s. A viewer named Bill Shepard created a global affinity group, INSITE—International Network of *Somewhere in Time* Enthusiasts—that to this day hosts an annual *Somewhere in Time* weekend at the Grand Hotel.

It is hard to watch this movie today without wondering what possessed Vincent Canby and like-minded critics to dish out such scorn as they reviewed this film: *Somewhere in Time* possesses grandeur, a handsomeness of imagery, that perhaps was just dead on arrival with avant-garde critics at the time. But avant-garde standards are demonstrably transient. As to the plot—and the issue of its logic or illogic—the time travel theme can be construed as metaphysically suggestive rather than silly. It all depends upon the viewer's expectations and sensibilities.

There is a fundamental difference between *Berkeley Square* and *Somewhere in Time*: whereas the symbolic talisman of *Berkeley Square*, the *crux ansata*, stays put within the Standish residence, the corresponding talisman of *Somewhere in Time*, the silver pocket watch, changes hands between Richard and Elise. Elise, like Helen Pettigrew, comes to realize (in this case after her lover's disappearance) that she fell in love with a man from the future, so she scans the horizon later on in life for a glimpse of the young man she knew. When she finds him in the 1970s, she gives him the watch, says "come back to me" and . . . dies. Richard, after joining the youthful Elise, gives the watch to her, and she has it in her hands when the fatal accident occurs.[32]

This, together with the plot device of having Richard see his own signature in a guest register from 1912—a signature that could only have been written long before he was born—creates a circular plot: this story has no beginning.[33] During the 1991 *Somewhere in Time* weekend, Richard Matheson was asked the question: where did the watch come from? According to one account on the INSITE Web site, here was his answer: "At one of the early meetings over script changes, he [Matheson] tossed out the idea of an elderly Elise showing up to give him the watch, and as soon as he said it, he realized that it would cause a loop, that it would have no beginning. But it was too late, the others loved the idea, he couldn't retract it, and it was in to stay. It became a gag of sorts even during filming . . . with Jeannot [Szwarc] wearing a T-shirt that read, 'Ask me about the watch,' and Richard [Matheson] wearing one that read, 'What watch?'" [34]

Because of this plot complication, the time travel template of *Somewhere in Time* creates a twist with a very different precedent: the doctrine of eternal recurrence, though the film presents its own distinct version of the flexible idea.

In most versions of "eternal recurrence"—a doctrine of Pythagoras and others that Nietzsche revived—the cosmic cycle repeats itself forever. ("From world's end to world's end" was the way that Jennie Appleton put it.) But the pattern of recurrence in *Somewhere in Time* is very different: it suggests that every moment is *constantly* repeating in a never-ending pattern of flow. The notion is comparable to—and yet still not exactly the same as—the doctrines of some of the esoteric thinkers who contributed to the "Work" (Ouspensky, for instance, theorized that after we die we live the same life over again).

Elise dies after giving the watch back to Richard Collier. She had known him in 1912, yet the man to whom she is giving the watch had not been born yet in 1912. Through eternal recurrence, the man to whom she gives the watch will *become* the young man whom she remembers, in the very same manner that the young Elise who loses her lover will *become* the old woman with the watch. The story has no beginning.

It is constantly in motion—and constantly repeating itself—in a loop.

And it has to keep happening—every single instant—to work. [35] Every part of this story has *happened already*, as when Richard, when he sees his own signature from out of the past, sees a signature written before he was born. And this signature would have to have been written by an *earlier* version of Richard—would it not?—in the very same manner that the Richard who will travel back to 1912 will write *another* signature which, in the loop of repetition, yet *another* iteration of "Richard" will behold in the future. [36]

Each phase of this ongoing story is repeating a sequence that already happened. And a newer iteration of the very same sequence must be coming along right behind it. And there's a loop in this channel—a loop through which it doubles back forever.

Is this correct?

Attempts to successfully trace out the patterns of the time channel lead to paradox and nothing more. Or perhaps they lead straight to the doctrine that "Elise" and "Richard" are aggregates of multiple "selves," arranged seriatim in the channel and linked by the spiraling loop. They are "events"—these people are nothing less than pure *events*—in rhythmic repetition.

Perhaps it's all sorted out after death.

In the meantime, can any of us give a satisfactory account of what happened to the self that we experienced a brief moment ago? Is it "back there?" Did it perish? We are far from being able to give a satisfactory account of what time really is.

Any more than we can give a satisfactory account of what we ourselves really are.

NOTES

1. Saint Augustine, *Confessions*, R. S. Pine-Coffin, trans. (Harmondsworth and New York: Penguin, 1961), 253.

2. Thomas Aquinas, *Selected Philosophical Writings*, Timothy McDermott, trans. (Oxford and New York: Oxford University Press, 1993), *In Aristotelis Librum Peri Hermeneias*, 282.

3. Saint Augustine, *Confessions*, 264–70.

4. Conceptual thinking at the cutting edge of modern physics is flirting with notions that are comparable with the doctrine of Parmenides, at least in some respects. Physicist Brian Greene, in his book *The Elegant Universe*, has written that many physicists suspect the existence of "raw state" of the universe in which "there is no realization of space or time," but from which the space-time fabric somehow emanates. Greene acknowledges the obvious when he states that "we run up against a clash of paradigms when we try to envision a universe that *is*, but that somehow does not invoke the concepts of space or time." Nonetheless, he continues, the human mind may very well have to cope with such problems if continued scientific investigation tends to "show that space, time, and, by association, dimension are not essential defining elements of the universe," but rather "convenient notions that emerge from a more basic, atavistic, and primary state." Brian Greene, *The Elegant Universe: Superstrings, Hidden Dimensions, and the Quest for the Ultimate Theory* (New York: Random House, 1999), 2000 Vintage edition, 378–79. For meditations by a nuclear physicist on the convergence of scientific and religious thinking in regard to the problem of time, see Lawrence Fagg, *Two Faces of Time* (Wheaton, IL: Theosophical Publishing House, 1985); and Lawrence Fagg, *The Becoming of Time: Integrating Physical and Religious Time* (Atlanta, GA: Scholars Press, 1995). Physicists who have subjected the proposition of time travel to serious analysis in recent years include J. Richard Gott, Igor Novikov, Li-Xin Li, and Kip Thorne. See Gott's book *Time Travel in Einstein's Universe* (Boston: Houghton Mifflin, 2001), which suggests that multiple universes emerge from a single and eternal time loop.

5. Immanuel Kant, *Critique of Pure Reason* (1781), Norman Kemp Smith, trans. (New York: St. Martin's Press, 1929), 77. He said the same thing elsewhere in the *Critique*; for example: "If we take away from our inner intuition the peculiar condition of our sensibility, the concept of time likewise vanishes; it does not inhere in the objects, but merely in the subject which intuits them." Ibid., 79.

6. Martin Heidegger, *Being and Time* (*Sein und Zeit*, 1927), John MacQuarrie and Edward Robinson, trans. (New York: Harper Perennial, 2008), 474.

7. Heidegger, *Being and Time*, 488.

8. Alfred North Whitehead, *Process and Reality* (1929), David Ray Griffin and Donald W. Sherburne, eds. (New York: Free Press, 1978), 35, 283.

9. John William Dunne, *An Experiment with Time* (London: A. & C. Black, 1927).

10. The phrase "arrow of time" was coined by the British physicist Sir Arthur Eddington in his 1928 book *The Nature of the Physical World*. Eddington was writing of the "asymmetry" of time dynamics at the macrocosmic level.

11. John William Dunne, *Nothing Dies* (London: Faber and Faber, 1940), 63. Dunne's theory began with his belief that he had experienced precognition—premonitions of the future—in dreams. And in order to see the future "before it happens," he further reasoned that the future must in some way be "out there" already. So he convinced himself that the past, the present, and the future exist simultaneously in a sequence of

extended duration, and a traveling "now-mark," where our consciousness maintains a presentational vantage point, moves along this continuum during the course of our lives. Since he postulated free will, he also wrote that the future we see can be altered, which means we can *avoid* the future we foresee, at least to some extent—that is, the future consists of incipient *tendencies* that come true unless altered by our own intervention. An aeronautical engineer, Dunne tended to think in spatial terms. Following in the lead of Charles Howard Hinton (1853–1907)—a British mathematician whose essay *What Is The Fourth Dimension?* appeared in 1880—Dunne argued that the three forms of spatial extension that we visualize as length, width, and height are traversed by a fourth dimension of duration, time, in which the ever-shifting forms within the three dimensions are extended in succession. H. G. Wells had suggested something similar in his *Time Machine* (1895), mathematicians Henri Poincaré and Hermann Minkowski developed the concept systematically between 1905 and 1908, and then Einstein embraced the principle, which led to the concept of "space-time" as a four-dimensional construct. In 1919 the German mathematician Theodor Kaluza suggested the possibility of more than three spatial dimensions. Then in 1926, Swedish mathematician Oskar Klein proposed that the spatial fabric of the cosmos may contain both extended and circular (or "curled-up") dimensions. The so-called Kaluza-Klein theory was revived in the 1970s and is now fundamental to "string theory" among the physicists. In any case, by the 1920s, the concept of a time dimension was commonplace. Dunne called this dimension "time 1." He then reasoned that in order to conceive of the *speed* with which the "now-mark" travels in time 1—in his book *The Serial Universe* (1938) he theorized that it must travel at the speed of light—there has to be a larger time continuum against which to measure the speed of the travelling "now." This is the fifth dimension, which he called "time 2." Dunne further extrapolated that this fifth dimension (time 2) crosses the fourth dimension (time 1) *at a right angle* (so to speak), in the very same manner that length, width, and height traverse each other in geometry. Therefore the fifth dimension, time 2, presents a lateral *cross section* of time 1, creating a presentational field in which the sequence of past, present, and future in time 1 can be seen at once. Dunne theorized that our minds subconsciously extend themselves upward and outward into higher temporal dimensions, and that precognition—a glimpse of the future in dreams—occurs when our sleeping mind is no longer paying conscious attention to past and present events in time 1, and so it can glimpse some parts of the future from its vantage point in time 2. Two more points: (1) Dunne presumed that the elapsed succession within time 1 endures forever within time 2, notwithstanding our birth and death in time 1 (hence his doctrine that "nothing dies," that we are in some sense immortal); (2) he theorized that the dimensionality of time is also infinite, which means that time 2 is bisected by a larger time 3, which in turn is traversed by time 4, and so on to infinity. Hence his doctrine of "serial time." Against this background, the statement by Dunne that was quoted in the text should be intelligible: "What *has been* in time 1 must remain unchanged, though present, throughout the eternity of time 2. Nothing which has been passed by the time 1 'now-mark' dies in real time. A rose which has bloomed once blooms forever." Dunne's work became openly theological when he postulated that what we think of as the human mind is an "animus" or soul that merely uses the body and brain that we possess in time 1 to enhance its own growth in the higher time dimensions, where it continues to exist forever. Perhaps it goes without saying, but the ontic significations of Dunne's statements that "nothing dies" and that temporal contents "endure" must be unfathomable to us as any kind of a reality that we can grasp according to experience. For besides the kinesis of durational things at the "now-mark," how does temporal reality subsist once the now-mark has passed? Are our past states recorded in archival fashion, "frozen in place" like a photograph? If they "move," how exactly do they do it—like a film replaying every instant? Do our "selves" in the past have the very same self-conscious identity that we do? And the "animus" that goes on existing in higher time dimensions: what exactly is the content of its existence once the now-mark has completed its transition through our life in time 1? Dunne did (in his book *Nothing Dies*) suggest that our future existence after death may be grasped through analogy. Looking downward and backward upon our previous life in time 1 from the higher time dimensions, he suggested, is rather like reading the musical scale as a prelude to composing a symphony, or like reading through the alphabet, as a prelude to using the letters of that alphabet to write great poetry.

12. The "hermetic" tradition derived from some Egyptian-Greek "wisdom texts" from the second and third centuries AD, texts that represented late-blooming pagan heterodoxy and derived their name from the eponymous teacher in the texts, identified as "Hermes Trismegistus." See Garth Fowden, *The Egyptian Hermes: A Historical Approach to the Late Pagan Mind* (Cambridge, UK: Cambridge University Press, 1986). Latin translations of hermetic tracts appeared in the late Middle Ages and early Renaissance. Hermeticism has been vastly influential in modern heterodoxies.

13. Ouspensky wrote that "the three dimensions of time can be regarded as the continuation of the dimensions of space." He argued that "the six-dimensional form of a body is inconceivable for us, and if we were able to apprehend it with our senses we should undoubtedly see and feel it as three-dimensional." Of the three dimensions of time, the first is the time we experience. Like Dunne, Ouspensky argued that the next time dimension traverses the first in a way that makes its "now" moments perpetual, or, in his own word, "eternal." The doctrine of the "eternal Now" would be taken up more emphatically by a British participant in "the Work," Maurice Nicoll and also by the British scientist John G. Bennett and the Swedish-American astronomer Gustaf Strömberg. Ouspensky's final time dimension is "the line of actualization of other possibilities which were contained in the preceding moment but were not actualized in 'time.' . . . The line of time, repeated infinitely in eternity, leaves at every point unactualized possibilities. But these possibilities which have not been actualized in one time, are actualized in the sixth dimension, which is an aggregate of 'all times.'" Unlike Dunne, who visualized time dimensions traversing each other at right angles, Ouspensky saw them forming a spiral; he argued that time is circular. He wrote that "eternity is the curvature of time. Eternity is also movement, *eternal movement*. And if we imagine time as a circle or as any other closed curve, *eternity* will signify eternal movement along this curve, eternal repetition, eternal recurrence." Ouspensky's doctrine of "eternal recurrence" was applied to the issues of life and afterlife as follows: "*Life* in itself is *time* for man. For man there is not and cannot be any other time outside the time of his life. . . . If I die today, tomorrow will not exist *for me*. . . . All theories of the future life, of existence after death, of reincarnation, etc., contain one obvious mistake. They are all based on the usual understanding of time, that is, on the idea that *tomorrow* will exist after death. In reality it is just in this that life differs from death. Man dies because his time ends. There can be no tomorrow after death. But all usual conceptions of 'the future life' require the existence of 'tomorrow.'" Nonetheless, since in Ouspensky's doctrine a person's "life" and its "time" are synonymous, they move in repetitive circles, which Ouspensky delineated (that is, he depicted it in a series of illustrations) as a wave pattern consisting of a line of circular loops: "This means that if a man was born in 1877 and died in 1912, then, having died, he finds himself again in 1877 and must live the same life all over again." But this eternal recurrence was modified by the final dimension in which unactualized possibilities are played out to infinity, which in turn led to a doctrine comparable to karma in the Hindu religion: each recurrence is akin to reincarnation, and in each incarnation the overall life may improve. Peter D. Ouspensky, *A New Model of the Universe: Principles of the Psychological Method in its Application to Problems of Science, Religion and Art*, R. R. Merton, trans. (New York: Alfred E. Knopf, 1931), Dover Edition, 1997, 425–26, 429–30, 476–77, passim. Maurice Nicoll (1884–1953), a British participant in Gurdjieff's movement—and also a psychiatrist who studied and worked with Carl Jung—articulated the doctrine of "eternal Now" with greater force. In his book *Living Time* (1953), he wrote that all history, past, present, and future, is a "living Today," an ever-living "Now," and he invoked the theory of time dimensionality in ways that are comparable to the doctrines of Ouspensky and Dunne: "*Now* contains all time, all the life, and the aeon of

life. . . . We must understand that what we call the present moment is not *now*, for the present moment is on the horizontal line of time and *now* is vertical to this and incommensurable with it." Maurice Nicoll, *Living Time and the Integration of Life* (London: Vincent Stuart, 1952), 261, 262, 277. Another associate of Gurdjieff, the British mathematician and scientist John G. Bennett (1897–1974), similarly formulated the "eternal Now" as a fifth "eternity axis" perpendicular to the time axis in the four-dimensional structure of space-time. See John G. Bennett, *The Dramatic Universe* (London: Hodder & Stoughton, 1956). The Swedish-American astronomer Gustaf Strömberg (1882–1962), who worked at the Mount Wilson Observatory, formulated this concept as an "Eternity Domain" outside of physical space-time, though connected with it. See Gustaf Strömberg, *The Soul of the Universe* (Philadelphia: David McKay, 1940). The application of these doctrines to the ancient dispute between Parmenides and Heraclitus is obvious. It all resolves into the principle of Parmenides that "becoming" (the present moment) is but a veil over "being" (the eternal Now). It also bears noting that the concept of circular time is fundamental in the cosmology of J. Richard Gott and Li-Xin Li, whose paper "Can the Universe Create Itself?" was published in the journal *Physical Review D* in May 1998.

14. It is perhaps worth noting at this point that contemporary "superstring theory" in physics embraces the concept of multidimensionality in the space-time fabric. By the 1980s, physicists were using a six-dimensional concept worked out by mathematicians Eugene Calabi and Sing-Tung Yau as their point of departure. Physicist Brian Greene—who includes an approximate illustration of a "Calabi-Yau space" (approximate because it is represented on a two-dimensional piece of paper) in his book *The Elegant Universe*—comments that that "our universe has many more dimensions than meet the eye—dimensions that are tightly curled into the folded fabric of the cosmos." After explaining that contemporary "string" theorists believe that as many as ten or eleven spatial dimensions lay "coiled" within microcosmic space, imperceptible to us, Greene goes on say that multidimensional time as a concept is also under study: "If a curled-up dimension is a time dimension, traversing it means returning, after a temporal lapse, to a prior instant in time. This, of course, is well beyond the realm of our experience. Time, as we know it, is a dimension we can traverse in only one direction with absolute inevitability, never being able to return to an instant after it has passed. Of course, it might be that curled-up time dimensions have different properties from the familiar, vast time dimension that we imagine reaching back to the creation of the universe and forward to the present moment. But, in contrast to extra spatial dimensions, new and previously unknown time dimensions would clearly require an even more monumental restructuring of our intuition. Some theorists have been exploring the possibility of incorporating extra time dimensions into string theory, but as yet the situation is inconclusive. . . . But the intriguing possibility of new time dimensions could well play a role in future developments." With regard to the warping of space and time that is fundamental to Einstein's theory of general relativity, Greene presented a set of graphic illustrations to depict the warping of space. But with regard to the curvature of time, Greene found the explication more daunting. "Physicists have invented analogous images to try to convey the meaning of 'warped time,'" he wrote, "but they are significantly more difficult to decipher, so we will not introduce them here." Brian Greene, *The Elegant Universe*, 6, 205, 74. It bears noting that the multiple dimensions of time envisioned by the engineer Dunne and the occultist Ouspensky are macrocosmic in their nature; that is, they emanate "upward and outward" from us. The multiple dimensions of space as envisioned by the physicists developing the Kaluza-Klein theory are (at this point) conceived as being generally microcosmic; that is, they lay coiled far down within the fabric of creation. Some physicists believe that the "extended" dimensions—the "classical" three dimensions of length, width, and height—are also "curled," but on a macrocosmic basis, which is to say that each one of them extends in an arc across the universe and then rejoins itself in a circle.

15. I am grateful to my student Charles Hohman for this observation.

16. For commentary on the play, see Michael Kantor and Lawrence Maslon, *Broadway: The American Musical* (New York: Bullfinch Press, 2004); and Larry Stempel, *Showtime: A History of the Broadway Musical Theatre* (New York: W.W. Norton, 2010).

17. For quotations from this and other reviews of the play, see Stephen Suskin, *Opening Night on Broadway: A Critical Quotebook of the Golden Era of the Musical Theatre* (New York: Shrimmer Books, 1990), 103–7.

18. Gene Lees, *The Musical Worlds of Lerner and Lowe* (London: Robson Books, 1990), 49.

19. Alan Jay Lerner, *The Street Where I Live* (New York: W.W. Norton, 1978), 26.

20. A literary comparison here is telling in regard to the device of interpenetrating time channels in a literary work from the mid-twentieth century. J. R. R. Tolkien's *Lord of the Rings* trilogy, composed between the 1930s and the early 1950s, makes use of the device in volume one, *The Fellowship of the Ring*. In this case, the enchanted realm is Lothlorien, a paradisiacal elvish land that is immune from the evils of the outer world. Consider the following extracts from Tolkien's text: "As soon as he [Frodo] set foot upon the far bank of [the river] Silverlode, a strange feeling had come upon him. . . . It seemed to him that he had stepped over a bridge of time into a corner of the Elder Days, and was now walking in a world that was no more. . . . A light was upon it for which his language had no name. All that he saw was shapely, but the shapes seemed at once clear cut, as if they had first been conceived and drawn at the uncovering of his eyes, and ancient as if they had endured forever. He saw no colour but those he knew, gold and white and blue and green, but they were fresh and poignant, as if he had at that moment first perceived them and made for them names new and wonderful." After Frodo and his comrades leave this realm, they reflect upon its nature. Frodo wonders whether in Lothlorien "we were in a time that has elsewhere long gone by. It was not, I think, until Silverlode bore us back to Anduin that we returned to the time that flows through mortal lands." The elf Legolas replies, "Nay, time does not tarry ever . . . but change and growth is not in all things and places alike." J. R. R. Tolkien, *The Fellowship of the Ring* (London: George Allen & Unwin, 1954), 1994 Ballantine edition, 392–93, 436.

21. Gene Kelly, quoted in Clive Hirshhorn, *Gene Kelly: A Biography* (New York: St. Martin's Press, 1974), 206.

22. Hirshhorn, *Gene Kelly*, 206–7.

23. Pauline Kael, *5001 Nights at the Movies* (New York: Henry Holt, 1991), 103.

24. Michael Dunne, *American Film Musical Themes and Forms* (Jefferson, NC: McFarland, 2004), 115.

25. David Thomson, *Showman: The Life of David O. Selznick* (New York: Alfred A. Knopf, 1992), 480, 494–502.

26. Lee Kovacs, *The Haunted Screen*, 56. Kovacs has developed an interesting theory about one of the supporting characters in the story, an art dealer (played by Ethel Barrymore) named "Miss Spinney." This old lady becomes an important confidante of Eben Adams, and she is (as her surname gently emphasizes) a *spinster*—she "never found love in this life," which is exactly what Jennie Appleton feared would be her fate in her first incarnation. A subliminal connection between Miss Spinney and the ghost of Jennie is thus established. After observing that Jennie's appearances occur in the aftermath of conversations between Spinney and Eben, Kovacs suggests that Spinney plays the role of a *medium*: that is, she plays a role in *summoning* Jennie, albeit unconsciously.

27. As Richard Collier browses amid the historical displays in the hotel, his first-person narrative includes this account of the photographs on display, photographs of some celebrities who visited the hotel: "There's Gloria Swanson in her furs. There's Leslie Howard; how young he looks. I remember seeing him in a movie called *Berkeley Square*. I recall him time-travelling back to the eighteenth century." Richard Matheson, *Bid Time Return* (New York: Ballantine Books, 1975), 9. The hotel in Matheson's novel was the "Hotel del Coronado" in San Diego, the very same hotel that achieved immortality on screen when Billy Wilder used it in the Marilyn Monroe classic *Some Like It*

Hot. The makers of *Somewhere in Time* initially intended to use this same hotel in the film, but chose the Grand Hotel on Mackinac Island, Michigan instead for a number of reasons.

28. In *Bid Time Return*, Richard Collier's narration includes a long and explicit reference to Priestley that serves as the grounding for the time-travel experiment. In a San Diego bookstore, Collier encounters the Priestly magnum opus: "Went to Wahrenbrock's again. Immediate good luck. J. B. Priestley authored and compiled a giant book on the subject, *Man and Time*." In the course of the following pages, Collier distills Priestley's book, chapter by chapter. A sample: "The final chapter. After this, I'm on my own. Priestley speaks of three Times. He calls them Time 1, Time 2, and Time 3. Time 1 is the time into which we are born, grow old, and die; the practical and economic time, the brain and body time. Time 2 leaves this simple track. Its scope includes co-existent past, present, and future. No clocks and calendars determine its existence. Entering it, we stand apart from chronological time and observe it as a fixed oneness rather than as a moving array of moments. Time 3 is the zone where 'the power to connect or disconnect potential and actual' exists." Matheson, *Bid Time Return*, 52, 55. As these extracts from Matheson's novel make clear, Priestley had chosen a theory of time-dimensionality comparable to Ouspensky's: three-dimensional time. While acknowledging his intellectual debt to Dunne, Priestley rejected "serialism" with its theory of infinite time dimensions as implausible. Instead, wrote Priestley, "let us make do with Times One, Two, and Three, remembering that we live in all three of them at once." He continued: "As visible creatures of earth we are ruled by Time One. We are born into it, grow up and grow old in it, and die in it." Following Dunne, he then postulated "another Time order, which we can call Time Two" to account for precognitive glimpses of possible futures via dreams. But "in Time Two, where the dreams belong, there is no distinction between the possibilities that are actualized and those that are not. . . . Therefore another time is necessary, Time Three." As to the nature of this third time dimension, which presumably contains the power to determine different futures, Priestley wrote: "I refuse to answer questions . . . about these possibilities in Time Three . . . because I do not know." But he was willing to speculate, like Dunne, about the higher time dimensions containing extensions of our self-hood beyond the grave: "I believe with Dunne that when we have come to an end in Time One, we go forward—spatially and geometrically, we may say, at a right angle—in Time Two, no longer concentrating our attention on the physical world, but now having in place of it all that accumulation of mental events . . . left to us from our Time-One lives." And "one feature of this Time-Two afterlife" might be the power not only to view all our deeds in Time One but to "put them right." Based upon Priestley's structure of time dimensions, however, such a power might be better relegated to Time Three. Regardless, Priestley conjectured that "our lives are not contained within passing time, a single track along which we hurry to oblivion. We exist in more than one dimension of Time. Ourselves in Times Two and Three cannot vanish into the grave; they are already beyond it even now. We may not be immortal beings. . . . We have not unlimited Time, though what limits will be in Time Two and Time Three I do not know. . . . I suspect, however, that in Time Two we begin by being more essentially ourselves than in Time One but end by being less ourselves, personality as we know it vanishing altogether in Time Three." J. B. Priestley, *Man and Time* (Garden City: Doubleday, 1964), Dell edition, 265–94, 315–54.

29. Laurent Bouzereau, "Back to *Somewhere in Time*," documentary supplement, *Somewhere in Time* DVD edition, Universal Studios Home Video, 2000. See also Bill Shepard, *The Somewhere In Time Story: Behind the Scenes in the Making of a Cult Romantic Fantasy Motion Picture* (LaGrange, IL: Somewhere In Time Gallery, 2004).

30. The afterlife conclusion made explicit references in its iconography to *The Ghost and Mrs. Muir*. In some notes from early script conferences in June 1978 there is the following entry: "We discussed the necessity of having Collier and Elise reunited at the very end of the movie (after Collier's death) somewhat in the manner of *The Ghost and Mrs. Muir*." In one of Richard Matheson's screenplay treatments he wrote, "dying,

he leaves behind his mortal body and walks out onto the beach where, in a *Ghost and Mrs. Muir* climax, which, hopefully, will leave not a dry eye in the house, he is reunited with Elise." Bill Shepard, *Somewhere In Time Story*, 26, 90. Over time, this treatment was changed to the cloudy "somewhere" that was actually closer to the imagery of *The Ghost and Mrs. Muir*'s conclusion. The cloudy conclusion was initially longer than it was in the film's final version. Director of Photography Isador Mankofsky explained that "it was an amazing shot. It was all done on the soundstage at the MRA studio [an existing film studio on Mackinac Island built years earlier by an evangelical group, which called itself "Moral Re-Armament," or MRA]. In the shot, we started filming on the ceiling, and tilted down past the windows to Reeve's stand-in on the bed. We then had a dimmer change, where we switched from one set of lights to another. We started dollying toward the window. At this point, the curtains had to part, and the set divided for us to go through in one continuous shot. The background was a white cyclorama, the floors were painted white, and Jane Seymour was standing there. . . . We had everybody working in that shot—pulling walls, rolling back the ceiling, pushing the dolly, changing the lights—it was all done in one continuous shot." Shepard, *Somewhere In Time Story*, 72–73.

31. Vincent Canby, "No Generation Gap," *New York Times*, October 3, 1980. Jeannot Szwarc wrote that "we couldn't understand it. The reviews were so nasty, and it's such a gentle film." Richard Matheson theorized that "maybe it was the wrong time for such a picture. Who knows? It *is* known that its release pattern was incorrect. It should not have been mass released but shown in one theatre in each city and given a chance to catch on." Some of the reviews, though not many, were positive; *Variety* called the film "a charming, witty, passionate romantic drama about a love transcending space and time. *Somewhere in Time* is an old-fashioned film in the best sense of that term—which means that it's carefully crafted, civilized in its sensibilities, and interested more in characterization than shock effects. . . . Made with impeccable style and intelligence . . . extraordinarily attractive cast, subtly detailed writing, and the sumptuous production values of the period hotel setting." Notwithstanding its box office failure, the film made money for Universal. Stephen Simon noted that "the picture wound up grossing about twelve million dollars domestically, and having cost only five million, Universal did rather well out of it." And the aftermarket sales later on (when the film had developed its cult following) were even better. A vice president for marketing and sales at MCA Universal Home Video stated that "*Somewhere in Time* has become a blockbuster right up there with the top all-time titles. . . . All those people fascinated by a film that went nowhere when it originally came out. Sales of the sound track are as popular as the video." All quoted in Shepard, *Somewhere in Time Story*, 101, 106, 107.

32. A similar plot device was used in *Portrait of Jennie*. When Jennie first appears (and then disappears), she leaves behind several items including a scarf. As the story unfolds, this scarf attains greater significance as an "au revoir" symbol, a promissory token that the bond between the lovers will remain unbroken. After the tidal wave sends Jennie to her death the second time, Eben's rescuers find him unconscious on the rocky island. And the scarf is lying next to him.

33. The idea of a never-ending circular flow has other antecedents in philosophy. The doctrine of Hegel, for example—to the extent that we are able to educe it from his terrible writing—is that "Geist," or "Absolute Spirit," sends forth its creative emanations and, through a dialectical interaction with something that is antithetical, something that is "not-self" (i.e., nature), it achieves a new synthesis that proceeds to recirculate, and the process starts again—indeed, it is always in motion. Whitehead proposed a comparable doctrine in *Process and Reality*. God creates actuality and then receives it in some ineffable way "into Himself." As to time travel fantasies, it could be argued (depending upon one's metaphysical presuppositions) that an element of circularity is inherent in any time travel plot. Explicit work-ups of circular or spiraling time travel were produced by the science fiction writer Robert Heinlein in his stories "By His Bootstraps" (1941) and "All You Zombies" (1958–1959). Other films involving

time travel romances are *Time After Time* (1978) starring Malcolm McDowell and Mary Steenburgen; *The Two Worlds of Jennie Logan* (1979, made for television) starring Lindsay Wagner and Marc Singer; *Bill and Ted's Excellent Adventure* (1989) starring Keanu Reeves, Alex Winter, and George Carlin; *Groundhog Day* (1993) starring Bill Murray and Andie MacDowell; *Frequency* (2000) starring Dennis Quaid, Jim Caviezel, Elizabeth Mitchell, and Melissa Errico; *Kate and Leopold* (2001) starring Meg Ryan and Hugh Jackman; *Déjà Vu* (2006) starring Denzel Washington and Paula Patton; and *Edge of Tomorrow* (2014) starring Tom Cruise, Emily Blunt, Bill Paxton, and Brendan Gleason. A time loop is fundamental to the plot of *Groundhog Day*, and the theme of progressive amelioration of one's spiritual condition in successive versions of the loop—improving karma—is also fundamental to the film. As to time travel theory among physicists, J. Richard Gott has explored the possibility of "time travel" in several different senses. As an astrophysicist, he writes about the principle of "visiting" the past by looking through a telescope and realizing that the view of the stars that you see shows those stars as they existed thousands of years ago, since their light has taken thousands of years to reach us. But this "visit" is only a *view* of certain things that came and went long ago and are no longer present except for the trace that they emitted in light waves (or photons). He also writes about the familiar principle of special relativity through which if you hopped aboard a rocket that could travel at speeds approaching light speed, you would return to find that the earth had aged thousands of years in your absence. But you never really left "your own time" in this particular version of a "visit to the future." It's just that "your own time" underwent a change. As you and the earth both continued to age, the rate at which you aged slowed down compared to the earth's rate of change since the passage of time slows down when your position accelerates. But Gott also writes about the principle of traveling to an earlier moment and actually *being there* by dint of the fact that you are traveling through warps in the bending fabric of space-time—taking "shortcuts." Here's an example: "If you found an Earth-Alpha Centauri wormhole, you could dive from earth through it in the year 3000 and emerge at Alpha Centauri. But when? You might emerge not in the year 3000 but perhaps in the year 2990 instead." And then "you could travel back to earth at 99.5 percent of the speed of light and arrive back at Earth approximately four years later—in 2994. Thus you would arrive back at Earth six years before you left. You could wait on earth for those six years, so you could shake hands with yourself when you took off in 3000." Gott, *Time Travel in Einstein's Universe*, 120–21. This radical version of time travel raises the obvious ontological problems. If you could somehow "meet yourself" in the past, that earlier version of you would not be "you" as you currently experience yourself. Presumably, this earlier version of you would possess a self-conscious identity distinct from your own, even though this earlier version of yourself would exist in a continuum that feeds directly into the center of conscious awareness that you currently possess, that you currently feel to be "yourself." We normally sense that as our consciousness extends itself from moment to moment, the consciousness we possessed a brief moment ago no longer exists. We exist and develop in a "now-coefficient" (Dunne called it a now-mark) that moves in chronological flow within the coordinates of space-time. But to travel to the past and then "meet yourself" implies that the cosmos is filled with endless versions of yourself—each of them possessing a now-coefficient but all of them moving in a sequence through which every version of yourself is morphing into the next one, constantly, over and over: as one moves forward, the next is coming up behind it. In other words, the "history of you" is ever-present—ever-subsistent—and is always being somehow *replenished*. The ontological question: how does this happen? Do continuous iterations of yourself get created every moment (how?), so that every instant of your previous existence springs forward to live and move again? Does this ever-active replenishment of "you" (if it truly takes place) reveal that continuous "being" can be reconciled with "becoming," since every moment of this endless flux is "always there"—which is to say, it is always represented by a newly emergent "copy" with a center of consciousness that replicates one you possessed in the past but is still distinct from the one that you possess this instant? No doubt the heterodox but scientific theorists of an "eternal Now" such as Nicoll, Bennett, and Strömberg would offer their collective theory as an answer to this unanswerable question. But the metaphysics through which every previous instant remains forever in motion, animate, *alive,* must be left to the imagination.

34. Jo Addie, "Frequently Asked Questions about *Somewhere in Time,*" http://www.somewhereintime.tv/articles.htm. A photograph showing Stephen Deutsch and Richard Matheson wearing these shirts appears on page 95 of Shepard's *The Somewhere in Time Story.* See also Ibid., 23–26.

35. This situation shows an interesting trend in the history of "eternal recurrence" as an idea, specifically: the scope of the recurrence has progressively shrunk in duration as the concept was successively modified in the twentieth century. In the classic version of "recurrence," handed down from Pythagoras to Nietzsche, the cosmic cycle plays out and then begins again, to be repeated in every detail the next time. In Ouspensky's doctrine, the scope of recurrence is comprised by the lifetime of the individual: after someone dies, the whole pattern of the life that just ended begins again. In *Somewhere in Time,* the recurrence appears to consist of a continuous flow of events in which a circular stream feeds *continuously* from "1912" to "1979" and then back again to 1912 without interruption, which in turn suggests that "Richard," "Elise," and their surroundings are nothing more (or less) than flowing *events* that get replenished, somehow, every instant as the loop of recurrence proceeds on its endless path. Ouspensky—a speculative occultist who made provision for alternative possibilities—wrote a passage that encompasses both aspects of the time loop in *Somewhere in Time*: its cyclical nature and its ever-instantaneous replenishment, though he saw them as separate and alternative concepts. He wrote that if eternity is construed as repetition, then "*some time* everything will be repeated or is repeated, either immediately after the completion of a particular cycle . . . or after every moment. The latter, that is, the immediate repetition of every moment again and again, brings this idea near the idea of co-existence." Ouspensky, *A New Model of the Universe,* 477.

36. In Matheson's novel, Collier perceives the pattern of eternal recurrence but believes that he can alter it via the dimension of time—Time 3—which, in his reading of Priestley, has convinced him that the possibility of altering future contingencies should be matched by a power to alter *past* contingencies. He puts it this way: "Why then should I not be able to go back, just as before, but, instead of causing sorrow in her life, cause only joy? Surely that sorrow was caused not by her meeting me or by anything I did to her but by her somehow losing me to the same phenomenon of time that brought me to her. I know this sounds mad but I believe it. I also believe that, when the moment comes, I can alter that particular phenomenon." Richard Matheson, *Bid Time Return,* 77.

FIVE

The "Second Wave" of Plays and the Milieu of World War II

Supernatural romances on stage—and the film adaptations of the early plays—proved significant. A second wave of love-death-afterlife plays were created and performed by the end of the 1930s, and the trend continued without interruption in the early 1940s. Meanwhile, World War II had begun, and so a new wave of supernatural romance *screenplays*—a distinctly war-based development—were written as well. Several of the resulting films were set (at least in part) within the combat zones of World War II.

Perhaps the supernatural romance tradition became powerfully associated with World War II—as powerfully linked to the war as the films that would be dubbed "film noir"—because the magnitude of death in World War I led many to anticipate a comparable level of mortality the second time around. And so the filmmakers were ready to go with their tales of consolation. Supernatural romances offered commentary on the theme of death—the war's cost—just as film noir offered commentary on the war's cause: human evil.

THE PLAYS AND THEIR FILM VERSIONS

Before proceeding further, a development should be noted: the love-death-afterlife formula began to be extended by the middle of the 1930s into other genres. An example is the huge thematic leap of supernatural romance from melodrama to comedy with *Topper*, a 1937 production of the Hal Roach Studio directed by Norman Z. McLeod. A few comic touches had been present already in *Death Takes a Holiday*. But *Topper* was made exclusively for laughs, and it was a box office success.

61

Based upon a novel by Thorne Smith, the film tells the story of a happy-go-lucky couple named George and Marion Kerby who die in a car crash. They want to be together in the afterlife, but they have to do a good deed for a mortal to gain admittance—in this case teach a mousy banker named Cosmo Topper how to have fun. This film, starring Cary Grant and Constance Bennett (as the Kerbys) and Roland Young (as Topper) was a great hit in 1937.[1] Supernatural romance would develop intermittently in hybrid forms: in movie musicals, in horror films, and in film noir (all as previously noted), and in other genres as well. Indeed, the next major supernatural romance departed slightly from the love–death formula as previously established.

Lawrence Edward Watkin's 1937 novel *On Borrowed Time* was dramatized and brought to the stage by Paul Osborn in 1938. The love theme in this love-death-afterlife story is significantly intergenerational: the loving couple, an elderly couple named Julian and Nellie Northrup, find that they have to raise their grandson, "Pud," when his parents (Julian and Nellie's physician son and his wife) are killed in a car crash. Death personified (and given a name, "Mr. Brink") thumbs a ride with Doctor and Mrs. Northrup. Their car veers off the road and they die. So their little son Pud, who was not in the car, is an orphan. Old Julian and Nellie take him in. But then Mr. Brink pays a call upon Nellie, and off she goes. So Julian has to raise the little boy himself.

A nasty and officious aunt named Demetria Riffle tries to take away the boy and adopt him for the purpose of getting her hands on his inheritance. Julian sees exactly what the harridan is up to. But his age and his health make it easy for the aunt to complain to the authorities and claim that he is not a fit guardian. And then Mr. Brink pays a call upon Julian.

Julian has already discovered that he got a magic wish in return for a good deed. For a long time he tried to chase away kids who were filching apples from the large old tree that stands in his yard, and so he made the following wish: anyone who climbs up the tree has to stay there until Julian agrees to let them go.

Julian tricks Mr. Brink in granting him a last request—an apple from the tree—and he further tricks the Grim Reaper into climbing up to fetch it himself. So Death becomes trapped in the tree, and in the meantime—for the duration—Julian is safe, for there is no way to die.

No one can die.

Julian puts a high fence around the tree, for he discovers that anyone touching it will perish (when a dog bites the dust after bumping into the tree, the deadly truth is apparent).

When Julian is forced to explain the presence of the fence—Demetria sees her chance to get him locked away in an insane asylum—no one believes it. But then the family doctor discovers that no one in the whole world has died in the past few days. So he enlightens Julian, explaining what awaits him (and millions of others) if Brink is kept trapped in the tree: infinite misery. Julian's resolution wavers. And Mr. Brink figures out a method to hasten this process.

Death finds a way to trick Pud into climbing the fence (he dares him to do it); the boy falls, and is horribly crippled. So Julian releases Mr. Brink and then requests him to "take us both." Mr. Brink—who is actually a very kind Reaper who reveals that Pud himself was destined to be "taken" in any case—wafts them both into pastures of bliss, and old Julian hears Nellie calling.

MGM produced the film version and released it in 1939. Lionel Barrymore played Julian, Beulah Bondi was cast as his wife Nellie, "Bobs" Watson played Pud, and Eily Maryon was superb as the sanctimonious and aggressive prig Demetria. Harold Bucquet was the director. Barrymore, because of the onset of a crippling illness that confined him to a wheelchair, was almost replaced by Frank Morgan. But the decision-makers kept him after Barrymore himself made the case that he was up to it (it also dawned upon the decision-makers that Julian in a wheelchair would be just fine). The music by Franz Waxman—creating eerie effects with remarkable devices—and the camerawork by Joseph Ruttenberg were excellent.

This film as a whole was well done, and the reviewers liked it. Frank S. Nugent of the *New York Times* deemed it "a mighty pleasant film, with a deal of warmth and sentiment and just enough ornery human acidity to keep it off the alkaline, or mawkish, side." He noted with regret, however, that "the Hays code required the toning down of the salty dialogue that was at once the most comically shocking and endearing virtue of crotchety old Julian Northrup" and that "those who treasured the play" were bound to miss it. He also wrote that "Lionel Barrymore is always too mannered to be anyone but himself"—a complaint that could easily be lodged against a great many movie stars—but that it was "probably unfair to hold his Lionel Barrymorism against him."[2]

One of the standout performances was Sir Cedric Hardwicke as Brink: clad in a top coat and fedora, intoning his lines with slow and exquisite upper-class British poise, he created what was perhaps his most memorable role. He reportedly called it his favorite.[3] It bears noting that the Osborn play has been revived a number of times, most recently in 1991 on Broadway with George C. Scott in the role of Julian Northrop.[4]

In 1938, a far more important play was written and performed: *Our Town* by Thornton Wilder. Just as Hitchcock's *Vertigo* will always be a *sui generis* Hitchcock film, so the Thornton Wilder play *Our Town* must be understood first and foremost within the oeuvre of Wilder: it's a Wilder play, pure and simple. As with *Vertigo*, however, the influence of powerful artistic movements infiltrated Wilder's creation, and one of them was supernatural romance.

The play is set in a small fictitious town in New Hampshire called Grover's Corners. The play depicts three days in the life of the town as glimpsed through events in the daily lives of two families who are next-door neighbors, the Gibbses and the Webbs. These particular days are set years apart: in 1901, 1903, and 1913. While the events depicted in the first two-thirds of the play are mundane, there is an aura about them that becomes overtly spiritual by the conclusion, which is based in the love-death-afterlife formula.

Wilder explained that his intention was "to find a value above all price for the smallest events of our daily life," and that he deliberately "made this claim as preposterous as possible, for I have set the village against the largest dimensions of time and space."[5] Surely Wilder was attempting to be arch when he called his own work "preposterous." No doubt he kept a wary eye on the critics who would balk at anything that struck their jaded sensibilities as "corny."

The supernatural element in the play is introduced by the presence of a "stage manager" who appears as a principal character. He introduces the characters, introduces the action, stops or speeds up the action, interacts with the characters, and teleports the action years forward (or backward). He is folksy and quaint. In some ways he performs the function of the announcer whom Shakespeare called "Chorus" in *Henry V*, but he partakes of a longer and "metatheatrical" tradition that flows from the ancient Greek chorus to the German theatrical experiments of the 1920s.

Before long we begin to sense him as a supernatural being, not least of all because the play employs the device of different time channels. He steps in and out of the time-continuum containing the town in any of the three years in question. He—and consequently we—stand outside of the time frame containing the town from 1901 to 1913. We stand apart from it, but we enter into it at will, with the manager's assistance. Several of the characters die within the time span in question, yet the stage manager can make them speak, both before their deaths and in the afterlife. Like Prospero in Shakespeare's *Tempest*, he can brag in effect that "graves at my command / Have waked their sleepers, oped, and let 'em forth / By my so potent art" (5.1.55–7). There is a romantic love drama in this play: the courtship and marriage of George Gibbs and Emily Webb. We see them as flirting teenagers, and we see their wedding day in 1905.

Then Emily dies in childbirth. The play shows her funeral in 1913 and we listen as she and all the other ghosts—the ghosts of all the town's folk who have been buried in this graveyard—comment on life, the plight of the living, and the prospect of immortality for those who have left the confines of this earth.

The play was first performed at the McCarter Theater in Princeton, New Jersey, on January 22, 1938. Then it moved to Boston and then to Broadway where, as a Jed Harris production, it opened on February 4. The play became famous, winning the Pulitzer Prize for drama. It was performed on the radio in 1939 with Orson Welles as the stage manager.

Producers Jed Harris and William K. Howard then sold the rights to producer Sol Lesser, who wished to use the play as a vehicle for a new independent filmmaking enterprise that would distribute in partnership with United Artists. "Principal Artists Productions" released the film version of *Our Town* in 1940, and the result was extremely impressive.[6]

Wilder declined to write the screenplay single-handedly, but he did agree to collaborate with Harry Chandlee and Frank Craven, who had played the stage manager. Craven agreed to reprise this role in the film. Sam Wood, who had directed the film version of *Goodbye, Mr. Chips*, was chosen as director and the cinematographer was Bert Glellon. The score for the film was composed by a major figure in the American music world, Aaron Copland. And the lead role of Emily Webb was played by Martha Scott, who had also played the role on stage.

Lesser talked Wilder into a major change in the plot: Emily would recover from her struggles in childbirth, and so the funeral and grave-yard scenes would constitute (depending upon one's theoretical proclivities) either a fantasy in her fevered brain as she hovered at the brink of death or else a brief stint as a "half-way" spirit in the afterlife.[7]

The aesthetics of *Our Town* in its 1940 film version have been frequently called superb. Glellon's camerawork, Copland's music, the screenplay, and the performances: all combine to create the ethereal beauty that critics had praised in earlier supernatural romances on screen such as the 1930 version of *Outward Bound*.

Here are some samples of the love-death-afterlife finale. As the third act begins, the stage manager is soliloquizing on a hilltop above Grover's Corners:

> This is an important part of Grover's Corners, up here on this hilltop.
> Lots of sky and lots of clouds—often lots of sun and moon and stars....
> I often wonder why people like to be buried in Woodlawn or Brooklyn
> when they might pass the same time up here in New Hampshire.

Yes, this is a graveyard, and the stage manager is warming up for what follows. One of the characters whom we have previously seen in action, Mrs. Gibbs, is buried in this cemetery. "Yep, Doc Gibbs lost his wife three years ago about this time," the stage manager observes. And then the big theme begins:

> An awful lot of sorrow has sort of quieted down up here. . . . All those
> important things—mother 'n daughter, husband 'n wife, enemy 'n ene-
> my, money 'n miser—all those terribly important things . . . the earth
> part kind-a burns away, *burns out.* . . . And what's left when your
> memory's gone and your identity, Mrs. Smith? . . . We all know that
> *something* is eternal, and that something has to do with human beings.

Then we learn that something is wrong with Emily Webb, who is struggling in childbirth. We hear the voices of the dead, high up on the hill as she succumbs. Rain and mist are blowing through the cemetery, and people in the funeral procession are advancing with massed umbrellas. The rain ceases, the stars appear, and we see the dead, in rows.

Mrs. Gibbs tells Emily to "rest yourself," since she and the others must "think only of what's ahead, and be ready for what's ahead." But Emily says it is hard to forget her mortal life and the loved ones in it. She wants to revisit a happy time and then she finds herself actually doing it, soaring over Grover's Corners on a wintry day. She revisits her sixteenth birthday, the first day she knew she loved George. She sees him—and she sees herself, as she used to be, gliding down the stairs to the party.[8] She sees her mother and she tries to communicate with her, to no avail:

> Oh, mama, just look at me one minute as though you really saw me. Mama, twelve years have gone by. I'm dead. . . . I married George Gibbs, mama. Wally's dead, too. Mama, his appendix burst on a camping trip to Crawford Notch. . . . But just for a moment now, we're all together.

But this is more than she can bear; these people, though happy enough in their lives, have no idea of what miraculous gifts they are holding in their hands, no conception of the numinous meaning that is immanent in every single instant:

> I can't go on. It goes too fast. Goodbye, world. Goodbye, Grover's Corners. . . . Mama and Papa. Goodbye to clocks ticking. . . . To my butternut tree and mama's sunflowers. And food and coffee. And new-ironed dresses and hot baths. And sleeping and waking up. Oh, earth, you're too wonderful for anyone to realize you! Do any human beings ever realize life while they live it—every, every minute? I want to live, I want to live, I want

She wakes up. In the movie, it's all been a dream. But in the play, she's really dead, and so she goes back up to her grave at the top of the hill.

Emily: "Mother Gibbs?"

Mrs. Gibbs: "Yes, Emily?"

Emily: "They don't understand, do they?"

Mrs. Gibbs: "No, dear, they don't understand."

Critics loved this movie, which was nominated for the following Academy Awards: best actress, best picture, best art direction, best original score, and best sound recording.

Bosley Crowther of the *New York Times* was bowled over. The stage version of the play, he wrote, "seemed almost too spiritual for transference to the screen [but] now that Producer Sol Lesser has had the insight to put it onto film—and to do so almost scene for scene and word for word—it is apparent that a finer original screen play could scarcely have been written." Crowther was particularly taken by the cinematic tricks that were used to give the stage manager his power: "Once he places his hand before the camera lens to stop a sequence and introduce another. The camera thus becomes animate, not just a recording machine. It is an exciting technique . . . and it enhances the scope of the screen tremendously."[9]

The influence of Wilder's play was enormous; Michael Powell, for instance, was deeply moved by a wartime production of *Our Town* and it possibly influenced several aspects of the Powell-Pressburger film *A Matter of Life and Death*.[10] Film scholar Philip Horne has suggested the influence of Wilder's play on the Frank Capra classic *It's a Wonderful Life*:

> Philip Van Doren Stern recorded that he had the idea for his short story "The Greatest Gift" (1943), the basis of Frank Capra's film *It's a Wonderful Life*, in February 1938, which, one can note, was eight days after the New York opening of *Our Town*. The notion of a man slowly realizing the value of his own life only when granted a vision of his world from the perspective of lifelessness seems traceable to . . . *Our Town*.[11]

It is also possible that the *film* version of the play—the version in which Emily does not really die—had an influence on the 1955 Danish film *Ordet* (produced and directed by Carl Dreyer), an explicitly religious love-and-death fable in which a woman who dies (or who seems to die) in childbirth is resurrected: she returns to the living.

Wilder's play was also a modest though significant demonstration of the mythical method. The literary device of allowing the dead to speak is ancient. Odysseus visited the underworld and spoke with the shades of the departed in the *Odyssey*, and Virgil used the same device in the *Aeneid*. In Aristophanes's *Frogs*, Dionysos visits the underworld for satirical conversations with Aeschylus and Euripides. The *Divine Comedy* of Dante is grounded in the method, and Wilder himself claimed inspiration for *Our Town* from the *Purgatorio*.[12] He might also have been inspired by Edgar Lee Masters's *Spoon River Anthology*, a 1913 collection of poems in which the souls of the dead from a fictitious Midwestern town tell their stories.

Meanwhile, two other supernatural romances appeared that were written for the stage: Harry Segall's *Heaven Can Wait* and Lynn Root's *Cabin in the Sky*. The latter play appeared on Broadway before it was adapted as a film. But the former play was snapped up for screenplay conversion before it was ever performed. It appeared on screen in 1941 under the title *Here Comes Mr. Jordan*.

This film is one of the most influential in the genre of supernatural romance. A sequel to the film was produced (*Down to Earth*, 1947) and the original was remade twice, as *Heaven Can Wait* (1978) and as *Down to*

Earth (2001). *Here Comes Mr. Jordan* was an obvious influence in the creation *of A Matter of Life and Death* (1946), which reverses its plot conceit. And the 1941 film has played a key role in the sequence of supernatural romances that use the theme of reincarnation.

The play by Segall told the story of a boxer named Joe Pendleton who is an amateur aviator as well: he likes to fly a single-seater plane. Flying to a boxing match, he is caught in an emergency when a cable snaps and his plane starts to hurtle downward.

He suddenly finds himself walking through a cloudy "somewhere" with a companion. This companion identifies himself as Conductor 7013, and he tells Joe that his soul was removed from the doomed plane and brought to this way station, from which he will be sent to his "final destination." Joe is dead. A spectral airliner is waiting in the clouds with a queue line of other passengers who are boarding for this final trip.

But Joe gets angry when he learns that his soul was taken before his plane hit the ground; he is convinced that he could have pulled out of the dive. Conductor 7013 gets flustered and summons the top bureaucrat, Mr. Jordan, and asks him to reason with Joe so he will calm down and cooperate.

But Jordan sides with Joe. It turns out that Joe was not destined to die for another half-century, and Conductor 7013 (who is new at this job) jumped the gun. Mr. Jordan tells the conductor to take Joe back and put him back in his mortal body.

But there's a problem: his body has been cremated.

So they talk it over and Jordan hits upon a plan: they will give Joe the use of a different man's body for the rest of his life on earth. They will travel the earth at supernatural speed and inspect the physiques of men who are at the brink of death: those who are really destined to die. Jordan, as opposed to his subordinate flunkies, has a better list of the doomed. And once the soul of the doomed man in question has been taken, Joe can have the free use of his body. Joe says that he intends to get the replacement body into shape so he can resume his career as a boxer.

After several comic scenes in which Jordan and Joe take a look at men mere seconds before they bite the dust, they arrive at the mansion of a sleazy investor named Bruce Farnsworth who is lying unconscious in a bathtub, drugged: his wife and his crooked executive secretary, lovers, are murdering him. Joe is disgusted by the prospect of using the body of this low-life, but then something changes his mind: a young woman named Bette Logan arrives at the mansion of Farnsworth, seeking restitution for a swindle.

Joe is suddenly seized by the power of Eros: Bette is the love of his life.

So he will take the body of Farnsworth on a "trial" basis—Jordan agrees to this—to help Bette Logan by transforming Bruce Farnsworth into a decent human being. Jordan tells him that once he is in the Farnsworth torso, he will speak with the authentic voice of Farnsworth so no

Figure 5.1. "Joe Pendleton," played by Robert Montgomery (center) in the 1941 hit film *Here Comes Mr. Jordan*, is shown after death in a cloudy "somewhere" arguing with celestial bureaucrats. He convinces them that he was cheated out of what should have remained of his life because a heavenly escort, played by Edward Everett Horton (left), made a mistake. So "Mr. Jordan," played by Claude Rains (right), a uniformed version of the Grim Reaper, fixes things through reincarnation. Joe gets a new body and then, in his new mortal version, meets the love of his life, Bette Logan, who is played by Evelyn Keyes. Courtesy of Photofest.

one else will be able to tell the difference. Meanwhile, Jordan will look for a long-term replacement body and Joe . . . well, Joe will see where things lead with Bette Logan.

Joe and Bette fall in love. She tells him there is something in his eyes that she has always been looking for. And with comic assistance from his old boxing trainer—who is gradually informed of the supernatural truth through a series of slapstick gags—Joe gets the Farnsworth cadaver into shape for a heavyweight bout. But then Jordan reappears. His information, though a great deal better than that of his subordinates, apparently is not quite perfect in regard to the ways of destiny. Or else he had been holding out on Joe from the beginning. Regardless, he tells Joe that Farnsworth's wife and her lover will succeed on their second murder attempt. Indeed, their success is imminent. So Joe must give up the Farnsworth body and consider a different one.

Joe, with only minutes to spare, tells Bette that if anything should happen, she should keep her mind open to merits of other men with "something in their eyes."

Here is the gist of what follows: Joe vacates the Farnsworth body, the world is mystified by Farnsworth's disappearance, the police investigate, Bette is stricken, and Jordan and Joe resume their search for a replacement body. In the midst of a police interrogation at the Farnsworth mansion, a radio broadcast of a boxing match brings some grim news: the favorite, a boxer named Ralph Murdoch, has suddenly collapsed, dead in the ring. Then just as suddenly—weirdly—he springs back to life and wins the fight. Joe (of course) has found his new body, and the world presumes that he is Murdoch.

Then Jordan tells Joe that this latest incarnation is his last; he will finish out his life as Ralph Murdoch. There's more: his memories of being Joe Pendleton will vanish. Joe protests, but Jordan tells him this is simply fate: "Eventually all things work out," Jordan says. "There's design in everything. . . . Don't worry, Joe. You'll have everything that was ordained for you."

Bette appears, now in mourning over Farnsworth, whose body has been discovered. Bette meets "Ralph Murdoch" in the corridor as he is leaving the match. She sees "something in his eyes," and he experiences déjà vu, to put it mildly. The two of them leave to get acquainted. Jordan says, "Goodbye, champ."

Jed Harris had planned on bringing the Segall play to Broadway, but Columbia bought the rights and a screenplay was produced by Sidney Buchman and Seton I. Miller. Alexander Hall was tapped as director. Robert Montgomery was cast as Joe Pendleton, Evelyn Keyes was cast as Bette Logan, James Gleason was the nonplussed boxing trainer who has to be informed about the supernatural truth, Edward Everett Horton played Conductor 7013, and Claude Rains played Mr. Jordan. The film was released on August 7, 1941, and it was a big hit, winning Oscars for best story and best screenplay and garnering Oscar nominations for best picture, best director, best actor, best supporting actor, and best cinematography.[13]

The *New York Times*'s reviewer found the film entertaining, calling it "a delightful and totally disarming joke at heaven's expense," and singling out a number of participants for praise:

> Sidney Buchman and Seton Miller, who wrote the script, and Alexander Hall, who directed it, have had the rare sense to keep the comedy where it belongs—in the characters and situations rather than in a series of double exposures and process shots of ectoplasmic spooks. The performances, with the exception of the distaff side, are tops. Robert Montgomery's dazed prizefighter keeps his place secure as one of the screen's deftest comedians. Jimmy Gleason again steals the film's most comic scene as the manager with cosmic premonitions. Claude Rains,

as Mr. Jordan, has all the kindly authority of an archangel. And save a line for Edward Everett Horton, the peripatetic Messenger 7013, who started it all.[14]

Variety's reviewer was also pleased. Montgomery, he wrote, surpassed himself in a performance that was "a highlight in a group of excellent performances." Keyes displayed "plenty of charm," James Gleason was effective as "the fast-gabbing fight manager, who is bewildered by the proceedings," and the director, Alexander Hall, sustained "a fast pace throughout."[15]

The mythical method was rife in *Here Comes Mr. Jordan*. Pythagorean myths about the transmigration and reincarnation of souls became central to the philosophic doctrines of Plato, who featured at the end of his *Republic* a vision of souls choosing new bodies for their next lives on earth. In Virgil's work, Aeneas's tour of the underworld includes a glimpse of souls "for whom a second body is in store: their drink is water of Lethe, and it frees them from care in long forgetfulness."[16]

The ancient doctrine of reincarnation had been given a new vogue by the late nineteenth-century theosophists, and then the theme began to infiltrate modernist literature. In 1913, Robert Frost presented this vision, which is now in the public domain:

> From a cliff-top is proclaimed
> The gathering of souls for birth,
> The trial by existence named,
> The obscuration upon earth. . . .
> The pure fate to which you go
> Admits no memory of choice,
> Or the woe were not earthly woe
> To which you give the assenting voice.[17]

In addition to its great cinematic influence, *Here Comes Mr. Jordan* might have influenced a novel by Jean-Paul Sartre, *Les Jeux Sont Faits*, written in 1943 and published in 1947, which tells of lovers who meet after death and who get a second chance to achieve love on earth through reincarnation.[18] This theme, in its turn, would reappear in the supernatural romances *Made in Heaven* (1987) and *What Dreams May Come* (1998).

Lynn Root's play *Cabin in the Sky* was produced on Broadway, where it opened in October 1940. With an all-black cast, this production is a fable that is set in the rural Deep South. The hero and heroine, "Little Joe" Jackson and his wife Petunia, are a poor and humble black couple. Petunia is deeply religious while her husband is easily tempted and intermittently shiftless: he gambles at a local den of sin, John Henry's, and he flirts with a winsome young hussy, Georgia Brown.

After Joe gets shot at John Henry's—in a fight with a gambler named "Domino" Johnson—he hovers at the brink of death. Petunia prays. The minions of heaven and hell arrive (invisible to all but the Little Joe, whose soul is floating in an out-of-body state) and they argue about Joe's fate. A messenger arrives with news from the Lord: Joe will get a last chance to be saved. The angelic and infernal agents will prompt him, but he will determine his own fate through his behavior. And he will remember nothing of this supernatural interlude.

After many plot complications, Joe and Petunia both wind up dead, and Petunia is saved right away: a twisting stairway to heaven appears. But Joe is damned. Petunia prays again, telling God she loves her husband so much she will stay with him, come what will (a theme to be reprised in *What Dreams May Come* years later). And her love triumphs: Joe is granted salvation, and the two of them climb the stairway.

It turns out, however, that the whole thing has been a dream from start to finish.

Like contemporaneous films such as *Stormy Weather*, this production was a showcase for African-American talent. In the Broadway version, Ethel Waters played Petunia, Dooley Wilson played Little Joe, and Katherine Dunham was Georgia Brown. Albert Lewis was the stage director and the choreography was by George Balanchine.

The MGM film version was directed by Vincente Minnelli; the screenplay was written by Joseph Schrank and Marc Connelly. Ethel Waters reprised her role as Petunia, but Eddie "Rochester" Anderson (Jack Benny's radio sidekick) was cast as Little Joe, Lena Horne (in her screen debut) played Georgia Brown, John William "Bubbles" Sublett was Domino Johnson, and Duke Ellington and his orchestra appeared. Louis Armstrong was given an engaging role as one of the devils. Some of the original music from the stage version, composed by Vernon Duke with lyrics by John LaTouche, was retained, but some new music by Harold Arlen and E. Y. Harburg was added.

Critical reactions to the film have understandably focused on its racial issues and its merits as a song-and-dance production. Some have condemned the elements of racial stereotyping in scathing terms while others have defended them as folklore.[19] The film's chief significance for supernatural romance is its clear iteration of the love-death-afterlife formula and its overt religious structure.

The last of the second wave of plays was a classic: Nöel Coward's *Blithe Spirit*. One of Coward's finest mordant comedies, it was in its nature a wartime production—for Great Britain. The Battle of Britain had raged from the summer of 1940 onward and when Coward conceived of this play, much of London lay in ruins. Coward biographer Philip Hoare has observed that when Coward departed from bombed-out London for a seaside resort in May 1941, he came up with "a black comedy . . . daringly dwelling with humor on the notion of death in a world in which death was just around the corner."[20] The play opened at the Manchester Opera House in June 1941, moving on to the West End. Coward himself directed it. It ran in London for a record 1,997 performances, notwithstanding mixed reviews. Then the play moved to Broadway and ran for 657 performances.

The play tells the story of a novelist, Charles Condomine, and his wife Ruth. Charles is planning on writing a novel about spiritualism, so he and Ruth throw a party where the guest of honor is a daffy medium, Madam Arcati. It's all for fun—everyone presumes as a matter of course that Arcati is deluded or a fraud—and a séance will top off the evening. But in the course of the séance, Charles is visited by the ghost of his deceased first wife, Elvira.

In a long and complicated series of plot twists, the truth—which is ghoulish or deeply entertaining, depending on taste—finally emerges: Elvira is lonely and she wants to kill Charles, turn him into a spirit like herself, and then marry him again on her own "astral plane"—notwithstanding the element of "astral bigamy" that would presumably be involved.

But her plot goes wrong, and it's Ruth who gets killed instead. So the ghosts of the women have cat fights, compete with each other, then come to terms as collaborators since both of them conclude (after comparing

Figure 5.2.   Ghostly mischief in the 1945 British screen adaptation of Noël Coward's *Blithe Spirit* **as the ghost of Charles Condomine's dead wife Elvira (played by Kay Hammond) creates an astral love triangle with Condomine, played by Rex Harrison, and his wife Ruth, played by Constance Cummings. Courtesy of Photofest.**

notes) that Charles was never really a good husband to begin with. Lots of hitherto unsuspected infidelities emerge from all quarters, and Charles, who eventually decides to try and exorcise the two ghosts, finds a way to trap them in his house and depart for a solo vacation.

The J. Arthur Rank organization created the film version of the play, which was released in 1945. David Lean, who directed the picture, wrote the screenplay in collaboration with Anthony Havelock-Allan and Ronald Neame. The film was a Technicolor production—Neame was cinematographer and Natalie Kalmus was the color director—and the film possesses the brilliant color palette and the crisp definition of form that were typical of 1940s Technicolor. The score for the movie was composed by Richard Addinsell.

Rex Harrison played the role of Charles Condomine, Constance Cummings was Ruth, Kay Hammond (rendered through gauzy and translucent special effects) was Elvira, and Margaret Rutherford played Madame Arcati.

Reactions to the movie spanned a very broad range. Coward told David Lean to "just photograph it, dear boy." He was unhappy with the screen kinetics. Turning to Lean at an early screening of the film, he said, "My dear, you've just fucked up the best thing I ever wrote."[21]

Coward biographer Philip Hoare believes the playwright's response was unreasonable, arguing that the film was successful, even brilliant.[22] Others have agreed: Lean scholar Michael A. Anderegg has written that Lean "smoothly disguises the play's more overt theatrical aspects without entirely denying its stage origins." A number of devices were employed: point-of-view shots, the transposition of scenes from indoor to outdoor locations, the extension of repartée from one locale to several. Above all, the casting was intelligent and the performances were outstanding, especially Rutherford, who gave one of the most inspired comic performances of her career.

In the context of supernatural romance, Coward's play was important for a special reason: its use of the love triangle. Earlier productions had employed the device—*The Mummy*, for example—but after the stage success of *Blithe Spirit*, an important wartime supernatural romance employed it: *A Guy Named Joe*. And a long succession of supernatural romances on screen would employ the theme of supernatural rivalry between a mortal lover and a ghostly rival: *Kiss Me Goodbye* (1982) and *Truly, Madly, Deeply* (1990), for example. Many supernatural romances are based in the highly romantic supposition that one love (and one love alone) is destined for each of us: the "love of our life." The alternative view is that each of us can love many times—either in this life, in the afterlife, or in successive reincarnations.

THE WAR-BASED SUPERNATURAL ROMANCES

The film *A Guy Named Joe* was based upon a story by Chandler Sprague and David Boehm. It was carefully produced and released by MGM during 1943 for presentation to a home-front audience; it opened at Christmastime. This is the story of a flyer who gets killed in combat, becomes jealous when he sees (from his vantage point in the afterlife) his fiancée fall in love with someone else, and then sees the larger picture. At end of the film he stops being possessive and helps the woman he had loved to find love with a different man. This movie had therapeutic potential for all the war widows who would face the challenge of grieving, adjusting, and moving on with life.

The hero of the film is Pete Sandidge, an American pilot stationed in England. His girlfriend Dorinda Durston is also a flyer, though her job is to ferry planes between America and Great Britain. Pete is a daredevil flyer, and Dorinda pleads with him (to no avail) to be cautious. She fears that his "number may be up," and it certainly is.

After Pete exceeds his orders and gets killed attacking a German naval task force, he finds himself in a cloudy "somewhere" that replicates the *mise-en-scène* created for the afterlife interludes in *Here Comes Mr. Jordan*. His escort is a buddy named Dick Rumney who was shot down in combat. Some dialogue:

Pete: "Say, there's something cock-eyed here."

Dick: "What?"

Pete: "You don't belong here, I saw you shot down over Brest, your plane was on fire, nobody could have got out of it."

Dick: "That's right."

Pete: "But you got out of it."

Dick: "No, I rode her down, Pete."

Pete: "Now wait a minute . . . either I'm dead or I'm crazy."

Dick: "Well, you're not crazy, Pete."

Dick takes Pete to a heavenly official, "the Boss"—it bears noting that all of these spirits wear military uniforms—who explains that the departed have work to do among the living: they offer guidance. Dick and Pete are assigned to an Army Air Force training base in Arizona. Their task: to serve as aviation mentors by beaming helpful thoughts into the minds of novice pilots. Pete is assigned to a pilot named Ted Randall and he gives him all sorts of advice, not only on flying but also on romance.

Randall and the other new pilots ship out to the combat zones in the Pacific. And their ghostly mentors go along. But then Pete sees Randall encounter Dorinda, who has also been sent to the Pacific. A new romance begins and Pete doesn't like it. So he starts to send pernicious suggestions to the mind of Ted: suggestions that are meant to constitute sabotage.

The Boss summons Pete for the helpful and predictable reprimand. "No man is really dead," he tells Sandidge, "unless he breaks faith with the future." Pete is being given a chance "to pay off to the future what you owe for having been part of the past. It's just another way of saying, 'I'm glad I lived . . . now let me give you a hand.'"

Pete is of course transformed and so he helps Dorinda and Ted. He tells Dorinda (though telepathy) that his love for her "should have been the kind that filled your heart so full of love that you just had to go out and find someone to give it to. . . . Go on—I'm setting you free. Goodbye, my darling."

The screenplay for this film was written by Dalton Trumbo and Victor Fleming was director. The producer, Everett Riskin, had produced *Here Comes Mr. Jordan*. Spencer Tracy played the role of Pete, Irene Dunne played Dorinda, Van Johnson was cast as Ted Randall, and Lionel Barrymore played "the Boss."[23] This film would be remade in 1989 as *Always*.

A Guy Named Joe got mixed reviews. Bosley Crowther wrote that "the people at Metro-Goldwyn-Mayer had a dandy idea by the tail"—an idea with "blithesome implications, as well as spiritual ones, and it looked for a while as though Metro and its people were going to play it well. But somehow, as often happens, they yanked it around too much; they let it go slack at the wrong spot and then jerked up on it too hard. And the consequence was that the fleet thing got completely away from them." Crowther liked the spirituality; when Pete Sandidge arrived "where all good dead pilots go," it seemed as if "the people at Metro had themselves a film." In his mood of anticipation, he felt as if "a more delightful metaphysical visitor has not been around since Mr. Jordan was in town." But then, in his view, it went wrong, and the part that bothered this reviewer the most was the love triangle: "They yanked in a very tricky rivalry between Mr. Tracy and Mr. Johnson . . . and then they let go in a finish that is as foolish as anything we've seen."[24]

Variety's reviewer agreed, arguing that "in taking a fling at the spirit world, Metro doesn't quite succeed in reaching the nebulous." What the film needed, the reviewer continued, was more "sharp wit" and less "spiritual counseling."[25]

Outward Bound was remade during World War II, thus linking the two world wars as generators of early supernatural romance. The Warner Brothers remake was given a different title—*Between Two Worlds*—and the film, directed by Edward A. Blatt, was released in 1944. The cast included Paul Henreid and Eleanor Parker as Henry and Ann, John Garfield as Prior, and Sydney Greenstreet as the Examiner.

In 1945, the British government commissioned filmmakers Michael Powell and Emeric Pressburger to produce a film that would hopefully ease Anglo-American relations. The obvious emergence of the United States as a superpower during World War II was hard to take by people in Britain and France who could see their nations slipping as America and Russia emerged as the arbiters of post-war politics. To make matters worse, two British and American commanders—Field Marshall Bernard Montgomery and General Dwight D. Eisenhower—got into a quarrel over strategy in the autumn of 1944, and Ike threatened to quit unless "Monty" backed down.

Monty was made to back down.

Powell and Pressburger (who called their studio "The Archers") decided to create a supernatural romance involving an Anglo-American love affair. The resulting film, called *A Matter of Life and Death* in Great Britain and released as *Stairway to Heaven* in the United States, is a major item for supernatural romance, not least of all because of its thematic relationship to *Here Comes Mr. Jordan*.

The film, created and directed by Powell and Pressburger, was released in 1946 by the J. Arthur Rank organization. Like the 1945 Rank production of *Blithe Spirit*, the Technicolor values of the Powell and Pressburger film (developed by their cinematographer, Jack Cardiff) were stunning: rich hues and hard-edged super-realist articulation of form. And the music by Allan Gray was powerful.

The film begins with a glimpse of the cosmos: via animation, we sweep past stars and nebulae, then we descend into the atmosphere of earth, where we see a dark bomber in the night sky—on fire. It's a British Lancaster, commanded by pilot Peter Carter (played by David Niven). He is doomed: the landing gear is gone, his parachute is torn, the other crew members are dead. So he has to make a simple choice: go down with the bomber or jump. Before he jumps, he makes radio contact with an American service woman named June (played by Kim Hunter), who is stationed at a British aerodrome.[26] Their conversation is mystical: they know (somehow) that they would fall in love if Peter could somehow live.

Peter jumps. Then he finds himself rolling in the surf on a beach, quite intact. And quite alive. Dazed, he wanders up the English Channel beach and encounters—who else?—June.

Cut to heaven (which is rendered throughout the film in sepia). A pretty woman angel in uniform is welcoming British and American war dead, who step laughing from the top of what appears to be an escalator. Heaven's "waiting room" is modernistic—an appealing rendition of contemporaneous styles of mid-twentieth-century modernism in architecture and décor. A clock on the wall with incomprehensible digits and multiple hands ticks away to strange chimes. A member of the bomber crew is loitering and waiting—waiting for Peter. But Peter is late.

The truth is that a heavenly escort, Conductor 71, tried but failed to snatch the soul of Peter as he fell. The conceit (of course) is here precisely the reverse of what happened in *Here Comes Mr. Jordan*. Conductor 71 (played by Marius Goring) is admonished to find Peter, inform him of the truth, and bring him up.

But Peter argues and refuses to come, for a simple and fundamental reason: he and June have fallen in love. He will not pay the price for a heavenly mistake, for *love changes everything, even death*. He demands an appeal, and is informed that the High Court of Heaven will consider his unprecedented request.

Then the plot turns ambiguous: June, when informed of these facts by Peter, believes that he is having hallucinations and the film contrives to keep the audience in doubt about this question for the remainder of the action. This ambiguity resulted from an argument between Powell and Pressburger, who disagreed as to whether the story's supernatural element should be real or a figment of Peter's imagination as he fell from the plane (or *imagined* that he fell from the plane). The partners therefore agreed to a compromise in which the answer is left up to the viewer.[27]

And so as Peter's trial begins in the High Court of Heaven—we see millions of ghostly onlookers watching from the benches of a courtroom that spans an entire galaxy—Peter undergoes brain surgery at the aerodrome hospital. When the members of the jury request to hear testimony from Peter and June, the judge, jury, and attorneys step onto an escalator that stretches all the way to planet earth and into the operating room.

Time is frozen for the mortals as the ghostly visitation occurs. Earlier in the film, Conductor 71 told Peter that they were talking "in space, not in time." Peter's soul steps out of his body and the soul of June is summoned. The upshot: after each of the lovers makes it clear to the court that they would die quite willingly for each other, the jury concludes that they are really in love, and so neither one of them has to die, at least for many years. Peter wakes up, informs June that "we won," and she replies, "I know."

This quirky movie makes an obvious use of the time channel device. Its relation to the wartime issues of life and death is direct. Its importance to supernatural romance as a genre is self-evident. But the film's ambiguity was difficult for its makers to sustain and the long-winded speeches of the lawyers in the heavenly trial belabor Anglo-American relations so much that even Powell and Pressburger admitted later on that they went overboard.[28] The British reviewer Dilys Powell complained that "*A Matter of Life and Death* remains an audacious, sometimes beautiful, but basically sensational film about nothing."[29]

As always, however, there is no accounting for the sensibilities of individual critics—unless one happens to know the person in question very well—and Bosley Crowther of the *New York Times* adored the film. "Had you harked," he began,

> you would have heard the herald angels singing an appropriate paean of joy over a wonderful new British picture, *Stairway to Heaven* [the American title of *A Matter of Life and Death*], which came to the Park Avenue Theatre yesterday. And if you will listen now to this reviewer you will hear that the delicate charm, the adult humor and visual virtuosity of this Michael Powell–Emeric Pressburger film render it indisputably the best of a batch of Christmas shows.

Though Crowther decided to accept the psychological explanation of Peter Carter's story, he let himself revel in the film's otherworldly dimensions. "If you wished to be literal about it," he wrote, "you might call it romantic fantasy with psychological tie-ins. But literally is not the way to take this deliciously sophisticated frolic in imagination's realm. For this is a fluid contemplation of a man's odd experiences in two worlds, one the world of the living and the other the world of his fantasies—which, in this particular instance, happens to be the great beyond."[30]

Years later, critic Roger Ebert called the movie "one of the most audacious films ever made." Aesthetics as always are a matter of taste, but the cinematography in this film is truly breathtaking and so are the special effects (including an eighty-five-ton heavenly escalator designed by Alfred Junge). Ebert was dazzled by some of the visions employed by Junge to depict the modernistic heaven: "vast holes in the sky with tiny people peering down over the edges," for example, and the way in the which Junge's mastery of special effects "creates a heavenly amphitheater that fills the sky, and fills it with infinite ranks of heaven's population" when the trial of Peter Carter is shown.[31] The editing was skillful and the point-of-view shots (including a view of what Peter sees as his eyelids start to close before the surgery) were often startling. Powell claimed that the film was his favorite and the film historian Ian Christie regards it as the Archers' "most spectacular production."[32]

Film scholar Philip Horne has perceived the connections between this film and earlier productions including *Our Town, Here Comes Mr. Jordan, A Guy Named Joe,* and *Blithe Spirit.* In a playful aside, he observes that "we could almost imagine that Peter Carter had seen *Here Comes Mr. Jordan* between bombing missions and seized on its portrayal of an incompetent heavenly emissary as a saving precedent in the projection of his own imaginative resistance to death."[33]

The 1946 classic *It's a Wonderful Life* is another unique and iconic film in which the influence of supernatural romance can be detected. The story of small-town banker George Bailey (played by James Stewart), who makes a wish that he had "never been born" and then *sees* (and participates in) a world in which his horrid wish has been granted—to see the world as it would have been without him—has other antecedents, not least of all the *Christmas Carol* of Dickens, which presents an alternative reality that is comparable: the world as it *will be* if Scrooge does not mend his ways before he dies.[34] There is also the precedent of Dante: George's ghostly sojourn in the loathsome counterfactual "Pottersville" is essentially a trip to hell and back.

But George's state (when he "has never been born") is in many ways a *surrogate for death* (like the state of Fiona Campbell in *Brigadoon*) since he remembers his loved ones clearly, just as he might in the afterlife if he were dead. It is also significant that Frank Capra created an opening sequence for this film that is identical to the opening sequence of *A Matter of Life and Death*: a glimpse of the cosmos.[35]

A few other films from this period partook of the love-death-afterlife theme. A 1943 Ernst Lubitsch film from 20th Century Fox, *Heaven Can Wait*—no relation at all to the Harry Segall play that inspired *Here Comes Mr. Jordan*—tells the story of a womanizer (played by Don Ameche) who arrives in hell all ready for admission because of his faithlessness to his wife in the first of their two marriages. But the infernal authorities decide that he behaved himself well enough the second time around to go to heaven instead, where the soul of his dead wife (played by Gene Tierney) is waiting.[36]

A 1944 Otto Preminger film that was also made by 20th Century Fox—*Laura*—has a love-death-afterlife twist that turns out to be a sham. A police detective (played by Dana Andrews) is romantically haunted by a portrait of the female murder victim, Laura Hunt (played by Gene Tierney). He is in love with a woman who is dead. But Laura isn't really dead at all; another woman was killed in her house while she was out of town. The moment she walks through her own front door is a great resurrection scene. And the murderer's speech at the end is a love-and-death classic: "Love is eternal. It has been the strongest motivation for human actions throughout centuries. Love is stronger than life. It reaches beyond the dark shadows of death."

Before the close of World War II, two novels had appeared that would generate more supernatural romances on screen. Robert Nathan's *Portrait of Jennie* had been published in 1940. And *The Ghost and Mrs. Muir* was published in 1945.

NOTES

1. This film was a great milestone for both its producer and one of its stars. The Hal Roach Studio produced this film in partnership with MGM. Roach, like Mack Sennett, had produced silent comedies in the 1920s, and he made the transition to sound very easily, producing Laurel and Hardy shorts for MGM well into the 1930s. But then Roach aspired to produce an "A" picture and with *Topper* he succeeded magnificently. *Motion Picture Herald* proclaimed in 1938 that "not so long ago Mr. Roach seemed firmly cast forever in the category of the two part comedy director, deep rooted in the traditions of an art of yesterday. Today he is to be discovered full

fledged and sure handedly engaged in first rank feature production, and production of a type unburdened by reminiscence. This constitutes a performance with few, if any, parallels in the annals of Hollywood. Few have had the elastic capacity." Quoted in Richard Lewis Ward, *History of the Hal Roach Studios* (Carbondale, IL: Southern Illinois University Press, 2005), 97. At one and the same time, *Topper* was a break-through for Cary Grant, whose contract with Paramount kept him playing straight romantic roles when he wanted to move to light comedy. Just after his contract with Paramount expired, Roach asked him to play George Kerby in *Topper*. There was no turning back for Grant, who moved swiftly on to some of his greatest comic roles in films such as *Bringing Up Baby*, *The Philadelphia Story*, and *His Girl Friday*. See Marc Eliot, *Cary Grant: A Biography* (New York: Harmony, 2004), 151–52. All of the perfor-mances in *Topper* were superb, and the performance of Roland Young as the dithering banker was one of the best in his entire career.

2. Frank S. Nugent, "The Screen in Review: Paul Osborn's fantasy, 'On Borrowed Time,' Reaches the Capitol's Screen under a Metro By-Line," *New York Times*, July 7, 1939,   accessible   via   http://www.nytimes.com/movie/review?res= 990CE4D9133AE532A25754C0A9619C946894D6CF&pagewanted=print.

3. Jay Robert Nash and Stanley Ralph Ross, *The Motion Picture Guide 1927–1983*, vol. 6 (Chicago: Cinebooks, 1987), 2244.

4. See Frank Rich, "George C. Scott has Death up a Tree in 'Borrowed Time," *New York Times*, October 10, 1991.

5. Thornton Wilder, preface, *Three Plays by Thornton Wilder* (New York: Bantam Books, Harper & Row, 1966), ix–xi.

6. Lesser courted various directors, including Ernst Lubitsch and William Wyler before settling on Sam Wood. He also considered Lillian Hellman as a scriptwriter. The production designer was Cameron Menzies and much of the shooting was done on location in Peterboro, New Hampshire. See Patricia King Hanson and Alan Gevin-son, eds., *The American Film Institute Catalog of Motion Pictures Produced in the United States* (Berkeley: University of California Press, 1993), Feature Films, 1931–1940, Film Entries, M–Z, 1590.

7. The correspondence between Lesser and Wilder on this and other matters has been preserved. For Wilder's commentary on (and approval of) the plot change, see Thornton Wilder to Sol Lesser, March 24, 1940, in *The Selected Letters of Thornton Wilder*, Robin G. Wilder and Jackson R. Bryer, eds. (New York: HarperCollins, 2008), 374–75. Some highlights: "Dear Sol: Sure, I see what you mean. . . . In a movie you see people so close that a different relation is established. In a theatre they are halfway abstrac-tions in an allegory; in the movie they are very concrete. So in so far as the play is a Generalized Allegory she dies—we die—they die; insofar as it's a Concrete Happen-ing it's not important that she dies; it's even disproportionately cruel that she dies. Let her live—the idea will have been imparted anyway."

8. The principle here is comparable to the experience of Ebenezer Scrooge with the Ghost of Christmas Past: in these particular fantasies of "time travel," the past as well as the characters in it cannot be influenced or changed by the visitation from the future. Neither Scrooge nor Emily can communicate with their family or friends in the past. "These are but shadows of things that have been," says the ghost to Scrooge; "they have no consciousness of us."

9. Bosley Crowther, "Our Town," *New York Times*, June 14, 1940.

10. Philip Horne, "Life and Death in *A Matter of Life and Death*," in Ian Christie and Andrew Moor, eds., *The Cinema of Michael Powell: International Perspectives on an English Film-Maker* (London: British Film Institute, 2005), 121.

11. Horne, "Life and Death in *A Matter of Life and Death*," 121.

12. Thornton Wilder, preface, *Three Plays by Thornton Wilder*, xi.

13. See John T. Soister, *Claude Rains: A Comprehensive Illustrated Reference to His Work in Film, Stage, Radio, Television, and Recordings* (Jefferson, NC: McFarland, 1999), 106. Columbia studio chief Harry Cohn was initially skeptical about the project, and so were his financial backers. But then, to his credit, he changed his mind, telling writer

Sidney Buchman to proceed. "All they want is what sold last year," he complained, and then told Buchman to "go ahead with the picture." See Jay Robert Nash and Stanley Ralph Ross, *The Motion Picture Guide*, vol. 4, 1210–11.

14. "'Here Comes Mr. Jordan,' in which Robert Montgomery Appears, Opens at the Music Hall—'Hold That Ghost' Arrives At Capitol—New Palace Film," *New York Times*, August 8, 1941, accessible via http://www.nytimes.com/movie/review?res= 9F02EED71530EF3ABC4053DFBE66838A659EDE.

15. "Review, 'Here Comes Mr. Jordan,'" *Variety*, December 31, 1940, accessible via http://variety.com/1940/film/reviews/here-comes-mr-jordan-1117791611/.

16. Virgil, *The Aeneid*, Robert Fitzgerald, trans. (New York: Random House, 1983), Vintage edition, 185. The theme of déjà vu as applied to the forgetfulness of past lives that is standard doctrine in theories of reincarnation has been applied in strictly "secular" fashion (via science fiction) to other film romances. In *The Eternal Sunshine of the Spotless Mind* (2004) the theme of memory erasure is employed without supernatural trappings.

17. Robert Frost, "The Trial by Existence," public domain, in *Selected Poems of Robert Frost* (New York: Holt, Rinehart & Winston, 1963), 16–17. Lines 17–20, 53–6.

18. I am indebted to my student Jan van Ewijk for calling my attention to this novel.

19. For a critical reaction to *Cabin in the Sky*, see Allen J. Woll, *The Hollywood Musical Goes To War* (Chicago: Nelson-Hall, 1983), 124–28. For a defense of the *"faux-naif"* Negro folklore in the film, see Pauline Kael, *5001 Nights at the Movies* (New York: Henry Holt, 1991), 112–13. See also Donald Bogle, *Toms, Coons, Mulattoes, Mammies, and Bucks: An Interpretive History of Blacks in American Films* (New York: Continuum, 2006), 81–82.

20. Philip Hoare, introduction, *Nöel Coward, Three Plays: Blithe Spirit, Hay Fever, Private Lives* (New York: Vintage Books, 1999), 6.

21. Philip Hoare, *Noel Coward: A Biography* (New York: Simon & Schuster, 1995), 353–54.

22. Hoare, *Noel Coward*, 354.

23. The production of this film was a harrowing experience for several reasons. For one thing, the stars, Spencer Tracy and Irene Dunne, were on very bad terms. The selection of Dunne had been one of the key factors in planning the production. As Tracy biographer Larry Swindell has explained, this film "needed a leading lady who was a good actress, one old enough to make her long involvement with Tracy plausible, but young enough to end up in the arms of a younger (and living) flyer, in a romance arranged by the dead pilot's spirit." Dunne was a good choice, but, as Swindell recounts the story, Tracy "was going through one of his bad times," drinking heavily and behaving badly toward Dunne on the set. Dunne complained to Louis B. Mayer and threatened to quit the picture if Tracy continued to misbehave. At the same time, Van Johnson suffered a serious head injury in a traffic accident, and Mayer was considering replacing him with Peter Lawford. Tracy, who liked Johnson, threatened to quit the picture if Johnson were removed from the cast. Mayer struck a deal: if Tracy behaved himself with Dunne, the production of the film would be adjusted to permit the recuperation of Johnson. See Larry Swindell, *Spencer Tracy: A Biography* (New York: World, 1969), 188–91. Much of the location shooting for this film took place at Army air bases, including Columbia Army Air Base in South Carolina; Luke Air Base in Glendale, Arizona; and Randolph Air Base in San Antonio, Texas. Shooting began in February 1943 and concluded in September. The film was a box-office success, one of the top ten box office hits in the 1943–1944 movie season. See Robert L. McLaughlin and Sally E. Parry, *We'll Always Have The Movies: American Cinema During World War II* (Lexington: University Press of Kentucky, 2006), 242–46.

24. Bosley Crowther, "The Screen: 'A Guy Named Joe,' A Variable Fantasy, With Spencer Tracy and Irene Dunne, Begins an Engagement at the Capitol," *New York Times*, December 24, 1943, accessible via http://www.nytimes.com/movie/review?res= 9C0DE3DC1238E33BBC4C51DFB4678388A659EDE.

25. "Review: 'A Guy Named Joe,'" *Variety*, December 31, 1943, accessible via http://variety.com/1943/film/reviews/a-guy-named-joe-2-1200414353/.

26. Powell and Pressburger knew from the outset that they wanted David Niven, just back from military service, to play Peter Carter, but it took some time to identify a suitable leading lady. Since the role called for an American woman, a talent search in Hollywood resulted. It was Alfred Hitchcock who called Kim Hunter to the attention of Powell and Pressburger. See Scott Salwolke, *The Films of Michael Powell and the Archers* (Lanham, MD: Scarecrow Press, 1997), 131–32.

27. Salwolke, *The Films of Michael Powell and the Archers*, 131–32.

28. Film historian Scott Salwolke has written that "once the two attorneys take up their positions [in the heavenly courtroom] the film is overwhelmed by dialogue and ideology. Even Powell concluded that he was not 'happy about the ending, but that's the relic of the propaganda period.'" See Salwolke, *The Films of Michael Powell and the Archers*, 138.

29. Dilys Powell, quoted in Salwolke, *The Films of Michael Powell and the Archers*, 132.

30. Crowther's encomium continued as follows: "We haven't space at this writing to give you any more, except to say that the wit and agility of the producers, who also wrote and directed the job, is given range through the picture in countless delightful ways: in the use, for instance, of Technicolor to photograph the earthly scenes and sepia in which to vision the hygienic regions of the Beyond (so that the heavenly 'messenger,' descending, is prompted to remark, 'Ah, how one is starved for Technicolor up there!'). We haven't space to credit the literate wit of the heavenly 'trial' in which the right of an English flier to marry an American girl is discussed, with all the subtle ruminations of a cultivated English mind that it connotes, or the fine cinematic inventiveness and visual 'touches' that sparkle throughout, notably in the exciting production designs of Alfred Junge." Bosley Crowther, "The Screen in Review: 'Stairway To Heaven,' a British Production at Park Avenue, Proves a Holiday Delight," *New York Times*, December 26, 1946, accessible viahttp://www.nytimes.com/movie/review?res=9E0CE0D61E3BE333A05755C2A9649D946793D6CF.

31. Roger Ebert, "Stairway to Heaven/A Matter of Life and Death," *Chicago Sun-Times*, April 21, 1995. The occasion for this retrospective journalistic review was the release of a restored Technicolor print. Accessible via http://www.rogerebert.com/reviews/stairway-to-heaven-a-matter-of-life-and-death-1995.

32. Ian Christie, *Arrows of Desire: The Films of Michael Powell and Emeric Pressburger* (London: Faber & Faber, 1994), 55.

33. Philip Horne, "Life and Death in *A Matter of Life and Death*," in Ian Christie and Andrew Moor, eds., *The Cinema of Michael Powell*, 122.

34. The link between *It's A Wonderful Life* and *A Christmas Carol* was the subject of commentary by Kenneth Turan, who compared the works in a 1989 issue of *TV Guide*: "In despair on Christmas Eve, the happiest night of the year, normally decent citizen George Bailey turns into a mini-Scrooge. . . . Brought to the brink of suicide by the possibility of financial ruin, Bailey, like Scrooge, is allowed to step outside the boundaries of space and time to see the truth about his life. But while Scrooge sees what a monster he's been, George Bailey sees that all the sacrifices he's made . . . have brought him the kind of love and respect mere money can never hope to buy." Cited in Stephen Cox, *It's A Wonderful Life: A Memory Book* (Nashville, TN: Cumberland House, 2003), 16.

35. Whether Capra was influenced (either consciously or unconsciously) by the opening sequence of *A Matter of Life and Death* is an interesting topic for conjecture. The British film was shot in the autumn of 1945 and premiered (in Great Britain) on November 1, 1946. Capra's *It's A Wonderful Life* went into production in in April 1946 and wrapped up in July. Capra himself described the origins of his heavenly/cosmic sequence as follows: "For a long time we were worried about how to show heaven. Heaven is never the same to any two people. . . . So, it just became ridiculous. I knew we wouldn't please everybody, and I knew we'd probably get some laughs with the thing that we naturally didn't want. So rather than getting laughs that we didn't want,

I used laughs that we did want. . . . This method of doing it with the stars and little cartoons and such came up after many sessions." Quoted in Stephen Cox, *It's A Wonderful Life: A Memory Book*, 49. An early script preserved in the library of the Academy of Motion Picture Arts and Sciences shows that Capra also considered a preliminary sequence of moving clouds, which MGM had used in *The Wizard of Oz*. See Cox, *It's a Wonderful Life: A Memory Book*, 89. There were other correspondences between *A Matter of Life and Death* and *It's a Wonderful Life*. In the British film, the heavenly messenger purloins a book about chess and then he tosses it from the heavenly dimension to the hero at the end of the film. In Capra's movie, the angel Clarence Oddbody is reading a Mark Twain novel and it suddenly shows up (inscribed) in the home of George Bailey at the film's conclusion.

36. The film got a so-so review in the *New York Times*. Bosley Crowther wrote that the movie "has utterly no significance. Indeed, it has very little point, except to afford entertainment. And that it does quite well." Except that "the character of the rakish hero is never clearly defined, nor is that of the girl who marries him. He remains an ambiguous changeling, and so does she. That may be one reason why Don Ameche and Gene Tierney are flat in the roles. Or rather, they lack the flexibility which such mannered comedy demands. But so many other characters are so amusingly written and played that the lack is not overpowering." Bosley Crowther, "The Screen: 'Heaven Can Wait,' An Amusing Comedy of Manners, with Don Ameche, Gene Tierney, and Charles Coburn, Opens at Roxy," *New York Times*, August 12, 1943, accessible via http://www.nytimes.com/movie/review?res= 9E07E3D81738E33BBC4A52DFBE668388659EDE. *Variety*'s review emphasized the directorial virtuosity of Ernst Lubitsch more than anything else: "Provided with generous slices of comedy, skillfully handled by producer-director Ernst Lubitsch, this is for most of the 112 minutes a smooth, appealing and highly commercial production. Lubitsch has endowed it with light, amusing sophistication and heart-warming nostalgia. He has handled Don Ameche and Gene Tierney, in (for them) difficult characterizations, dexterously." *Variety* staff, "Review: 'Heaven Can Wait," *Variety*, December 31, 1942, accessible via http://variety.com/1942/film/reviews/heaven-can-wait-1200414109/.

SIX

The Ghost and Mrs. Muir and the Applications of Theology in Supernatural Romance

In 1945, another literary venture in supernatural romance hit the shelves: *The Ghost and Mrs. Muir*, a novel by "R. A. Dick," which was the pseudonym of an Anglo-Irish woman author, Josephine Aimee Campbell Leslie. The heroine of the novel becomes an author, too—an author who employs a pseudonym.

The book tells the story of a young widow, Lucy Muir, who moves with her children, Cyril and Anna, to a house by the sea in the fictitious English town of "Whitecliff." The house turns out to be haunted by the ghost of a sea captain, Daniel Gregg, who manifests himself to Lucy in her dreams.

20th Century Fox bought the rights and producer Darryl F. Zanuck tapped Joseph Mankiewicz to direct the film, which was largely shot on location in California in places where the Pacific coastline would give the impression of the English Channel coast around Dover. Filming began in November 1946 and concluded early in 1947.

In the movie Lucy has only one child, her daughter Anna, and they move into "Gull Cottage" in the seaside town of Whitecliff along with Lucy's servant and friend, Martha Huggins. Unlike the book, the ghost of Captain Gregg in the film manifests himself to Lucy (intermittently) in her waking hours as well as in her dreams. Though an ectoplasmic presence, he appears corporeal enough to have a vivid relationship with Lucy, one that develops into a literary partnership when they co-author the story of his life. They call the book *Blood and Swash* and they foist it on the world as the production of a mysterious single author, "Captain X."

In the course of writing this book they fall in love. She calls him Daniel and he calls her "Lucia" to salute the feminine magnificence just beneath her quiet demeanor. But there's a problem, of course: he's dead. And so all of their erotic feelings lead to nothing more than frustration.

After much emotional turmoil and unfulfilled longing, he hypnotizes her one night as she sleeps and suggests to her that the whole thing has been an illusion. "You must make your own life amongst the living," he says, "and whether you meet fair winds or foul, find your own way to harbor in the end." Then he suggests to her hypnotized mind that she wrote the book herself—"a book you imagined from his house, from his picture on the wall, from his gear lying around in every room. It's been a dream, Lucia. And in the morning, and in the years after, you'll only remember it as a dream. And it will die, as all dreams must die, at waking."

He decides that he has to go away. But he describes the things he could have shown her. "How you would have loved the north cape," he exclaims, "and the fjords and the midnight sun . . . to sail across the reef

Figure 6.1.   Carnal frustration ensues in *The Ghost and Mrs. Muir*, a 1947 film about a love affair between a living woman, played by Gene Tierney, and the ghost of a dead sea captain, played by Rex Harrison. Resolution, of course, occurs at once when she dies and then the spirits walk hand-in-hand together into a misty horizon. Courtesy of Photofest.

at Barbados where the blue water turns to green." His voice rises gradually in pitch: "to the Falklands, where a southerly gale whips the whole sea white! What we've missed, Lucia . . . what we've both missed," he tells her. He begins to fade away as the camera pulls back to show him silhouetted by a window. "Goodbye—m'darling." The room is empty as Lucy sleeps on.

We sense again that "time made an error," as it did in *Portrait of Jennie*. We feel that Daniel and Lucy were obviously destined for love, but something happened—something went wrong—he died too soon.

The film tracks the rest of Lucy's life. Her daughter grows up and moves away. Lucy passes her time taking walks along the strand as she ekes out a brave, contemplative, and lonely life in the house atop the cliff above the sea.

At last she is old, and we see her on her last night alive. She is sitting in a chair and then is stricken, collapses, and is dead. A shadow approaches, and the unchanged spirit of Daniel, triumphant, lifts the ghost of Lucy from her body. She is in the full bloom of youth. Their eyes ravish one another as they walk without words down the stairs, out the door, and away into a misty horizon.

The screenplay for *The Ghost and Mrs. Muir* was produced by Philip Dunne, and the score for the film was composed by Bernard Herrmann. Charles Lang, Jr. was cinematographer. Gene Tierney played Lucy and Rex Harrison was cast as Captain Gregg.

The film got mixed reviews when it was released. The *New York Times* called it "gently humorous and often sparkling good entertainment, but only up to a point. It starts out so auspiciously and spins along so merrily as Mrs. Muir comes to speaking terms with Captain Gregg that we regret having to impart the news that it falls to pieces somewhere about halfway through."[1] *Variety*'s reviewer, however, called Tierney's performance her "best to date," adding that Harrison's presence on screen "commands the strongest attention."

Variety's reviewer said the movie "pulls audience sympathy with an infectious tug that never slackens."[2] The film won an Oscar nomination for best cinematography.

Film scholars have sometimes damned this film with faint praise. According to Frieda Grafe, Joseph Mankiewicz, the movie's director, regarded it as mediocre; "his statements about the film," she observes, "are sparse and monosyllabic: a piece of hack-work, taken on purely out of expedience."[3] Grafe herself viewed the film as inept, complaining that "the music at times gets the upper hand and determines the point of view of the scene more firmly than the camera's organization of the scene."[4]

Once again, such pronouncements can be shown to be hopelessly subjective; Lee Kovacs wrote just a few years after Grafe that the film was "a remarkable and beautiful achievement."[5] Indeed, the case can be made—on subjective grounds of artistic taste—that *The Ghost and Mrs. Muir* was perhaps the most accomplished supernatural romance at that point in the development of the genre. It is hard to find a scene in which the music and the visual composition are not congruent—to the point of perfection—and the lyricism of the imagery blends with the melodic values, which are based in part upon understated sea chantey themes.

It was a production with stunning coherence and unity, both in cinematic values and intellectual content.

As to the latter, the film's hint of a sensuous afterlife—an afterlife in which the carnal frustration of Daniel and Lucy will yield to blessed rapture—speaks to an age-old theological conflict. The ascetic tradition—the association of sex with original sin and the derivative vows of chastity that remain fundamental to monasticism and the celibacy that is mandated for priests within the Catholic Church—flowed from several influences with a powerful cumulative impact on early Christianity: the cult of Orphism in Greece and the ancient Persian religion, with its dualism between spirit (which emanates from and returns to the deity Ormazd or Ahura-Mazda) and the entrapment of spirit in matter by the evil Ahriman. This doctrine was reprised in the Manichaean movement that attracted St. Augustine before his conversion to Christianity as well as in the early Christian heresy of Gnosticism, which preached a release of spirit from the prison of gross flesh.[6]

Compare such notions to the vision of Milton in *Paradise Lost*. In the Garden of Eden, Adam talks with the angel Raphael about a number of topics and he asks about love among the "heav'nly spirits." Raphael gives him this answer:

> Let it suffice thee that thou know'st
> Us happy, and without love, no happiness.
> Whatever pure thou in the body enjoy'st
> (And pure thou wert created) we enjoy
> In eminence, and obstacle find none
> Of membrane, joint, or limb, exclusive bars:
> Easier than air with air, if spirits embrace,
> Total they mix, union of pure with pure
> Desiring; nor restrained conveyance need
> As flesh to mix with flesh, or soul with soul.[7]

We sense the likelihood that Lucy and Daniel will experience this (or something like it) in the afterlife. Indeed, according to Scripture, the possibilities for love are much greater in the afterlife, since monogamy is no longer binding.

However fundamental the sacrament of marriage is in this life, it binds no longer in heaven, according to the New Testament. In Matthew 22:30, Christ answers a group of Sadducees who ask him which of seven men who had been married to the very same woman should have her as a wife in heaven. Christ replied that "in the resurrection they neither marry, nor are given in marriage." Depending upon one's sensibilities (and proclivities) the implications might seem open-ended and perhaps quite permissive. But the vision of a sensuous afterlife is not to everybody's taste.

Years ago, the philosopher Arthur O. Lovejoy reflected on the states of mind he called "this-worldly" and "other-worldly" in regard to their visions of life after death. He put it this way:

> To be concerned about what will happen to you after death, or to let your thought dwell much on the joys which you hope will then await you, may obviously be the most extreme form of this-worldliness; and it is essentially such if that life is conceived, not as profoundly different from this, but only as more of much the same sort of thing . . . with merely the omission of the trivial or painful features of terrestrial existence, the heightening of some of its finer pleasures, the compensation for some of earth's frustrations.[8]

Theologian Christopher Deacy has recently said much the same thing in regard to the visualizations of the afterlife in cinema: "It is really not surprising," he writes, "that filmmakers as well as theologians should have resorted to employing this-worldly and present-oriented visions and metaphors to refer to what will happen after we die."[9]

Many supernatural romances partook of such a "present-oriented" outlook. In *Outward Bound*, for example, the "examiner" describes the pleasant work in heaven that awaits the souls who are saved—work that is similar enough to what they did when they were alive. A clergyman aboard the ocean liner is told that more spiritual work will await him in the afterlife: he will minister to the needs of other souls and his experience in life will be very useful. In *A Guy Named Joe*, the dead are given helpful work that will assist the living down below. In *Our Town*, however, Emily is told she must detach herself from her experience among the living in order to prepare for the very different kinds of things that are in store. And this is more in line with what Lovejoy called the "other-worldly" state of mind, which embraces the belief that "both the genuinely 'real' and the truly good are radically antithetic in their essential characteristics to anything to be found in man's natural life, in the ordinary course of human experience."[10]

And as far as love among the angels—or the blessed souls of the departed—is concerned, the otherworldly outlook was stated severely by Plato, who condemned erotic feelings as harmful to the soul's salvation. In *Phaedo*, Plato speaks this message through a conversation that is supposed to have taken place between the imprisoned Socrates and some admirers. Socrates says that he is eager to die, to have done with human pleasure and its grubbiness. He has nothing but scorn for "the soul which has been polluted, and is impure at the time of her departure, and is the companion and servant of the body always, and is in love with . . . the desires and pleasures of the body."

Such polluted souls are condemned to hang around the world as ghosts: they are "heavy and weighty and earthy." They keep "prowling around tombs and sepulchres, near which, as they tell us, are seen certain ghostly apparitions of souls which have not departed pure." [11]

Surely *The Ghost and Mrs. Muir* makes a powerful statement in response to such doctrines, whether Christian in their nature or pagan. The ghost of Captain Gregg haunts the earth, but he is not "polluted"—no matter how earthy and salty his sensibilities may be. He is waiting for the beauty that is destined. The triumph of love, death, and the afterlife in this movie is implied to be nothing less than a direct compensation for the unfulfilled longings on earth—a compensation for "what we've missed"—a paradise of Eros.

For this and other reasons, this film is an essential document for the genre of supernatural romance.

The theological implications of *The Ghost and Mrs. Muir* are implicit— never explicit. There are no references at all to God or even heaven in the picture. But many other supernatural romances—in fact, most of them— make religious implications crystal clear, at least to some extent. *Outward Bound* presents salvation and damnation very clearly, Peter Standish in *Berkeley Square* speaks of time as an idea in the mind of God; Little Joe and Petunia in *Cabin in the Sky* are involved in a war between heaven and hell; the plot of *Brigadoon* is centered in an explicit covenant with God; and the convent scenes in *Portrait of Jennie* play a crucial role in the plot as well as in the explication of the mystery. *Death Takes a Holiday* reflects overtly pagan antecedents—and so does *The Mummy*—but even pagan and polytheistic religions are, after all, religions.

Perhaps this is the place to make some observations regarding the content of supernatural romances in relation to the theological doctrines of established religions. Critics later on (especially in the 1990s) would complain that many Hollywood visions of the afterlife are often vague for commercialistic reasons: to avoid giving any offense that might diminish the revenue from box office receipts. It is hard to deny that commercial ventures are driven by marketing strategies. But complaints about the blandness of some—not all—supernatural romances is to give short shrift to the flip side of that situation: by leaving such matters open-ended, the movies open up the door to adventurous speculation that can be quite subversive to the theological doctrines of established orthodoxies. And they can usher in all sorts of innocuous-seeming heterodoxies (or outright heresies, such as reincarnation, vis-à-vis the Judeo-Christian tradition). They can challenge the faith-based creeds without appearing to challenge much of anything. And what better form of challenge can there be than a challenge that is hidden?

Perhaps the theological issue that figures in supernatural romances more than any other—indeed it shows up over and over again in these films—is the issue of "destiny," especially when its edicts are compounded with (or confounded by) "errors," chance occurrences, and "accidents." The issue of God's omnipotence vis-à-vis (or versus) human "free will" has vast theological importance especially concerning the doctrine of predestination. And this theological issue has its purely logical counterpart in metaphysical philosophy.

Among the ancient Greek philosophers, the Stoics were inclined to view everything as subject to fate—and they believed that the wise should submit to fate "stoically." The Epicureans, however, believed that the cosmos is subject to accidental and contingent events—subject to the chance "swervings" of "atoms" (a doctrine in some respects comparable to modern quantum mechanics among the physicists). Among the surviving Epicurean works is the book *On the Nature of the Universe* by the Roman poet Lucretius, who put the matter this way: "If the atoms never swerve so as to originate some new movement that will snap the bonds of fate, the everlasting sequence of cause and effect—what is the source of the free will possessed by living things throughout the earth?" [12]

The "everlasting sequence of cause and effect" has been the notion of "determinists" throughout intellectual history: the idea that "what goes before" inherently *compels* whatever comes after and *causes* it to happen. And the sequence of cause-and-effect takes place within the sequence of before-and-after, thus linking the determinism problem to time. One's "destiny" flows from the past. [13]

Immanuel Kant tried to "snap the bonds of fate" by trying to associate freedom with *timelessness*—with a state that is completely exempt from the process of before-and-after. He tried to argue on metaphysical grounds that "noumena," things in themselves, do not participate in time, which is nothing more than a quality of appearances ("phenomena"). [14] So they are "free." But the question still remains: if timelessness is a precondition of "freedom," how can the "noumena" *use* this putative "freedom?" The *use* of freedom is an *act*, and every act must surely take place in a sequence of *before and after*. Freedom minus action is an empty proposition—is it not?

In theology, the issue of "destiny" is related to the doctrine of God's "omnipotence" in most—if not all—of the monotheistic religions. Like "infinity," however—or "eternity," for that matter—the term "omnipotence" can be defined in different ways. Pantheists, for instance, believing that God is literally *everything*, construe his all-powerful nature as an all-pervasive and all-inclusive nature: God, in their view, is simply everything, with nothing excluded. Theists, on the other hand—those who distinguish between the heavenly creator and his cosmic creation—construe omnipotence as the *capacity to do anything*, though some would qualify the doctrine to mean anything that does not involve an internal contradiction.

So "destiny" in monotheistic religion tends to be equivalent to "God's will." But defining the nature and extent of "God's will" can be difficult, too. St. Augustine, for example, argued that since God is "outside time in eternity," it follows that he "does not will first one thing and then another, but that he wills all that he wills simultaneously, in one act, and eternally."[15] St. Thomas Aquinas agreed that "because God is altogether unchanging, he can't will something that he previously didn't, or start to know something new."[16] Such reasoning was subjected to ridicule by David Hume, who argued that such nominal "theists" were in fact "atheists without knowing it [because] a mind, whose acts and sentiments and ideas are not distinct and successive; one, that is wholly simple, and totally immutable; is a mind which has no thought, no reason, no will, no love or hatred; or in a word is no mind at all."[17]

So can *anything* be really "accidental"—subject to "chance"—if "God wills all that he wills simultaneously, in one act, and eternally"?

Aquinas had an answer: God's nature is miraculous. He acts in accordance with his nature. And his nature must include divine volition. Something similar is logically true of the cosmos that God created: freedom is based upon the miracle of *possibility*. It can all be understood logically, and the Scholastics knew how to present this through formal analysis: "*What can be* and *what must be* are variants of being," St. Thomas wrote, and so it stands to reason "that it is from God's will itself that things derive whether they must be or may . . . be."[18]

Alfred North Whitehead developed a comparable answer: building upon the so-called "vitalist" tradition in metaphysical philosophy—a tradition that views all "material" things as emanations from a deeper force of spirit—Whitehead wrote that while the force of "causal efficacy" is real, things are also in their nature to some extent *self-creating*, that the universe, as it were, can lift itself up by its own bootstraps.[19] There is an authentic element of *power* in "actual entities."

Enough: it is time to apply these issues of destiny, fate, and chance to a supernatural romance, specifically *Here Comes Mr. Jordan*—and also to the slightly different treatment of these issues in its 1978 remake, *Heaven Can Wait*.

In the 1941 film, the fate of Joe Pendleton *seems* to be clear, and the "cosmic error" results from the squeamishness (or the empathy) of the heavenly messenger who lifts his soul out of his plane before it actually crashes. Up in the clouds, Mr. Jordan is shown with a clipboard containing a list of all the souls who are scheduled to board the spectral airliner. "There's no Pendleton, Joseph listed," he muses as he looks over the names. Then he says, "I'll see if he's on any of the newer listings." Looking up at the pilot in the cockpit of the airliner, Jordan says, "Mr. Sloan, contact the registrar's office, will you? Ask them for whatever they have on Pendleton, Joseph." After several minutes, the pilot tells Jordan that "the official record says that both of his parents are happily withdrawn and awaiting his arrival. Joseph is scheduled to join them on the morning of May 11, 1991." There it is: "destiny." Except that we learned the interesting fact that "newer listings" are handed down sometimes from the registrar's office, for reasons we can only surmise. Perhaps other mistakes have been made by heavenly bureaucrats.

Just the same, Mr. Jordan can confidently reassure Joe that "there's design in everything. . . . You'll have everything that was ordained for you." But destiny needs a helping hand from time to time. Things are always put right in the end, as long as the *spontaneous* ideas and choices of beings, both mortal and supernatural—beings such as Joe and Mr. Jordan who can think up creative ideas like reincarnation—can support the work of destiny and help it along.

In the 1978 remake, *Heaven Can Wait*—starring Warren Beatty as Joe Pendleton (a football player in this version), Julie Christie as Bette Logan, and James Mason as Jordan—the scene in the clouds unfolds differently. This time the heavenly messenger has snatched Joe's soul from a different situation: Joe was riding a bike that might have collided with a car that was trying to pass another car in a no-passing zone in a dark tunnel. Joe assures Mr. Jordan that he—an athlete with perfect reflexes—would have reacted in time and missed the car. Jordan calls out, "I want a checkout on Joseph Pendleton. When is he due to arrive at this way station?" A heavenly official makes a telephone call. "Pendleton, Joseph, due to arrive 10:17 a.m., March 20 of the year 2025," he says. The messenger stammers his excuses, and Jordan angrily says, "You're supposed to wait for the outcome!"

Then the metaphysical rules of the game are presented in a different version. Jordan: "Is this your first assignment as an escort?" Messenger: "Yes sir." Jordan: "Haven't you learned the rules of probability and outcome? Aren't you aware that every question of life and death remains a probability until the outcome?"

A probability until the outcome. But how can it remain a probability and not a *certainty* when Joe's date to go to heaven is fixed: March 20, 2025 (at 10:17 a.m., no less). Here is one of the perennial attempts to solve the chance-versus-fate conundrum—determinism versus indeterminism—by having the matter both ways, by suggesting that destiny and chance coexist and that they somehow interpenetrate each other.

The task of supporting destiny by fixing an error is integral to many supernatural romances. The couple is destined for each other (or at the very least perfect for each other), but something goes wrong—for Peter Ibbetson and Mary, for John Carteret and Moonyeen, for Peter Carter and June, for Daniel Gregg and Lucy Muir, for Eben Adams and Jenny Appleton, for Richard Collier and Elise McKenna, even (perhaps) for Scotty Ferguson and Judy Barton. In many (though by no means all) of these tragedies, "time made an error" that is fixed through manipulating channels of time or else solved at last in eternity.[20]

A very different commentary on destiny and chance is offered by *Sliding Doors*, a British film released in 1998. While the afterlife does not figure in this movie, there is nonetheless the presence of either (1) alternating channels of time that suggest supernatural force or else (2) a sequence of destiny or chance that manifests itself in parallel universes. In any case, the issues are close enough to the theological and philosophic problems already considered to bear examination.

Sliding Doors—like *Somewhere in Time*—could be viewed as a hybrid that displays a fusion of supernatural romance and science fiction. And, like *Somewhere in Time*, *Sliding Doors* shows the possible influence of an Irish literary figure from the 1920s who entertained unorthodox visions of time. *Somewhere in Time* (as previously noted) shows the possible influence of John William Dunne. Dunne's influence on the "time plays" of J. B. Priestley was openly acknowledged. *Sliding Doors* seems to show the influence of Edward Plunkett, the Eighteenth Baron of Dunsany (1878–1957), whose production *If: A Play in Four Acts* (1921) possesses elements that are similar to the plot of *Sliding Doors*. Moreover, Priestley's first "time play," *Dangerous Corner* (1932) has a plot that in some ways prefigures *Sliding Doors*.

The film, a joint creation of Miramax, Paramount, Intermedia Films, and Mirage Productions, was written and directed by Peter Howitt. It tells the story of a young woman in contemporaneous London, Helen, played by Gwynneth Paltrow. Helen has a terrible day as the film begins: she gets fired, misses a subway train in the London Underground (the door slides closed in her face), and gets mugged. Then the uncanny part is introduced. The subway scene is played over, first in a reverse-motion sequence as the footage plays backward—Helen backs up the stairs from the street that she had descended just a few moments earlier in film-time—and then forward with a slight variation, to wit: she descends the stairs to the Underground again and this time *catches the train*. From this point onward, the film tells two simultaneous stories: the story of the Helen who missed the train and the Helen who caught the train. The plot alternates between these parallel (or not-so-parallel) lives.

Here is what seems to be a quirk of "pure chance," a variation in micro-cosmos that ramifies into macro-cosmic force as Helen's life unfolds in different ways depending on whether she caught the subway or missed it. A "sliding door" determines her fate. Lucretius would doubtless attribute it all to the "swerving of an atom."

The love-and-death part is very simple. In one of the parallel lives, Helen meets a wonderful guy named James (played by John Hannah). They are perfect for each other and they plan to be married. But then Helen gets hit by a car as she crosses the street and she dies on the operating table as James looks on—desolate. In the other life, Helen (who has not met James at all this time since she missed the subway), has an accident and suffers a concussion. She is taken to the very same hospital and this time she meets James there (he is visiting his sick mother).[21]

"Pure chance" is transcended by "destiny," providence, or fate. What would happen in the afterlife or via reincarnation in many other supernatural romances—destined lovers who are cheated out of their romance get a second chance to have it after death through supernatural processes—happens in a parallel universe (or in an alternate time channel) where the lovers get a *different* chance to be together.

And so destiny and chance coexist and interpenetrate each other. Or do they? Perhaps "chance" is not involved at all—and this is where the theological issues attain great relevance.

In the 1950s, an American scientist named Hugh Everett III proposed what others would later call the "Many Worlds Interpretation (MWI)" of quantum mechanics. Engineer Eugene Mallove has described the gist of it (for laymen) as follows: "The universe continually bifurcates . . . into a tree-like infinity of parallel and disconnected worlds. All possible things happen 'somewhere.' In one universe, a cat dies, and in another it continues to live."[22]

This secular and scientific theory has a theological equivalent. There was a doctrine, "the Great Chain of Being," that used to take the concept of God's omnipotence in a unique direction that was engrafted into some forms of Christian orthodoxy during the Middle Ages. In his definitive book on the subject, philosopher and intellectual historian Arthur O. Lovejoy summed it up this way: God's goodness is such that he can "begrudge existence to nothing that could possibly possess it," a doctrine that Lovejoy traced to the teachings of Plotinus in the third century AD, which in turn drew from Plato's *Timaeus*.[23] In other words, God is *driven* to create . . . every possible species of thing.

Alfred North Whitehead suggested something comparable in his book *Process and Reality*, a vision in which God is driven endlessly to create all possible things.

A small step from this doctrine to the notion that God will create every possible *sequence of events*, every possible . . . *universe*, spread to infinity.

If "all possible things happen somewhere," a deterministic proposition unfolds: if God is driven to create every possible sequence of events, how can chance be a genuine component in any single one of these schemes? It cannot. However minute the variations, these universes will be spread out seriatim—in an orderly array and in an infinite range—to complete God's work. There is no real contingency at all in this precise and everlasting pattern.[24]

The view that "all possible things happen somewhere" springs from the larger doctrine of a "full universe," meaning that everything that can possibly exist . . . exists, since God cannot begrudge existence to anything. Dunne's doctrine of "serial time," through which "nothing dies" — nothing that has happened can be "taken away" from reality since it goes on existing "somewhere" in the channels of time that are arranged in an infinite regress—is another variation of the theme. "Nothing dies." It is interesting to note that Whitehead's treatise, as much a venture in speculative theology as a venture in metaphysics, concludes with a vision of all created things "passing back" into God somehow. Though the process is not made clear, the emotional upshot is very clear: all the things that happen in the universe "perish and yet live for evermore." [25]

The human mind is capable of generating almost endless doctrines to console us in the face of death and loss.

One final theological issue—one that made its appearance in *The Mummy* and in *Here Comes Mr. Jordan*—will now be considered, a theme that often appeared in supernatural romances after World War II: the theme of reincarnation. Notwithstanding its importance among the ancient Greeks and Romans, this doctrine became heretical (or at least heterodox, as in nineteenth-century theosophy) in the Western organized religions. In the East, however, it remains fundamental to Hinduism and to some aspects of Buddhism.

The theme of reincarnation was given a sensational vogue in 1956, with the publication of *The Search for Bridey Murphy*, by Morey Bernstein. The central theme in this book was the use of regressive hypnosis to access "past lives." This device was used by Alan Jay Lerner in the play *On a Clear Day You Can See Forever*, which opened on Broadway in 1965. The music was composed by Burton Lane. This time, a reviewer noticed and commented on the presence in Lerner's plot of the *Berkeley Square* influence: *Time* magazine declared that John Balderston was as much an "unseen ally" as George Bernard Shaw—whose *Pygmalion* had of course inspired the plot of Lerner's play *My Fair Lady*. [26]

The play tells the story of a woman named Daisy Gamble, who has "ESP." She seeks the help of a psychiatrist, Dr. Mark Bruckner, to help her kick her smoking habit, and when Bruckner puts her under hypnosis, she starts to tell him all about her previous life in eighteenth-century England, where she was "Melinda Wells." In the course of the plot, Daisy and Mark (of course) fall in love.

The Paramount film version of the play was released in 1970. Directed by Vincente Minnelli, it starred Barbra Streisand as Daisy and Yves Montand as the psychiatrist, who in this version is named "Marc Chabot." [27]

Another supernatural romance that used the theme of reincarnation was *Made in Heaven*, a 1987 Lorimar Productions film that was directed by Alan Rudolph. A heavenly afterlife was included this time: the hero, Mike Shea (played by Timothy Hutton), goes to heaven and falls in love there with the spirit of a woman, Annie Packert (played by Kelly McGillis), who has not yet gone to earth to lead a mortal existence. The hero and heroine will be allowed to meet again on earth via reincarnation —

and to fall in love if this is destined—but (of course) they will not be allowed to remember the heavenly interlude.[28]

The 1991 film *Dead Again* was yet another cinematic hybrid: a salute to film noir that used reincarnation to superimpose the love-death-afterlife theme. The story was based upon a movie script by writer Frank Scott, who sent it to Kenneth Branagh—who admired the story so much that he directed the resulting picture himself and starred in it. Paramount produced it.

The film begins with an event from 1949: the execution of a German-born composer, Roman Strauss (played by Branagh), for the brutal murder in Los Angeles of his wife Margaret. Strauss is executed, but before he dies he proclaims that he will love his wife forever.

Fast forward some forty-odd years: a Los Angeles detective named Mike Church (also played by Branagh) gets involved in the case of a woman with amnesia who is wandering around. The woman was played by Emma Thompson. They visit a hypnotist (played by Derek Jacobi), who puts her under regressive hypnosis, and out comes the truth right away: in a past life she was the murder victim, Margaret.

The plot thickens as the mystery woman and Mike start to date—then fall in love. But what if he's the reincarnation of Roman Strauss, who killed her in a previous life?

The truth: Roman Strauss never murdered his wife. The true killer, a child at the time of murder, grew up to become none other than the hypnotist, who suspects that the dead woman's spirit is coming after him, seeking revenge. So he tries to convince both Church and the mystery woman that one of them will murder the other. His plan is to incite them to kill each other off. But the truth emerges, and Mike and the mystery lady (whose name in this life turns out to be Amanda Sharpe) turn the tables and kill the murderer.

The classic routine of supernatural romance is thus rolled out again: the lovers, who were robbed of their chance to be together the first time around, have a second chance now via reincarnation. Their love is destined.

Most of the reviews of this film, which was a box-office success, stressed its link to film noir as well as to the Hitchcock thrillers of the 1940s like *Suspicion* and *Notorious*. But film scholar Samuel Crowl at least noticed the theme of "cosmic karma," which he mentioned in his book about the films of Branagh.[29]

If *Dead Again* was to some extent a synthesis of film noir (or neo-noir) and supernatural romance, Nora Ephron's 1993 *Sleepless in Seattle* was a hybrid of screwball comedy (or romantic comedy) and supernatural romance, or so it could be argued. Reincarnation is the clue to the synthesis of content in this comedy-drama.

The movie *begins with death*, at a cemetery in Chicago where Sam Baldwin (played by Tom Hanks) and his eight-year-old son Jonah

Figure 6.2. In the 1991 thriller *Dead Again*, reincarnation helps a loving couple when the innocent husband, Roman Strauss, played by Kenneth Branagh, is wrongly executed for the murder of his wife, Margaret, played by Emma Thompson. A generation later, their reincarnated spirits turn the tables on the real murderer and get the love that they should have had the first time around. Courtesy of Photofest.

(played by Ross Malinger) are mourning Jonah's mother, Maggie, who has died of cancer. Stricken by grief, Sam decides that the two of them should start over somewhere else, in a city far-away from their memories. So they move to Seattle.[30]

Sam cannot get over Maggie, whose ghost (played by Carrie Lowell) appears to him from time to time, when he is alone, for brief epiphanies. Perhaps it is only his imagination, but the hint of supernaturalism—and with it the love-death-afterlife theme—gets introduced in this fashion.

At Christmastime, Jonah finds a way to get his dad on a talk-radio show. The host is a woman psychiatrist, and the show is broadcast nationwide. On the other side of the continent, Annie Reed (played by Meg Ryan), a reporter for the *Baltimore Sun*, listens on the radio in her car as Sam pours out his memories. It gives her the holiday blues, but something else is occurring (we can see it in a close-up of her face), something uncanny. It isn't quite déjà vu, yet she feels a definite but quite ineffable *bond* with this man whom she has never met.[31]

She writes him a letter (after using a journalistic pretext to elicit his address from the radio station), and Jonah opens it up. The boy quickly feels an uncanny *bond* with the woman who wrote the letter, and he tries to get his father interested. But Sam says that this kind of blind date is completely impractical, since Annie lives a continent away.

Annie tries to put the matter out of her mind, but she cannot let it go. And she cannot explain *why*. So she hires a detective in Seattle, gets a picture of Sam, and quickly hops a plane for the West Coast—only to chicken out and head back to Baltimore, feeling like a fool. But in the course of her very brief visit to Seattle, Sam, without knowing who she is, sees her twice. By coincidence (or fate) Sam and Jonah are at the airport when Annie arrives. She doesn't see him, but he sees her—and Eros results. For she seems like a goddess to him as she traipses down the "Arriving Passengers" corridor, lithe, blond, and winsome. He tries to follow her, but she disappears in the crowd.

Next day, she pays a visit to the Baldwin home. Sam, who is busy and distracted, pivots casually as she is crossing the street and then . . . *he sees her*, the goddess from the airport, standing right there in the middle distance like a delicate wraith. The feeling of déjà vu is communicated powerfully.

But Annie can't go through with it: she doesn't know what to say or how to begin, but when Sam says "hello," she says hello right back in a tone that confirms . . . the *bond*.

Sam hasn't the faintest idea that this woman is the very same "Annie from Baltimore" whom Jonah keeps nagging him about. But Jonah says to his father that he learned something interesting about reincarnation from a friend of his named Jessica. Their exchange of remarks is worth quoting:

Jonah: "Dad, I was talking to Jessica about reincarnation. She says you knew Annie in another life."

Sam: "Who's Annie?"

Jonah: "The one who wrote us. But Jessica says that you and Annie never got together in that life. So your hearts are like puzzles with missing pieces, and when you get together, the puzzle is complete. The reason I know this and you don't is because I'm younger and purer and more in touch with cosmic forces."

That's the only mention of reincarnation in the entire film, but it's enough. Because the direction by Ephron, the camerawork of Sven Nykvist, the music by Marc Shaimann, and the performances of Hanks, Malinger, and Ryan combine in just the right ghostly ways throughout the picture, notwithstanding the tone of light comedy. This remarkable synthesis is pulled off to perfection.

In his review of the film, Vincent Canby marveled at this. He called the movie "a stunt, but a stunt that works far more effectively than anybody in his right mind has reason to expect." It was a film that "you may hate yourself in the morning for having loved the night before." He went on, observing that Hanks and Ryan were

> terrifically attractive, each somehow persuading the audience of the validity of all the things that keep them apart and then miraculously bring them together. . . . No great effort is made to explain how Annie could have fallen in love with him in the first place. He's a plot function. . . . The film was made by the book, yet Ms. Ephron and her associates create a make-believe world so engaging that *Sleepless in Seattle* is finally impossible to resist.[32]

"A stunt" . . . more effective "than anybody in his right mind has reason to expect" . . . "a plot function" . . . "made by the book." Well yes, except that the plot structure that achieves this unity that no one has reason to expect is the hidden template of reincarnation, presented entirely through subliminal effects except for the single tip-off provided by Jonah to his dad.

The film's finale, which is set in New York for reasons too lengthy to recount, is another near-miss for these souls who have striven over who-know-how-many previous lives to "get together." In the nick of time—after much confusion—destiny wins, and the mystical effects of this scene are just subtle enough to be sustained.

Figure 6.3.   This poster for the 1993 romantic comedy *Sleepless in Seattle* advertises a story about a couple who are struggling through physical separation to reach their romantic destiny. But there is more: the story suggests (explicitly) that their spirits have been trying through countless incarnations in past lives to find their way to each other. Meg Ryan (left) plays journalist Annie Reed and Tom Hanks (right) plays architect Sam Baldwin. Courtesy of Photofest.

Jonah's doctrine—that he is younger and purer and "more in touch with cosmic forces"—is grounded in centuries of reincarnation theory. Plato in particular believed that despite our overall forgetfulness of previous lives (the oblivion of memory induced by the waters of Lethe), certain souls can recall some glimpses of what went before. In fact, Plato insisted in the dialogue *Meno* that learning is really "recollection" since "the soul has learned everything" already.[33]

The theme has persisted in Western heterodoxy, though the emphasis is typically forgetfulness. Wordsworth's *Ode: Intimations of Immortality from Recollections of Early Childhood* is surely the most famous poetic iteration (fortunately within the public domain) of the theme:

> Our birth is but a sleep and a forgetting:
> The Soul that rises with us, our life's Star,
> Hath had elsewhere its setting.
> And cometh from afar:
> Not in entire forgetfulness,
> And not in utter nakedness,
> But trailing clouds of glory do we come (58–64).

Alas, we soon forget, and then the glory starts to fade from our souls:

> There was a time when meadow, grove, and stream,
> The earth, and every common sight,
> To me did seem
> Apparelled in celestial light,
> The glory and the freshness of a dream.
> It is not now as it hath been of yore,—
> Turn wheresoe'er I may,
> By night or day,
> The things which I have seen I now can see no more (1–9).

All we can manage in moments of tantalizing déjà vu is to struggle with

> . . . questionings
> of sense and outward things,
> Fallings from us, vanishings;
> Blank misgivings of a Creature
> Moving about in worlds not realized,
> High instincts before which our mortal Nature
> Did tremble like a guilty thing surprised:
> But for those first affections,
> Those shadowy recollections,
> Which, be they what they may,
> Are yet the fountain light of all our day,
> Are yet a master light of all our seeing (141–152).[34]

In *Look Homeward, Angel*, Thomas Wolfe's hero sensed "that he had been sent from one mystery into another. . . . The ghost of memory walked through his mind, and for a moment he felt that he had almost recovered what he had lost." He "lived here a stranger, trying to recapture the music of the lost world."[35]

Even children's literature—appropriately, in light of this doctrine—bears the imprint. In P. L. Travers's first Mary Poppins book, the infants John and Barbara talk merrily away with a starling who is sitting on the windowsill in their nursery. Not only do they talk to the birds, they also talk in sophisticated language that their parents and older siblings hear as prattle. Only Mary Poppins and the starling know the truth.

The infants marvel that their older sister and brother, Jane and Michael, cannot talk to the birds, or to the wind, or the stars. "They did once," says Mary Poppins. John asks her to explain how they forgot. "Because they've grown older," she replies.[36]

NOTES

1. "*The Ghost and Mrs. Muir*, With Gene Tierney, Rex Harrison, and George Sanders, Opens at Radio City Music Hall," *New York Times*, June 27, 1947, accessible via http://www.nytimes.com/movie/review?res=
9A07E6DA123CE13BBC4F51DFB066838C659EDE.

2. Review, *The Ghost and Mrs. Muir*, *Variety*, December 31, 1947, accessible via http://variety.com/1946/film/reviews/the-ghost-and-mrs-muir-1200414980/.

3. Frieda Grafe, *The Ghost and Mrs. Muir* (London: British Film Institute, 1995), 10.

4. Grafe, *The Ghost and Mrs. Muir*, 40.

5. Lee Kovacs, *The Haunted Screen: Ghosts in Literature and Film* (Jefferson, NC: McFarland, 1999), 42.

6. See Homer W. Smith, *Man and His Gods* (Boston: Little, Brown & Co. 1953), 127–29, 213.

7. John Milton, *Paradise Lost*, William G. Madsen, ed. (New York: Random House, 1969), Modern Library Edition, 221. Lines 620–9.

8. Arthur O. Lovejoy, *The Great Chain of Being* (Cambridge, MA: Harvard University Press, 1936), 24.

9. Christopher Deacy, *Screening the Afterlife: Theology, Eschatology and Film* (London and New York: Routledge, 2012), 78.

10. Deacy, *Screening the Afterlife*, 25.

11. Plato, *Phaedo*, Benjamin Jowett, trans., in Scott Buchanan, ed., *The Portable Plato* (Harmondsworth and New York: Penguin Books, 1977), 226–27.

12. Lucretius, *On the Nature of the Universe*, R. E. Latham, trans. (New York: Penguin Books, 1951), 67.

13. For an excellent mid-twentieth-century symposium on these issues, see Sidney Hook, ed., *Determinism and Freedom in the Age of Modern Science* (New York: Collier Books, 1958).

14. Immanuel Kant, *Critique of Practical Reason* (1788), Lewis White Beck, trans. (New York: Macmillan, 1985), 98, 99–107. Kant wrote that "no other course remains than to ascribe to existence of a thing so far as it is determinable in time . . . merely to appearance, and to attribute freedom to the same being as thing-in-itself."

15. Saint Augustine, *Confessions*, R. S. Pine-Coffin, trans. (Harmondsworth and New York: Penguin, 1961), 253, 290.

16. Thomas Aquinas, *Selected Philosophical Writings*, Timothy McDermott, trans. (Oxford and New York: Oxford University Press, 1993), *Summa Contra Gentiles*, 276.

17. David Hume, "Dialogues Concerning Natural Religion (1776)," in Charles W. Hendel, Jr., ed., *Hume Selections* (New York: Charles Scribner's Sons, 1927), 321–22.

18. Thomas Aquinas, Selected Philosophical Writings, *In Aristotelis Librum Peri Hermeneias*, 283.

19. Alfred North Whitehead, *Process and Reality* (1929), David Ray Griffin and Donald W. Sherburne, eds. (New York: Free Press, 1978), 25, 88, passim. Whitehead wrote that "however far the sphere of efficient causation be pushed . . . there always remains the final reaction of the self-creative unity of the universe." He insisted on the reality of "causal efficacy" (47), yet he also insisted on the process through which all entities creatively *act*: they *receive* the forces that shape them and then they *transmit* these forces in an *altered state* into the unfolding future. We, for example, experience "a sense of emotional feeling, belonging to oneself in the past, passing into oneself in the present, and passing from oneself in the present towards oneself in the future; a sense of influx of influence from other vaguer presences in the past, localized and yet evading local definition, such influences modifying, enhancing, inhibiting, diverting, the stream of feeling which we are receiving, unifying, enjoying, and transmitting" (178). This feeling emanates from what Whitehead called "prehensions," pulses of psychic force from which all other physical forces, from subatomic particles upward, constantly emanate. In many ways, this formulation owes much to the metaphysics of Leibniz, who argued that the fundamental units of existence are "monads," indivisible centers of percipient force. Emanations from the monads lead to conscious states of perception.

20. A somewhat minor film deserves to be mentioned in this connection: *Heaven Only Knows* (reissued as *Montana Mike*), an independent film made in 1947 by Nero Films and released by United Artists. Directed by Albert Rogell, the film tells the story of a man (played by Brian Donlevy), who, due to a clerical error in heaven, is born without a soul and thus misses out on the love he was destined to have. A guardian angel, played by Robert Cummings, descends and fixes everything.

21. Roger Ebert panned this movie as follows: "'Sliding Doors' uses parallel time-lines to explore the different paths that a woman's life might take after she does, and doesn't, find her lover in bed with another woman. I submit that there is a simple test to determine whether this plot can work: Is either time-line interesting in itself? If not, then no amount of shifting back and forth between them can help. And I fear they are not." Roger Ebert, "Sliding Doors," April 24, 1998, *Chicago Sun-Times*, accessible via http://www.rogerebert.com/reviews/sliding-doors-1998. Stephen Holden of the *New York Times* was also unimpressed, though he did like Paltrow's performance: "As slight as it is, 'Sliding Doors' provides Ms. Paltrow, who adopts a Minnie Driver-style English accent to play Helen, with her most winsome star turn since 'Emma.'" Stephen Holden, "Film Review: A Second Chance at Love," *New York Times*, April 25, 1998, accessible via http://www.nytimes.com/movie/review?res=9c06eed7123ff936a15757c0a96e958260.

22. Eugene F. Mallove, "The Universe as Happy Conspiracy," *Washington Post*, October 27, 1985, B-2. The comparability of Everett's and Ouspensky's doctrines should be apparent.

23. Lovejoy, *The Great Chain of Being*, 50. The theological implications of a "many worlds" cosmos began to be explored in a serious way during the eighteenth century, when the cumulative impact of post-Aristotelian cosmology from Galileo to Newton (the discarding of the geocentric view of the universe) hit with particular force and speculation in regard to life on other worlds forced devout Christians to re-assess some theological assumptions. The doctrine of the Chain of Being proved useful in assimilating Christian orthodoxy and the insight that other lifeforms probably exist on other worlds. The Puritan minister Cotton Mather, for instance, exclaimed in his book *The Christian Philosopher* (1721), "Great God, what a Variety of Worlds thou hast created! How stupendous are the Displays of thy Greatness . . . in the Creatures with which thou hast replenished those worlds." A different kind of doctrinal synthesis occurred in the twentieth century when J. R. R. Tolkien, a devout Catholic, responded to criticism from fellow Catholics that the parts of his fictional "legendarium" (in his *Lord of the Rings* trilogy and also in the contextual work, *The Silmarillion*) regarding the crea-

tion of the world by a deity named Eru were at odds with Christian orthodoxy. Tolkien replied that God's use of one particular creative method did not preclude his use of others, either simultaneously or seriatim, and that the imaginary world of which he wrote in his fiction was "a tribute to the infinity of His potential variety." See Humphrey Carpenter, ed., *The Letters of J. R. R. Tolkien* (Boston: Houghton Mifflin, 1981), accessible via http://www.e-reading.ws/bookreader.php/139008/The_Letters_of_J.R.R.Tolkien.pdf.

24. As of this writing, the science of physics suggests that in certain respects (though not in others) the indeterminists may have it right and that the universe is authentically contingent. In his discussion of quantum mechanics, Brian Greene has explained that by the 1920s the work of Erwin Schrödinger and Louis de Broglie suggested that subatomic "particles" partake of wave-like properties that render the movement of the "particle" merely "probable," that is, make it subject to genuine contingency. Greene elaborates: "It was not long before Schrödinger's equation and the probabilistic interpretation were being used to make wonderfully accurate predictions." By "predictions" Greene meant predictions in the aggregate, that is, predictions as to where individual "particles" might appear *most* of the time. Greene continues: "By 1927, classical innocence had been lost. Gone were the days of a clockwork universe whose individual constituents were set in motion at some moment in the past and obediently fulfilled their inescapable, uniquely determined destiny. According to quantum mechanics, the universe evolves according to a rigorous and precise mathematical formalism, but this framework determines only the probability that any particular future will happen—not which future actually ensues. . . . Everyone agrees on how to use the equations of quantum theory to make accurate predictions. But there is no consensus on what it really means to have probability waves, nor on how a particle 'chooses' which of its many possible futures to follow, nor even on whether it really does choose or instead splits off like a branching tributary to live out all possible futures in an ever-expanding arena of parallel universes. These interpretational issues are worthy of a book-length discussion in their own right, and in fact, there are many excellent books that espouse one or another way of thinking about quantum theory. But what appears certain is that no matter how you interpret quantum mechanics, it undeniably shows that the universe is founded on principles that, from the standpoint of our day-to-day experiences, are bizarre." Greene then presents the truly bizarre theories of physicist Richard Feynman, who suggested in the 1950s that every electron "traverses every possible trajectory simultaneously." According to this version of quantum mechanics, every particle in the universe in some ineffable manner goes everyplace at once, or so Feynman's theory would suggest. Physicists called this the "sum-over-path" theory. However, Feynman asserted (in Greene's paraphrase) that "all paths but one cancel each other out when their contributions are combined," which thus accounts for the fact that in *this* universe only one outcome ensues, though other possibilities may be realized in parallel universes. Einstein was disturbed by the implications of quantum mechanics, and he famously quipped that "God does not play dice with the universe." But the British physicist Stephen Hawking asserted in the 1980s that "Einstein was confused, not the quantum theory." Since the 1980s, "string theory" in physics has offered an explanation of quantum phenomena. The string theorists argue that elementary particles like electrons are not really "point particles" at all, but rather extended things that are composed of oscillating and spinning loops—loops composed of some filament or "string"—and if this assumption is granted, all the strange dynamics of quantum mechanics sort out into mathematically cogent phenomena. "String theory" has expanded to encompass the probability of multidimensional strings that vibrate within and also wrap around the multiple dimensions of a "Calabi-Yau space." But this still begs the question of determinism. It is interesting to note that Greene, having summarized the way in which quantum mechanics leads only to probabilities rather than inevitabilities, cautioned that quantum mechanics "does not leave the concept of determinism in total ruins." A doctrine of "quantum determinism," he reasoned, was tenable at least in conjectural terms. He

continued: "Wave functions—the probability waves of quantum mechanics—evolve in time according to precise mathematical rules." Consequently, "knowledge of the wave functions of all the fundamental ingredients of the universe at some moment in time allows a 'vast enough' intelligence to determine the wave functions at any prior or future time. Quantum determinism tells us that the *probability* that any particular event will occur at some chosen time in the future is fully *determined* by a knowledge of the wave functions at any prior time." All cited in Brian Greene, *The Elegant Universe: Superstrings, Hidden Dimensions, and the Quest for the Ultimate Theory* (New York: Random House, 1999), 107–12, 135–65, 341. "Chaos theory," which argues for a determinism whose effects can never be predicted due to the complexity of the interacting forces at work, dates to the 1880s but began to gather force in the 1960s through the work of mathematician and meteorologist Edward Lorenz. Physicist Paul Davies occupies the middle ground between determinism and indeterminism, arguing that universal processes are not random, but that the cosmos has a built-in potential to "self-organize." His theorizing links scientific method with metaphysical and theological speculation. See his books *Cosmic Blueprint* (New York: Simon & Schuster, 1988) and *The Mind of God: The Scientific Basis for a Rational World* (New York: Simon & Schuster, 1993). One of the classic works from the relatively recent past to relate modern physics to religious issues—in this case the belief systems of Eastern religions—is *The Tao of Physics* (1975) by physicist Fritjof Capra.

25. Whitehead, *Process and Reality*, 351. In Whitehead's scheme, God is presented (conjecturally) as a "dipolar" being, which means that one of the divine "poles" is unconscious and the other one is conscious. The unconscious pole of God is driven to create endless new variations of eternal forms or ideas, a doctrine that Whitehead of course borrowed from Plato. The conscious pole of God sees it all, absorbs it all, and then, when appropriate, *suffers* right along with us. From this doctrine emerged an influential and trans-denominational movement of "process theology." It bears noting that in Whitehead's scheme God's never-ending creation of novelty is at odds with St. Augustine's edict that God creates in one single, unchanging, and eternal act. The idea that all things emanate from God and eventually "return" to God is in some respects borrowed from Hegel.

26. "Theater: Please Don't Pick on Daisy," *Time*, October 29, 1965, accessible via http://content.time.com/time/magazine/article/0,9171,941500,00.html?promoid= googlep.

27. Vincent Canby gave the film a mixed review, calling it "a movie of fits and starts, but because the fits are occasionally so lovely, and the starts somewhat more frequent than Fifth Avenue buses, I was eventually hypnotized into a state of benign though not-quite-abject permissiveness." He averred that the film's supernatural component provided "some attractively romantic ideas about love and the mystery of the life force. 'On a Clear Day' may be the only comedy to end on the happy note that its lovers will be reunited in 2038 in, of all strange sites for reincarnation, Virginia." Vincent Canby, "Screen: 'On a Clear Day You Can See Forever' Begins Its Run," *New York Times*, June 18, 1970, accessible via http://www.nytimes.com/movie/review?res= 9C06E4D6103EE034BC4052DFB066838B669EDE.

28. An interesting feature of this film that connects it to the afterlife template of *What Dreams May Come* (both the Richard Matheson novel and the film adaptation) is the malleability of heaven as shaped by the dreaming or visualizing powers of the human mind after death. Reviewers reacted to the film in very different ways. In her review for the *New York Times*, Janet Maslin wrote that the film "has a disarming gentleness and a light, buoyant charm, not to mention a penchant for surprises." Still, it fell short by her standards. She wrote that the movie "again confirms the director [Alan Rudolph] as one of the American cinema's most fascinating also-rans. Mr. Rudolph has yet to make a film that really goes anywhere, but there's every reason to expect that he eventually will." Janet Maslin, "Film: 'Made In Heaven,' A Love Story," *New York Times*, November 6, 1987, accessible via http://www.nytimes.com/movie/ review?res=9B0DE5DC1439F935A35752C1A961948260. Roger Ebert's review was

more severe. He complained that "the movie blows most of its opportunities to have fun with heaven, in order to strand us on earth in a plot so humdrum you can hardly believe the movie was directed by Alan Rudolph." Ebert regretted that the metaphysical presuppositions of the film were not sufficiently explored. Rudolph's heaven, wrote Ebert, is one in which "the operative principle is that all you have to do is think of someplace, and you're there, and think of something, and it happens, and think of somebody, and they appear in front of you." But "if you can think of somebody and they instantly appear, what happens if they don't like you and don't want to appear?" Since Ebert disliked the overall plot, he wrote that if the film "had stayed in heaven, exploring the contradictions and paradoxes of its heavenly laws, it might have been more fun." But it "doesn't head in those directions . . . and what it tries to do was done before, and better, in Beatty's 'Heaven Can Wait.'" Roger Ebert, review of *Made In Heaven*, November 6, 1987, accessible via http://www.rogerebert.com/reviews/made-in-heaven-1987.

29. Samuel Crowl, *The Films of Kenneth Branagh* (Westport, CT: Praeger, 2006), 54, 51. See also Marcia Landy and Lucy Fischer, "Dead Again or A-Live Again: Postmodern or Postmortem?" *Cinema Journal* 33.4 (Summer 1992): 3–22.

30. After coauthoring the preliminary script of *Sleepless in Seattle*—with Jeff Arch and Audrey Gochinour—Nora Ephron recruited her sister Deliah to join the team of writers in response to a critique of the screenplay by Tom Hanks, whom Ephron had already approached to play the male lead. In the earliest version of the plot, the predestined lovers were both living in Chicago. Then Annie was relocated to Pittsburgh. At last Deliah Ephron proposed that they should live on opposite sides of the continent, which led to the corollary vision of an animated credit sequence—reprised at key moments throughout the film—of sunlight spreading from east to west across a map of the United States. Nora and Deliah Ephron, "Audio commentary," *Sleepless in Seattle*, Columbia TriStar Home Video, Tenth Anniversary DVD Edition.

31. Sometimes the perspective of a student shines brilliant light upon the work of a teacher, and such is the case with an essay by my student Marissa Marino-White—an essay she wrote for a course in film genres that I offered in spring semester 2014. In her paper "Time in Supernatural Romance," Ms. Marino-White commented on the way that many supernatural romances turn death from a tragedy into a blessing not only through the afterlife's consolations—a theme of conventional religion that is quite familiar—but also by dint of the fact that *death is the plot device that brings the two lovers together*. This represents a flip-side dimension to the theme in so many of these movies that death is a *tragedy* that *separates* the lovers until their eventual reunion in heaven. But consider the following. It is the *death of Sam's first wife* in *Sleepless in Seattle* that brings him to Annie Reed's attention, since without the loss and grieving he would never have been on the radio when she switched it on. In *A Matter of Life and Death* it is death—or in this case the *threat* of death—that brings Peter and June together, because "had Peter not been in the falling plane, and therefore about to die, he would never have contacted June and would never have known about her." In *The Ghost and Mrs. Muir*, it was the death of her first husband, Edwin, that caused her to move away from London to the town of Whitecliff, thus bringing her within the orbit of Daniel in both terrestrial and supernal dimensions. In *Here Comes Mr. Jordan* (and of course in its remake, *Heaven Can Wait*), it is the *death* of Joe Pendleton that causes him to meet Bette Logan. Would he have ever encountered her otherwise in the course of his athletic career? Two other outstanding student papers from my genre course in spring semester 2015 merit comment as well. Each of these papers illuminated the use of a particular recurrent motif in a number of supernatural romances as a structural element within the plot templates. Holly Chisholm's paper, "Portrait of Romance: Connecting Souls and Immortalizing Love in Art," showed how visual depictions in studio artwork (or photography) figured as symbolic and literal bonds between the lovers in *Portrait of Jennie*, *The Ghost and Mrs. Muir*, *Somewhere in Time*, and *What Dreams May Come*. Leonard Witt's paper, "Walls That Breathe: The Significance of Architecture in Supernatural Romance," presents a parallel view of how buildings (or physical struc-

tures such as the Land's End Light) serve as elements in the plots of *The Ghost and Mrs. Muir*, *Portrait of Jennie*, *Somewhere in Time*, *Sleepless in Seattle*, *What Dreams May Come*, and *Just Like Heaven*. All of these papers have significant potential for adaptation as journal articles.

32. Vincent Canby, "When Sam Met Annie, Or When Two Meet Cute," *New York Times*, June 25, 1993, accessible via http://www.nytimes.com/movie/review?res= 9F0CE5DA123EF936A15755C0A965958260.

33. Plato, *Meno*, W. K. C. Guthrie, trans., in *Protagoras and Meno* (New York: Penguin Books, 1956), 129–30.

34. William Wordsworth, "Ode: Intimations of Immortality from Recollections of Early Childhood (1804)," public domain, in David Ferry, ed., *Wordsworth* (New York: Dell, 1959), 113–18. (Lines 58–64, 1–9, 141–152).

35. Thomas Wolfe, *Look Homeward, Angel* (New York: Scribner, 1929), 2006 edition, 32, 454.

36. P. L. Travers, *Mary Poppins* (New York: Harcourt, Brace & World, 1934), 1962 edition, 139–40.

SEVEN

The Tradition Evolves

It emerged from the 1910s and 1920s, and developed for the rest of the century. Supernatural romance had completed its formative stage during World War II and its aftermath.

Those who have previously noticed the love-death-afterlife films of the 1940s—Frank Rich, for example, who once mentioned the "Hollywood wartime fantasies . . . that patriotically promised an afterlife to an audience increasingly primed to sustain heavy casualties overseas"—have not known that the genre started earlier.[1] Compared to film noir—a genre that is also associated with the Zeitgeist of the 1940s (though it too has earlier antecedents)—supernatural romance has been neglected by critics and historians, and the full dimensions of its significance have remained obscure. Film noir, by contrast, was recognized and studied right away.

After World War II, supernatural romance continued to develop in different directions. Remakes of early supernatural romances commenced in 1944 with *Between Two Worlds*, which revived *Outward Bound* with only slight modifications, and the trend continued: *Berkeley Square* was remade in 1951 as *The House on the Square* (released as *I'll Never Forget You* in the United States) starring Tyrone Power and Ann Blyth.[2] *Here Comes Mr. Jordan* reappeared in 1978 as *Heaven Can Wait*, starring Warren Beatty and Julie Christie, and again (with greater modifications) in 2001 as *Down To Earth*, starring Chris Rock and Regina King. *A Guy Named Joe* was remade in 1989 as *Always*, starring Richard Dreyfuss and Holly Hunter.[3] And *Death Takes a Holiday* was brought back with a crucial plot change in 1998 as *Meet Joe Black*, starring Brad Pitt, Claire Forlani, and Anthony Hopkins.

Several distinctive plot devices introduced in the early stages of the genre—love triangles, for example, as in *Blithe Spirit* and *A Guy Named*

Joe—were extended in interesting ways. In *Kiss Me Goodbye* (20th Century Fox, 1982), a widow engaged to be married moves back into the home where she and her deceased husband lived. His ghost haunts the house, and the woman soon becomes the object of a tug-of-war between the spirit and his mortal rival. Inspired by a 1976 Brazilian film, *Dona Flor and Her Two Husbands* (*Dona Flor e Seus Dois Maridos*), which in turn was based upon a 1966 novel of the same name by Jose Amado, the American film was directed by Robert Mulligan and starred Sally Field, James Caan, and Jeff Bridges.[4]

A similar story was featured in *Truly, Madly, Deeply* (BBC/MGM, 1990), a British film directed by Anthony Minghella. A widow is joined by the spirit of her deceased husband, whom she adored. He has no idea why he returned. But he brings with him certain aggravating habits that the widow had forgotten, along with new ghostly friends who have their own annoying proclivities. The widow is therefore tempted when she meets a pleasant new fellow. Feeling guilt and ambivalence, she nonetheless commits to the new romance as her ghostly ex-husband and his friends look on in sadness. The film starred Juliet Stevenson, Alan Rickman, and Michael Maloney.[5]

Another tendency in early supernatural romances was extended after World War II: hybridism. As previously noted, supernatural romance had infiltrated other genres, such as horror (*The Mummy*), comedy (*Topper*, *Blithe Spirit*), film noir (*Laura*), and musicals (*Cabin in the Sky*, *Brigadoon*). The trend continued. Another musical supernatural romance, *On a Clear Day You Can See Forever*, was created by Alan Jay Lerner. An auteur production with an element of supernatural romance, Thornton Wilder's *Our Town*, was succeeded by a newer one, Hitchcock's *Vertigo*. Film noir combined with supernatural romance in *Dead Again*, and romantic comedy embraced the love-death-afterlife trinity in *Sleepless in Seattle*. Time travel—introduced in *Berkeley Square*, reprised in *Somewhere in Time*, and employed with a number of modifications in *Portrait of Jennie* and *Brigadoon*—was by no means the only theme from science fiction that could incorporate elements of supernatural romance, as *Solaris*, to be considered momentarily, would show. And a more complex form of hybridism would emerge in *Down To Earth*, the 1947 sequel to *Here Comes Mr. Jordan*.

Down To Earth (Columbia, 1947) made a number of back-references to the 1941 film. But this time the plot involved a romance between a mortal and a heavenly being, one of the classical Greek muses, Terpsichore, who descends to earth and gets involved with the producer of a musical for reasons too lengthy to summarize. In any case, she goes back where she came from and then Mr. Jordan consoles her that she and her boyfriend will meet again in heaven. The film starred Rita Hayworth and Larry Parks.[6]

This film was obviously unusual and distinctive for several reasons. To be sure, *Death Takes a Holiday* had already set the precedent (building upon the myth of Hades and Persephone) for romance between a mortal and a divinity: in this case Hades, the lord of the underworld (or, if one pleases, the earlier Greek proto-deity Thanatos, death personified). Of course Greek mythology was rife with stories of liaisons between the denizens of Olympus and mortals, both male and female. But except for *Death Takes a Holiday*, all ghostly romances thus far on screen had involved a romance between a person and a *ghost*, that is, the spirit of *another mortal*—one who is deceased.

Down to Earth, with its romance between a man and a muse, was different. But it was building upon another trend in comedy established in the 1938 Rodgers and Hart musical, *I Married An Angel*, which was brought to the screen by MGM in 1942. This particular story did not involve death or the afterlife. And this play spawned a rapid-fire dialectical counterpart, *I Married A Witch* (1942), which perhaps in its turn was an inspiration for the 1948/1949 John van Druten play—and the subsequent 1958 film—*Bell, Book, and Candle* as well as the 1960s television series *Bewitched*.[7]

In 1980, *Down to Earth* was remade as *Xanadu*, starring Olivia Newton-John, Michael Beck, and Gene Kelly.

Love between an angel and a mortal was depicted in the Franco-German film *Wings of Desire* (*Der Himmel über Berlin*), directed by Wim Wenders and released in 1987. This film tells the story of an angel, Damiel (played by Bruno Ganz), who longs to partake of human passions and is ready to give up immortality in exchange. After becoming human, he falls for a female trapeze artist, Marion (played by Solveig Dommartin).[8]

In the American remake, *City of Angels* (Warner Brothers, 1998), this story was fused with the love-death-afterlife formula. Seth, an angel, falls in love with a woman named Maggie, and decides to give up his angelic status to love her. But she dies, and he has to console himself that he will join her in heaven after his now-mortal existence has run its course. The film, directed by Brad Silbering, starred Meg Ryan and Nicholas Cage.[9]

Also worthy of note in this regard is the 1951 film *Pandora and the Flying Dutchman* (MGM and Romulus Films), which tells the tale of a woman in a Spanish town who falls in love with a Dutch sea captain who turns out to be the *Fliegende Holländer* himself, cursed by Satan to sail the seas forever. Love changes this situation, but only via death. The film, which was directed by Albert Lewin, starred Ava Gardner and James Mason.[10]

Out of this evolving trend of hybridism came the gothic supernatural romances of recent years such as *Twilight* (2008–2012), which built upon the horror lore of vampirism to encompass an engaging (especially for teens) pattern of romance with the "un-dead."[11]

The most ambitious fusion of supernatural romance and science fiction is *Solaris*, based upon a 1961 novel by Stanislaw Lem. The story, with alterations that greatly displeased the author, became a Soviet-era film by Andrei Tarkovsky in 1972.[12] The film tells the story of a cosmonaut, Kris Kelvin, who is sent to investigate events aboard a space station that is orbiting a planet called Solaris. This mysterious planet appears to be an *organism* that communicates mentally with other beings in the vicinity and intervenes in their lives. Solaris has read the minds of humans aboard the station and turned their wish-fulfillment fantasies into weird realities.

When Kelvin arrives, Solaris creates a new "replica" version of his dead wife, Hari, and Kelvin falls in love with this woman all over again, but the question remains . . . is it "her?" This meditation on the problem of identity has obvious correspondences with the religious issue of the "soul." The original version of *Solaris* starred Donatas Banionis and Natalya Bondarchuk. The film was remade by in 2002 by 20th Century Fox: directed by Steven Soderbergh, the new version starred George Clooney and Natascha McElhone.

The original film won the British Film Institute's award for best film of the year and it also won a prize at the Cannes Film Festival. Reviews in the United States were mixed; Jay Cocks in *Time* wrote that "the effects are scanty, the drama gloomy, the philosophy . . . thick as a cloud of ozone." But Jack Kroll in *Newsweek* called the film "engrossing and gravely beautiful."[13] The 2002 remake was hailed by critic Roger Ebert as "a workshop for a discussion of human identity."[14]

Generally speaking, supernatural romance fell into a relative lull for roughly a generation after its formative period. The productions (including hybrids) from the early 1950s to the early 1980s total ten: *Pandora and the Flying Dutchman* (1951), *The House on the Square/I'll Never Forget You* (1951), *Brigadoon* (1954), *Vertigo* (1958), *On A Clear Day You Can See Forever* (1970), *Solaris* (1972), *Heaven Can Wait* (1978), *Somewhere in Time* (1980), *Xanadu* (1980), and *Kiss Me Goodbye* (1982).

But beginning in the late 1980s, a surge of new supernatural romances began. Some of them used the theme of reincarnation, perhaps demonstrating the influence of the 1960s/1970s counterculture and its "new age" spirituality. The 1970s novels of Richard Matheson in particular—*Bid Time Return* and *What Dreams May Come*—come directly from the period in question, and both played important roles in the evolution of supernatural romance. Previously noted examples of the new wave (including hybrids) are *Made in Heaven* (1987), *Always* (1989), *Truly, Madly, Deeply* (1990), *Dead Again* (1991), *Sleepless in Seattle* (1993), *Sliding Doors* (1998), *What Dreams May Come* (1998), *City of Angels* (1998), and *Meet Joe Black* (1998). Others (to be considered momentarily) are *Beetlejuice* (1988), *Rouge* (1988), *Ghost* (1990), *Defending Your Life* (1991), and *To Gillian On Her 37th Birthday* (1996).

Perhaps it also bears noting that the James Cameron blockbuster film *Titanic* (1997) featured a conclusion in which the hero and heroine, Jack and Rose, who are parted by death, meet again in the afterlife aboard the great ship.

What accounted for this new wave of supernatural romances must remain conjectural. For some reason, 1998 was a particularly rich year. To some extent (perhaps) the trend reflected the typical *fin-de-siècle* mentality: the tendency to look backward and reflect as the century sputters to its end, to breathe new life into older forms—by way of revival—thereby creating a cultural transition from the old century to the new one. The 1990s was also a rich time for film noir and screwball comedy revivals. It also bears noting that critical reactions to the new supernatural romances were generally negative—itself, perhaps, a commentary on different *fin-de-siècle* sensibilities, those of disillusioned burn-out.

Regardless, several of the newer supernatural romances have special interest as one-of-a-kind productions.

The film *Beetlejuice* drew the love-death-afterlife theme into a comedy and horror pastiche by dint of the fact that a husband and wife get killed together at the outset of the story and they enter the afterlife together. Adam and Barbara Maitland, played by Alec Baldwin and Geena Davis, die in a car crash and return to their home, which is quickly sold to a family they find insufferable: the Deetzes, played by Jeffrey Jones, Catherine O'Hara, and Winona Ryder. To help them exorcise the awful Deetzes, the spirits of the Maitlands recruit an obnoxious fellow ghost named Beetlejuice, played by Michael Keaton. The film, which was a box office success, was directed by Tim Burton.[15]

Based upon a novel by Lilian Lee, *Rouge* was a Hong Kong film that was directed by Stanley Kwan. Starring Leslie Cheung and Anita Mui, it tells the story of a suicide pact: like Henry and Ann in *Outward Bound*, these lovers expect to be together in the afterlife. But it doesn't work because only one of them dies. When the woman, "Fleur," comes back to visit earth as a spirit, she discovers that her lover has cheated on her, so she departs. This film swept the eighth annual Hong Kong film awards, and it was praised around the world. *Los Angeles Times* critic Kevin Thomas called it "exquisite."[16]

The 1990 film *Ghost* was a huge commercial success, and it fused supernatural romance with a suspense thriller plot. This Paramount film was directed by Jerry Zucker and it starred Demi Moore and Patrick Swayze. It tells the story of a loving couple who are separated when the husband is murdered. His ghost, with the help of a zany medium (played by Whoopi Goldberg), intervenes from the afterlife to save his wife from the killers, who intend to murder her as well. And with the help of the medium, the lovers come close to achieving an erotic union. At the film's conclusion, the ghost of the husband is summoned to heaven in a nimbus of sensuous light and he tells his wife that they will meet again on the other side. This film was nominated for five academy awards, including best picture, and it won Oscars for best supporting actress (Goldberg) and best original screenplay (by Bruce Joel Rubin).[17]

Defending Your Life was a 1991 romantic comedy set in the afterlife. After a man gets killed he finds himself in "Judgment City," a way station containing a court in which his life will be judged. If his life on earth was satisfactory, he gets to proceed to the next phase of existence. If not, he will be sent back (via reincarnation) to try again. In the process—of course—he falls in love (with a female spirit), and in risking everything to be with her, he proves his worthiness to move on. The film, produced by Geffen Pictures and distributed by Warner Brothers, was directed by Albert Brooks, who also starred as the leading man, opposite Meryl Streep.[18]

The 1996 film *To Gillian On Her 37th Birthday* was based upon a play by Michael Brady, which was converted to a screenplay by David E. Kelley. Produced by Triumph Films, it was directed by Michael Pressman and it starred Michelle Pfeiffer and Peter Gallagher. This film is the story of pure grieving. The title character plunges to her death from the mast of a sailboat, ironically on her birthday, and every year on the very same date her husband, David, stages an elaborate celebration of her life. Her ghost joins him from time to time. David's friends are concerned about his mental health, and they keep trying to help him to get over the loss so he can find someone new. At the end of the film he finally agrees to make the attempt—but viewers never find out what happens.[19]

The 1998 film *What Dreams May Come* is in a class by itself in this genre—without a doubt one of the most important of the supernatural romances, not least of all because its exploration of the conjectural afterlife is the most elaborate and the most artistically accomplished to date. Like *Somewhere in Time*, it was based upon a novel (in this case with the same title) by Richard Matheson. But this time, Matheson did not participate in the making of the film (notwithstanding the fact that the same producer, Stephen Simon, did the honors in getting the story on screen), and the author was displeased with the result, thus joining the roster of writers such as Nöel Coward, Stanislaw Lem, and others who repudiated the screen version of their work. Matheson did not like the changes to his plot that emerged in the screenplay, which was written by Ronald Bass.[20]

This film was created by a corporate consortium of the kind that was typical by the late twentieth century: in this case, DreamWorks, Polygram Filmed Entertainment, Metafilmics, Gramercy Pictures, and Universal Pictures. The director was Vincent Ward. *What Dreams May Come* was a demonstration par excellence of the new possibilities of digital imaging—simultaneously transforming science fiction films through a special-effects revolution—as applied to supernatural romance. The depiction of the afterlife was as stunning and literal as the imaginative scenes in *A Matter of Life and Death* that were set in the "waiting room" of heaven.

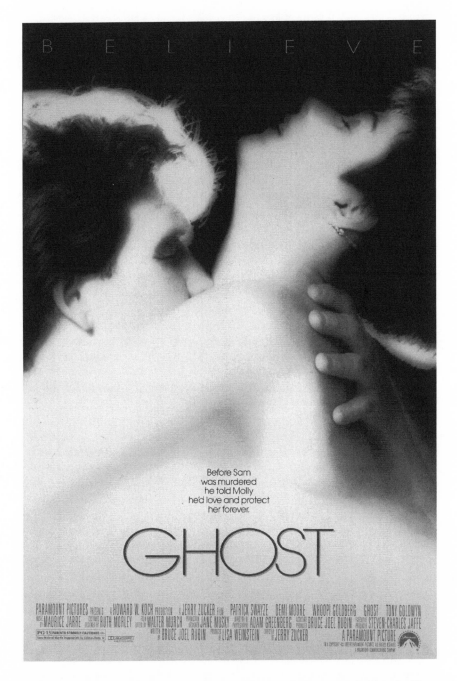

Figure 7.1. Another movie poster, this one for the 1990 smash hit *Ghost*, a film about a man who reaches back from the afterlife to save his wife from the murderers who killed him. The film's stars, Demi Moore and Patrick Swayze, are shown here in an ectoplasmic embrace. Courtesy of Photofest.

But heaven (and hell) as shown in *What Dreams May Come* were much, much more extensive—and more pervasive as a setting for the plot. Due to the fact that the wife in this story is (in her mortal life) an artist, the afterlife is an art-historical blend of some related painterly styles from masters as diverse as the Limbourgs, Giotto, Sasetta, Michelangelo, Raphael, Botticelli, Bosch, Monet, Van Gogh, and even Maxfield Parrish. Some of the location shooting was done in Montana's Glacier National Park, but its landscapes are transformed in a way that prefigured the cinematic style of Peter Jackson's *Lord of the Rings* trilogy, which transformed New Zealand into Tolkien's Middle Earth.[21]

The film tells the story of Chris and Annie Nielson, played by Robin Williams and Annabella Sciorra, a loving couple who are devastated by the deaths of their son and daughter in a car crash. Annie sinks into clinical depression, but Chris helps her find her way back to sanity. But then he, too, is killed in a car crash.

Most of the story is seen from the point of view of Chris, who finds himself a spirit and who haunts the earth for a while, trying vainly to communicate with Annie. He is guided by the soul of a deceased colleague, Albert (played by Cuba Gooding, Jr.), who explains the ways of the afterlife in a series of lessons. Chris then moves on to heaven and he finds himself in the middle of one of his wife's paintings. Albert explicates it all: heaven is an open-ended place where each soul creates its own realities, based upon fantasy.

In the course of this plot, Chris is reunited with the spirits of his children, both of whom have taken on different racial appearances, for complicated reasons. Then he finds out that Annie has committed suicide and is relegated to hell. Chris is determined to find her and rescue her again, and this rescue reprises the time in their mortal existence when he helped her back to sanity. For just as heaven is a place that is based upon dream-like fantasies, hell is created by each damned soul from its own nightmares, and Annie's nightmares spring from depressive delusion. It was madness that drove her to take her own life, and it is madness that plunges her to hell. Chris is guided to hell by a "tracker," played by Max von Sydow.

Chris rescues his wife a second time through self-surrender. He loves her so much that he will stay with her—right there in hell—where of course he will lose his own mind. The enormity of this sacrifice snaps Annie out of her spell, and the two of them are quickly resurrected to the painted landscape, where the souls of their children (this time appearing as they did in their past life on earth) join them in a euphoric reunion. Chris and Annie decide to go back to earth through reincarnation—to meet and fall in love all over again, but this time making "better choices."

The mythical method is back at work in this film, for the scenes in hell are decidedly Dantesque. In addition to Dante's *Divine Comedy*, *Paradise Lost* provides some provenance, since Milton depicted the afterlife as to a

Figure 7.2. An iconic afterlife scene from *What Dreams May Come*, the ambitious and technically dazzling 1998 film about a man named Chris Nielson, played by Robin Williams, who goes to heaven and then rescues his wife, Annie, played by Annabella Sciorra, who, because she killed herself, has gone to hell. Here, perhaps, is a variation on the myth of Orpheus and Euridice, but with a happy ending. **Courtesy of Photofest.**

large extent a place of mental projection, through which "The mind is its own place, and in itself / Can make a Heav'n of Hell, a Hell of Heav'n" and in which Satan can reflect quite mournfully that "Which way I fly is hell / myself am Hell."[22]

Since Annie calls her husband "Christie" in this tale (rather than Chris), another theme with direct Christian provenance is suggested—though this one is never mentioned in scripture: Christ's "harrowing of Hell." This story—which is derived from the Apostles' Creed and the Athanasian Creed—of Christ's descent to fetch the souls of the righteous who had died before His birth, suggests other miraculous rescues, the retrieval of Alcestis from the underworld by Herakles, for instance, and the ill-fated mission of Orpheus. *What Dreams May Come* presents to us the vision of an Orpheus who succeeds: he descends into "Hades" (in Christianized form) and rescues his wife.

Reincarnation increases the heterodoxy of the film's religious feeling, notwithstanding the heavy use of traditional Christian themes—not least of all the humbling of pride through self-abnegation as the key to salvation, on earth and also . . . beyond. Chris's rescue depends upon a gesture of such utter self-sacrifice that it approaches martyrdom. And it works.

"When you lose, you win," says Annie when she joins Chris and her children.

What Dreams May Come won an Oscar for visual effects as well as an Art Directors Guild award for excellence in production design. Reviews of the film were not surprisingly mixed. Owen Gleiberman wrote in *Entertainment Weekly* that "the film may preach to the audience about matters of the spirit, but its bejeweled special-effects vision of the afterlife can't help but come off as aggressively literal-minded."[23] Roger Ebert, writing in the *Chicago Sun-Times*, praised the film while acknowledging some arguable shortcomings. "This film . . . shows how movies can imagine the unknown," he wrote, adding that the film "contains heartbreakingly effective performances by Robin Williams and Annabella Sciorra."[24]

Stephen Holden's review of the film for the *New York Times* was deeply ambivalent. Calling the film "one of the most elaborate metaphysical love stories ever tackled by Hollywood," he described its impressive visual qualities as a significant achievement in aesthetics; it was a film which

> at its most visually evocative portrays its characters' lives and afterlives as a kind of hall of mirrors, in which the lines between dream and reality, memory and eternity are continually blurring as one gives way to another. At its most seductive, the film portrays heaven as a magical, hallucinatory extension of the physical world that has been left behind. It is a place flooded with dim golden light and thick with flowers, of misty peaks and crags, where people and objects float through the sky and great distances can be breached with a single leap (of faith, of course).

Correspondingly,

> The underworld he visits with the help of a grim-faced guide played by (who else?) Max von Sydow is a grim but PG-13–looking place (when it comes to punishment and suffering) surrounded by burning shipwrecks. In the most powerful image of hell, one that is intensely claustrophobic, Chris is forced to run across a sea of muttering heads all craning up through an endless expanse of mud.

On the other hand, Holden could not resist the scorn that was so typical of the critical responses to supernatural romance in the 1990s. The following excerpts from his coverage reveal the same hopelessly subjective judgments that are always applied by the standards of different sensibilities to art. Holden complained that the screenplay was "so clotted with slogans, riddles and dime-store psychobabble that Chris and Annie never coalesce into anything more than a pair of idealized greeting-card parents with terrible luck."

He wrote that the message of the film "represents the uncomfortable collision of two ideas about filmmaking, one commercial, the other eccentrically, ambitiously dreamy. On the commercial level, it is an ecumenically canny exercise in pop inspiration that's smart enough to drop the name 'God' only once, in a vague, nondogmatic reference."

This makes the film's heterodoxy sound contrived—or even cynical. But surely Matheson's original story sprang from genuine and deeply felt reflections. And any venture in performing arts must after all calibrate its effects to achieve the right audience response.

But Holden's scorn was even more comprehensive. Along with his contemporaneous fellow reviewer at the *Times*, Janet Maslin, Holden seemed to believe that almost *any* production with optimistic theological implications is tantamount to gush:

> It's often been said that baby boomers think they can live forever. "What Dreams May Come" is the movie that tells them, yes, it's possible, at least in a solipsistic New Age sense, to attain eternal life. That's because eternity, the movie soothingly suggests, is whatever you imagine it to be. If you can conjure it up, then on some level it must be reality. Just like "Peter Pan." Close your eyes, snap your fingers and you can fly.[25]

In any case, many no doubt found the power of *What Dreams May Come* impressive and the film remains a landmark in the evolution of supernatural romance. And in the very same year, the remake of *Death Takes A Holiday* developed great power.

This time Death, who is played by Brad Pitt—he will be known as "Joe Black" for the duration of his earthly visit—takes a mortal body and imposes on a media magnate, played by Anthony Hopkins, whose number is up due to heart disease. The magnate will get an extended reprieve if he agrees to show Death around. "Joe" falls in love with the magnate's daughter, played by Claire Forlani, but, rather than take her with him, he makes a sacrifice instead and departs without her.

As Joe and the daughter embrace the last time, she stares deeply into his eyes and starts to grasp that he is . . . "someone else." We sense that she has grasped the full truth at this point, but she adores him notwithstanding. And vice versa. "Thank you for loving me," he says gently. The music, composed by Thomas Newman, has a great deal to do with the haunting effect—at least for those who are susceptible to the film's pathos. Produced by City Light Films and distributed by Universal, *Meet Joe Black* was directed by Martin Brest.

Supernatural romance in the early twenty-first century has not abated as a trend. To the contrary: its range continues to expand. Indeed, the fast recitation to follow—a summation of the new additions to the genre—is a stunning demonstration of the impact this cinematic tradition continues to exert upon the world of contemporary film.

Dragonfly, directed by Tom Shadyac and produced by a consortium of production companies, was released and distributed by Universal in 2002. It tells the story of a doctor played by Kevin Costner, whose deceased wife, played by Susannah Thompson, communicates to him via patients who return from near-death experiences.[26]

In 2003, a Disney film, *The Haunted Mansion*, used the love-death-afterlife theme as a device for an Eddie Murphy comedy. Eddie and his co-star Marsha Thomason play a husband-and-wife team of realtors, Jim and Sara Evers, who are invited (with their kids) to pay a visit to an old mansion. The invitation is a pretext, since the owner of the house, "Master Gracey"—a ghost—believes that Sara is the reincarnation of his long-lost love. She isn't: Gracey's murdered lover haunts the house as a disembodied spirit. The ghostly lovers are at last reunited after lots of scary-but-funny complications for the Evers family. This film was directed by Rob Minkoff.

In 2004, *De-Lovely*, an MGM film directed by Irwin Winkler, served up a biography of the composer Cole Porter, who is played by Kevin Kline. The film argues that Porter's bisexuality prevented a full consummation of his love for his wife, who is played by Ashley Judd, until the afterlife. Just before Porter's death, Death himself is the producer of a musical play about Porter, who is watching the play from the audience. So Porter's life is made to "pass before his eyes," in this play within a play, before he goes.

In the same year, *Birth*, a New Line cinema film that was directed by Jonathan Glazer, presented the story of a woman, Anna, played by Nicole Kidman, whose marriage plans are interrupted by a child named Sean, played by Cameron Bright, who claims to the reincarnation of her deceased former husband, who was also named Sean. The evidence is ambiguous, and so is the film's conclusion.[27]

In 2005, Dreamworks released *Just Like Heaven*, directed by Mark Waters. The plot of this movie was in basic terms *The Ghost and Mrs. Muir* reversed, but with ancillary variations: this time it's a *guy* who moves into a pad that is haunted by the ghost of a *woman*, and of course they fall in love. Except that there's a "half-way" twist to the story this time: the woman is not fully dead, not yet. She's lying in a hospital comatose and her wandering spirit is suffering amnesia. The woman, played by Reese Witherspoon, was herself a doctor before the car crash that put her into a coma and she knew the people at the hospital. As she realizes the truth— recovering from her amnesia through déjà vu experiences—she guides her new boyfriend, played by Mark Ruffalo, to the hospital just in time to interfere with the plans of a callous physician (and professional rival) to remove life support.[28]

Another light variation on the themes of supernatural romance was released in the same year, 2005, by Tim Burton, who produced the digitally animated children's films *The Nightmare Before Christmas* and *James and the Giant Peach*. The new film, *Corpse Bride*, was another love-triangle version of supernatural romance. Johnny Depp supplied the voice of the hero, Victor van Dort, who is engaged to marry Victoria Everglot (whose voice was supplied by Emily Watson). But Victor gets waylaid in a forest as he practices his wedding vows. When he puts the wedding ring around the upturned root of a tree, he discovers that the root is the finger of a dead girl, Emily (voice supplied by Helena Bonham Carter), who takes him off to the Land of the Dead, where she intends to marry him. After many complications, Victor winds up back with Victoria. Burton directed this film with Mike Johnson and the film was distributed by Warner Brothers. Roger Ebert called it "a sweet and visually lovely tale of love lost."[29]

In 2006, *Wristcutters: A Love Story* was produced by a consortium of No Matter Films, Crispy Pictures, and Halcyon Pictures. Based upon a story by Etgar Keret, this very dark comedy directed by Goran Dukić tells the story of "Zia," played by Patrick Fugit, who commits suicide and finds himself in an afterlife reserved for suicides—a bleak and desolate country. He learns that his former girlfriend, Desiree (played by Leslie Bibb), has also decided to end it all, and so he hits the road with a new male friend in the hope of finding her. Along the way they pick up a girl hitchhiker, Mikal (played by Shannyn Sossamon), who claims that she is there by mistake and is seeking the "people in charge." Zia and Mikal hit it off. At last, after many plot complications, they wind up back on earth—and alive—together . . . in hospital beds.[30]

In 2010, the film *Hereafter* told the story of several characters who have near-death experiences or other glimpses of the afterlife. Romance ensues when some of these characters meet.

One should also consider the love-death-afterlife link in the *Harry Potter* films (2001–2011), based upon the J. K. Rowling books. Harry communes with the souls of his parents (and others) throughout the series until the "resurrection stone" (one of the "deathly hallows") permits him to summon the spirits more directly.

Supernatural romance remains a potent formula with limitless plot possibilities. Does it seem as if the many permutations of this genre are finally exhausted?

Don't bet on it.

NOTES

1. Rich made this observation in the course of a review of a stage revival of *On Borrowed Time* in 1991. See Frank Rich, "George C. Scott Has Death Up A Tree In 'Borrowed Time,'" *New York Times*, October 10, 1991.

2. The remake of *Berkeley Square* got poor reviews. Bosley Crowther complained that while the film *I'll Never Forget You* contained "obvious intimations of the lovely play *Berkeley Square* . . . there is little of its poetry or magic in this latest rendering of it on the screen." Instead, the 20th Century Fox remake was afflicted by such "ponderous crudity that all the fragile charm and wistful pathos of the original are crushed beneath the mass." Bosley Crowther, "The Screen in Review: 'I'll Never Forget You,' with Tyrone Power, Ann Blyth, New Bill at the Roxy," *New York Times*, December 8,

1951, accessible via http://www.nytimes.com/movie/review?res= 9C05E5DA1E3BE23ABC4053DFB467838A649EDE.

3. Ironically, in light of the mixed reviews that *A Guy Named Joe* elicited in 1943, the original film was viewed as exemplary or even perfect later on by some movie reviewers who criticized the remake, *Always*. Janet Maslin, for instance, complained that while "'Always' is bigger and busier than 'A Guy Named Joe' in every way," the newer film "lacks the intimacy to make any of this very moving. Though Ms. Hunter should be perfectly cast as the strong-willed, self-possessed Dorinda and Mr. Dreyfuss sounds ideal for the gruffly affectionate Pete, the two characters never interact convincingly, without a lot of excess baggage in their way. Mr. Dreyfuss, in fact, only comes to life after Pete is dead, when the opportunities for back-seat driving suit him very well. The film's occasional moments of sweetness—Audrey Hepburn appearing briefly as an angel gently alerting Pete to his new status, Pete's hovering tenderly beside a Dorinda who only barely senses his presence—are too easily upstaged by clutter and silly, implausible gags." Janet Maslin, "Review/Film: 'Always,' Love and Death in a Wilderness," *New York Times*, December 22, 1989, accessible viahttp://www. nytimes.com/movie/review?res=950de4db103ef931a15751c1a96f948260. Roger Ebert, after observing that director Steven Spielberg had watched *A Guy Named Joe* many times as a child—and after adding that Richard Dreyfuss supposedly watched the 1943 film no less than thirty-five times—lamented that the remake was no comparison to the original. Ebert called *Always* "Spielberg's weakest film since *1941*." Roger Ebert, review of *Always*, *Chicago Sun-Times*, December 22, 1989, accessible viahttp://www. rogerebert.com/reviews/always-1989. It bears noting that Spielberg laced his film with period references in an effort to establish subliminal connections to the 1940s, including the use of Fats Waller music and the song "Smoke Gets In Your Eyes," which was sung by none other than Irene Dunne (the original Dorinda Durston) in the 1934 Astaire-and-Rogers film *Roberta*.

4. This film elicited a scathing review by Vincent Canby, who wrote that this "consistently lugubrious comedy" was rather like "a Nassau cruise ship with eight bars, seven discos, five swimming pools and no compass. It sails out of New York, turns left instead of right at the Ambrose Lightship and heads confidently toward sunny Iceland." Comparing the film to the earlier Brazilian film that inspired it, Canby observed that "much of the humor of the Brazilian film was based on the fact that the widow, played by the beautiful and frequently unclothed Sonia Braga, continued to enjoy an active sex life with the ghost of her husband who, in all respects except lovemaking, had been a boor. In Mr. Mulligan's glossy visitation, in which people don't undress very often, the ghost can't—as they say—'do' anything. Visible only to his wife, he just sits around and makes snide remarks as Mr. Bridges attempts to make love to the distracted Miss Field. This is, I think, the film's only joke." Vincent Canby, "Movie Review: 'Kiss Me Goodbye,'" December 22, 1982, *New York Times*, accessible viahttp://www.nytimes.com/movie/review?res= 9F0CE1D8123BF931A15751C1A964948260.

5. Vincent Canby was also disgusted by Minghella's attempt at a love triangle that intersects the afterlife in *Truly, Madly, Deeply*. The film "should be enchanting," he wrote, "but it isn't. Everyone pushes too hard, especially Mr. Minghella, the writer and director. There are a few amusing lines and a lot of terrible ones." Vincent Canby, "Review/Film: Living or Dead, Too Good to be True," *New York Times*, May 3, 1991, accessible via http://www.nytimes.com/movie/review?res= 9D0CE1D7143AF930A35756C0A967958260. Roger Ebert was more charitable, joking that "for some time now I have been complaining about movies in which people return from the afterlife. My complaint is always the same: If the afterlife is as miraculous as we expect it to be, why would anyone want to return? I have my answer. They come back to watch movies on video. . . . My information about the afterlife comes from Anthony Minghella's 'Truly, Madly, Deeply,' a truly odd film, maddening, occasionally deeply moving." Despite its quirks, he concluded, the film leads "toward some truths that are, the more you think about them, really pretty profound." Roger

Ebert, review, *Truly, Madly, Deeply, Chicago Sun-Times*, May 24, 1991, accessible via http://www.rogerebert.com/reviews/truly-madly-deeply-1991. Ebert's response a year earlier to the blockbuster *Ghost* was quite similar.

6. Bosley Crowther was gently dismissive in his review. An extract: "Eventually, Mr. Jordan—he's that heavenly superintendent, you recall, who first juggled fate and time so kindly for Bob Montgomery in a film a few years back—is going to become a nuisance, if Columbia and others persist in making a series character of him and of his supernatural powers. One piece of Jordan hocus-pocus in a theatrical lifetime is nigh enough. But, at least, one more genial interference by the gentleman in "Down to Earth," which came yesterday to the Music Hall, gets a pretty good musical under way." Bosley Crowther, "'Down To Earth,' Columbia Film in which Rita Hayworth and Larry Parks Share Honors, Is New Feature at Radio City," *New York Times*, September 12, 1947, accessible via http://www.nytimes.com/movie/review?res= 940DE5D8153AE233A25751C1A96F9C946693D6CF.

7. The gist of *I Married An Angel* was the *perfection* of the angel, which made her "too good for this world," and unfit for the imperfections of marriage unless she becomes more human, that is, flawed. This is essentially the gist of Disney's self-spoofing *Enchanted*, where a goody-goody cartoon princess with a personality like Snow White is wafted into this world, where she becomes fit for marriage only by losing her näivété through learning how to feel and project anger and other human "vices."

8. Wenders' film, though it won international recognition, got mixed reviews. Janet Maslin assessed it in the *New York Times* as follows: "Startlingly original at first, 'Wings of Desire' is in the end damagingly overloaded. The excesses of language, the ceaseless camera movement, the unyielding whimsy have the ultimate effect of wearing the audience down. The flashes of real delight that spring out of Mr. Wenders's visionary methods grow fewer and fewer as the film proceeds, and they are long gone by the time it nominally comes to life. Mr. Ganz, who conveys great yearning before reaching his decision 'to take the plunge' and a charming eagerness thereafter, is left in a kind of limbo, and the film is, too. This comes as a relief of sorts, but it's also far less effective than must have been intended. 'Wings of Desire' is Mr. Wenders's most ambitious effort yet, and certainly radiates immense promise. But there's a relentlessness to the direction, which won the best-director award at Cannes last year, that keeps it earthbound." Janet Maslin, "Review/Film: The Rage of Angels, According to Wim Wenders," *New York Times*, April 29, 1988, accessible viahttp://www.nytimes. com/movie/review?res=940DEFDE153DF93AA15757C0A96E948260. In 2009, reviewer Bill Weber hailed the film in *Slant* magazine as a "cultishly adored fantasy" that constitutes a "cinema souvenir of a moment in culture and Western history." Accessible viahttp://www.slantmagazine.com/film/review/wings-of-desire.

9. *City of Angels* did not stand a chance among reviewers in comparison to the Wenders film. Critic Stephen Holden, in his *New York Times* review of what he called an "ultra-slick Hollywood production" that "smoothes out the quirks in Mr. Wenders's loopy romance," found it hard to repress sarcastic excess: "Miscast as Seth, Mr. Cage looks more like a serial killer than an angel, and in the scenes when he steals up behind people and lays invisible hands on their bodies, it often looks as though he were contemplating slitting their throats. Even when he's making cow eyes at his beloved and wearing the insipid little smile of a lovesick puppy, there is something deeply creepy in Mr. Cage's celestial vibrations. Most of his dialogue is intoned in a hushed, gee-whiz semi-whisper that's meant to convey profundity but that given the banality of what he says sounds like the shallow come-on of a cult leader recruiting candidates for brainwashing." Stephen Holden, "Film Review: Heaven, He's From Heaven, But His Heart Beats So . . . ." *New York Times*, April 10, 1998, accessible via http://www.nytimes.com/movie/review?res= 9D02E2D9143DF933A25757C0A96E958260.

10. Looking back from 2010, critic Andrew Pulver called *Pandora and the Flying Dutchman* "part folk-myth, part deranged love story, part flamenco documentary . . .

one of those unclassifiable efforts that threaten permanently to topple over the edge of ridiculousness, but somehow manage to avoid it." Andrew Pulver, "Pandora and the Flying Dutchman," *The Guardian*, May 13, 2010, accessible via http://www.theguardian.com/film/2010/may/13/pandora-and-the-flying-dutchman-review. In this version of the Flying Dutchman story, the cursed captain murdered his wife in a rage and is doomed to sail the seas until he finds some woman who is *willing* to sacrifice her life for him.

11. See Victoria Nelson, *Gothicka: Vampire Heroes, Human Gods, and the New Supernatural* (Cambridge, MA: Harvard University Press, 2012).

12. See Vida T. Johnson and Graham Petrie, *The Films of Andrei Tarkovsky: A Visual Fugue* (Bloomington, IN: Indiana University Press, 1994), 98–110; and Nathan Dunne, *Tarkovsky* (London: Black Dog, 2008), 58–79. Tarkovsky decided to adapt the science fiction novel in 1968 after several previous projects had been vetoed by Soviet authorities. He began casting in 1970 before he had permission to proceed with the project, though that permission was finally granted in October of the same year. Shooting began in March 1971 and the completed film was released in 1972.

13. Jay Cocks and Jack Kroll, cited in Johnson and Petrie, *The Films of Andrei Tarkovsky*, 101.

14. Ebert continued as follows: "When I saw Tarkovsky's original film, I felt absorbed in it, as if it were a sponge. It was slow, mysterious, confusing, and I have never forgotten it. Soderbergh's version is more clean and spare, more easily readable, but it pays full attention to the ideas and doesn't compromise. Tarkovsky was a genius, but one who demanded great patience from his audience as he ponderously marched toward his goals. The Soderbergh version is like the same story freed from the weight of Tarkovsky's solemnity. And it evokes one of the rarest of movie emotions, ironic regret." Roger Ebert, review of *Solaris*, *Chicago Sun-Times*, November 22, 2002, accessible via http://www.rogerebert.com/reviews/solaris-2002.

15. Roger Ebert gave this film faint praise, overall, in his review. "'Beetlejuice' gets off to a start that's so charming it never lives it down," he wrote. "The movie is all anticlimax once we realize it's going to be about gimmicks, not characters." To be sure, he continued, "there has never before been a movie afterworld quite like this. Heaven, or whatever it is, seems a lot like a cruise ship with a cranky crew. The newly-deads find a manual, which instructs them on how to live as ghosts, and they also find an advertisement from a character named Betelgeuse, who specializes in 'exorcisms of the living.'" But "one of the problems is Keaton, as the exorcist. Nearly unrecognizable behind pounds of makeup, he prances around playing Betelgeuse as a mischievous and vindictive prankster. But his scenes don't seem to fit with the other action, and his appearances are mostly a nuisance." Roger Ebert, review of *Beetlejuice*, *Chicago Sun-Times*, March, 30, 1988, accessible via http://www.rogerebert.com/reviews/beetlejuice-1988.

16. Kevin Thomas, "Movie Review: 'Rouge,' A Supernatural Fable Filled With Romantic Visions," *Los Angeles Times*, October 10, 1990, accessible via http://articles.latimes.com/1990-10-10/entertainment/ca-1762_1_hong-kong.

17. Roger Ebert could not resist equating the plot of this film to pulp fiction. "The thing about ghost stories," he wrote, "is that they usually have such limited imaginations. If a spirit were indeed able to exist in two realms at the same time—to occupy the spirit world while still involving itself in our designs here in the material universe—wouldn't it be aghast with glory and wonder? Wouldn't it transcend the pathetic little concerns of daily life? To put it another way: If you could live in the mind of God, would you still be telling your wife she's wearing the T-shirt you spilled the margarita on? 'Ghost' is no worse an offender than most ghost movies, I suppose. It assumes that even after death we devote most of our attention to unfinished business here on Earth, and that danger to a loved one is more important to a ghost than the infinity it now inhabits. Such ideas are a comfort to us." In light of the storyline of this movie, such a view seems glib, to say the least: equating a rescue from beyond the grave to a trivial pursuit. Roger Ebert, review of *Ghost*, *Chicago Sun-Times*, July 13,

1990, accessible via http://www.rogerebert.com/reviews/ghost-1990. Janet Maslin was equally dismissive. "Current Hollywood thinking extends into the next world, but not very far," she wrote. "Being dead has lately been presented on screen as a character-building experience, but beyond that the current ghost films hedge their bets. The questions of just what ghosts can do, of what effect ghosts may have on others or even of how ghosts regard their new status are seldom even addressed. What seems most important is that ghosts come to the aid of their loved ones, and that the ghost film manages, at least on its own terms, to be sincere." Janet Maslin, "Review/Film: Looking to the Dead For Mirth and Inspiration," *New York Times*, July 13, 1990, accessible via http://www.nytimes.com/movie/review?res=9C0CE2DB1439F930A25754C0A966958260.

18. Roger Ebert was in a good mood when he reviewed this supernatural romance. He wrote that "the movie is funny in a warm, fuzzy way, and it has a splendidly satisfactory ending, which is unusual for an Albert Brooks film (his inspiration in his earlier films is bright but seems to wear thin toward the third act). The best thing about the movie, I think, is the notion of Judgment City itself. Doesn't it make sense that heaven, for each society, would be a place much like the Earth that it knows? We're still stuck with images of angels playing harps, which worked fine for Renaissance painters. But isn't our modern world ready for images in which the angels look like Rotarians and CEOs?" Roger Ebert, "Defending Your Life," *Chicago Sun-Times*, April 5, 1991, accessible via http://www.rogerebert.com/reviews/defending-your-life-1991. Caryn James's review in the *New York Times* was also favorable, and for the same telling reasons; this supernatural romance was sardonic, jaded, and at times overtly satirical: "Here is the bad news about the afterlife, according to Albert Brooks," she wrote: "it is just as annoying as this life, at least for the first few days. There are lawyers after death and people who get better hotel rooms than you do and little old ladies on buses who talk your ear off about their pet poodles. When you die you go to Judgment City, an earthlike place where they have dead-Kiwanis meetings and stand-up comics in plaid sport jackets." In all, "this comically sour view of earth makes Mr. Brooks's 'Defending Your Life' the most perceptive and convincing among a recent spate of carpe diem movies," films in which "stars grapple with life and death in oversized terms." Unlike most of these films, she concluded, "'Defending Your Life' is savvier and, despite its white-robed characters, more realistic than most carpe diem movies because it does not depend on melodrama or old-fashioned idealism. It rests on the timely philosophy that earth is a banal place." Caryn James, "Film Review: Carpe Diem Becomes Hot Advice," *New York Times*, April 21, 1991, accessible via http://www.nytimes.com/movie/review?res=9D0CE7DA1339F932A15757C0A967958260.

19. Janet Maslin's review in the *New York Times* was bemused and noncommittal. "'To Gillian on Her 37th Birthday' begins with the sight of a couple, David Lewis (Peter Gallagher) and his wife, Gillian (Michelle Pfeiffer), frolicking in the surf," she wrote. "They wear matching khakis and white shirts, looking handsome and misleadingly happy, since Gillian is actually dead." And because of "David's habit of communing with Gillian's great-looking ghost, he has not really gotten on with his life." The mix of comedy and melodrama was uneasy in this film, at least in Maslin's opinion: "the actors don't easily vacillate between the flippant and the sincere. Mr. Gallagher has the toughest row to hoe, since David's grief is treated as a comic eccentricity and it is undermined by Gillian's looking none the worse for wear." Janet Maslin, "Movie Review: Gone But Not Forgotten," *New York Times*, October 18, 1996, accessible via http://www.nytimes.com/movie/review?res=9E04E7DF1331F93BA25753C1A960958260.

20. In a Web site interview, Matheson said, "I will not comment on *What Dreams May Come* except to say that a major producer in Hollywood said to me, 'They should have shot your book.' Amen." Richard Matheson interview, accessible via http://www.iamlegendarchive.com/matheson.htm/. Though Stephen Simon, who had worked in partnership with Matheson to turn his novel *Bid Time Return* into a film—*Somewhere In Time* was the result—worked closely with him in the similar effort to

adapt *What Dreams May Come,* the author bore him no ill will for the turn of events in the 1990s that left Matheson out of the final work on the film. Matheson stated, in the previously cited interview, that "the producer Stephen Simon tried to get my script filmed for many years so I can't fault him for finally having to go the route he did in order to get the film made." Simon has since gone on to other cinematic projects with spiritual implications. He has founded the Spiritual Cinema Circle to promote the production of films with theological implications and heterodox character. In 2006 he produced and directed the film *Conversations with God,* which was based upon a series of books by the same name written by Neale Donald Walsch. The book series (1995–2006) contains long self-help essays framed as dialogues that draw upon theological themes from Neo-Platonism to Hegel. The film is constructed as the life story of Walsch. See Simon's book *The Force Is With You: Mystical Movie Messages That Inspire Our Lives* (Newburyport, MA: Hampton Roads, 2002).

21. Eduardo Serra was the cinematographer and the digital special effects were created by Visual Effects Supervisors Joel Hynek, Nicholas Brooks, Kevin Mack, Joel Hunker, and Stuart Robinson under the guidance of Art Director Joshua Rosen and Production Designer Eugenio Zanetti.

22. John Milton, *Paradise Lost,* William G. Madsen, ed. (New York: Random House, 1969), Modern Library Edition, 15, 94.

23. Owen Gleiberman, *"What Dreams May Come," Entertainment Weekly,* October 9, 1998.

24. Roger Ebert, *"What Dreams May Come," Chicago Sun-Times,* October 2, 1998.

25. Stephen Holden, "Film Review: Apparently, The Afterlife Is Anything But Dead," *New York Times,* October 2, 1998, accessible via http://www.nytimes.com/ movie/review?res=9E00E1DA1438F931A35753C1A96E958260.

26. A. O. Scott's review of this film for the *New York Times* was, typically enough for this period, jaundiced. "This vehicle for Kevin Costner's unlimited talent for conveying self-righteous self-pity," wrote Scott, "takes a benevolent view of the great beyond. Apart from a few cheap horror-movie tricks—a dead boy's eyes suddenly pop open; otherworldly voices and dissonant musical effects rumble up from the bowels of the theater's Dolby system; sudden gusts of wind awaken the hero in the middle of the night—the director, Tom Shadyac, steers the material toward maudlin melodrama." A. O. Scott, "Film Preview; Paging the Doctor: It's Your Dead Wife, *New York Times,* February 22, 2002, accessible via http://www.nytimes.com/movie/review?res= 9A03E6DB123EF931A15751C0A9649C8B63.

27. Roger Ebert was quite impressed with this film. "'Birth' is an effective thriller," he wrote, "precisely because it is true to the way sophisticated people might behave in this situation. Its characters are not movie creatures, gullible, emotional and quickly moved to tears. They're realists, rich, a little jaded." The movie, he continued, "is a dark, brooding film, with lots of kettledrums and ominous violins in Alexandre Desplat's score. Harris Savides' cinematography avoids surprises and gimmicks and uses the same kind of level gaze that Sean employs. Echoes of 'Rosemary's Baby' are inevitable, given the similarity of the apartment locations and Kidman's haircut, so similar to Mia Farrow's. But 'Birth' is less sensational and more ominous, and also more intriguing because instead of going for quick thrills, it explores what might really happen if a ten-year-old turned up and said what Sean says. Because it is about adults who act like adults, who are skeptical and wary, it's all the creepier, especially since Cameron Bright is so effective as the uninflected and non-cute Sean." Roger Ebert, review of *Birth,* October 28, 2004, *Chicago Sun-Times,* accessible via http://www. rogerebert.com/reviews/birth-2004. A. O. Scott agreed, writing in the *New York Times* that the film was "both spellbinding and heartbreaking, a delicate chamber piece with the large, troubled heart of an opera." A. O. Scott, "A Visitor from Betwixt Shows Up in Between," *New York Times,* October 29, 2004, accessible via http://www.nytimes. com/2004/10/29/movies/29birt.html?_r=0.

28. Roger Ebert's reaction to this film was pleasantly arch: "Can one movie support these many coincidences and close calls and misunderstandings? Yes. The movie

works, and so we accept everything." Roger Ebert, review of *Just Like Heaven*, *Chicago Sun-Times*, September 15, 2005, accessible viahttp://www.rogerebert.com/reviews/just-like-heaven-2005. In some ways, *Just Like Heaven* could be taken as a salute to the genre as a whole, since, in addition to the plot conceit of reversing the dynamics of *The Ghost and Mrs. Muir*, the film also includes some elements suggestive of plot situations in *Portrait of Jennie*, *Vertigo*, and *Sleepless in Seattle*.

29. Roger Ebert, review of *Corpse Bride*, *Chicago Sun-Times*, September 22, 2005, accessible via http://www.rogerebert.com/reviews/tim-burtons-corpse-bride-2005.

30. Critic A. O. Scott argued that *Wristcutters* was "more likely to live on as a cult favorite than a consensus classic." He praised the film for its "offbeat, absurdist charm that turns a potentially creepy conceit into an odd, touching adventure." A. O. Scott, "Life's A Little Bit Worse Now That They're Dead," October 19, 2007, *New York Times*, accessible via http://www.nytimes.com/2007/10/19/movies/19wris.html?_r=0.

Conclusion

Underground Religion

In an age of resurgent intolerance and religious warfare, decent people are placed in a quandary: what can we do to fight back without fueling the sectarian hatred we abhor?

This book presents an answer that is only half-facetious: go to the movies.

The films that I call supernatural romances have subverted dogmatic forms of faith. They have prompted free-flowing speculation through plots that both challenge and amuse—plots about love, death, and the afterlife that draw upon faith traditions in a manner that is largely non-creedal.[1] They draw viewers gently into questions that famous theologians have pondered. They limber up the mind—set it free for independent reflection. Disarming and enticing, these films have played a civilizing role in the world.

And they demonstrate the interesting ways in which lofty ideas can play out in the form of recreation. Successful movies have resulted from migrations of ideas from the related and overlapping realms of religion, philosophy, and science to cinema, causing writers of screenplays to say, "I could turn that into a story."

On a purely intellectual level, this trend is fraught with significance. Several theologians have studied this pattern not only for its relevance to their ongoing work but also because it is fascinating in and of itself. Christopher Deacy, for instance, has hailed the "ever-growing field of theology and film," declaring that his fellow theologians should pay very close attention to movies such as these. "Any theology," he writes, "which fails to draw on agencies of popular culture simply misses the point about how and where theological reflection is already taking place."[2]

Perhaps most importantly of all at the moment, these films possess political significance. They illustrate the way in which democracies, unlike theocracies, encourage us to wonder about the mysteries of existence. They exemplify how the decent side of the religious sensibility—toleration of different points of view, free inquiry, free speculation in matters of the spirit—can make religious life humane and a force to be more fully integrated with feelings that all of us share, such as love in the face of mortality.

We live in an age of resurgent religious wars, as everybody knows. History is rife with the carnage of religious persecution, and we see it right now, to our fury and disgust, in the daily news: the mass-murder, the torture, the emotional tyranny, the stultification of selfhood, all of these monstrosities resulting from the unchecked force of religious fanaticism and its cruelty.

But religion of course can have its comforts. Every thinking person must sooner or later ask the following questions or some slight variations thereon: why is there anything at all instead of nothing, why is the cosmos organized the way it is, why is there so much suffering out there, what (if any) future do we have beyond the grave, what does God want, what does He intend, what (if any) are the limits of His power? We can also ask ourselves whether many gods exist instead of one. And if God does not exist . . . then what?

Candid thinkers will admit that we have no idea how to answer. Our minds are no more equipped to answer such questions than (for instance) a cold virus is equipped to understand this sentence. Yet we ask such questions—we have to, or else confess to being mindless (or to suffering from ennui).

So here we are, perplexed as we can be, in this state of irresolution. Except that prophets and oracles routinely arise and they claim to have definitive answers. Organized religions have resulted, based upon faith.

At their best, they supply great benefits: mercy, charity, forbearance. They offer emotional comfort and consolation to the stricken, and they do much more that is often quite admirable, even beautiful. But they can also prompt persecution and their dogmas are projected through mental enslavement: the indoctrination of the young, supplemented by many devices of control, such as guilt, fear of hell, fear of breaking away from tradition, and the pressure to conform.

Supernatural romances free the mind, if only for a while. They can stimulate philosophic thinking and provide all the mental liberation of heterodoxy—they are rather like popular science (or science fiction), as applied in this case to the ineffable, the unscientific, the unanswerable. They are democratic productions and they liberate.

A large claim, and yet it stands self-evident. So let's toast the feisty people who created this mass entertainment. Here's to them, wherever they may be.

NOTES

1. Films that prompt religious speculation must of course be distinguished from films explicitly designed to support religious orthodoxy, films such as Cecil B. De-Mille's two versions of *The Ten Commandments* (1923 and 1956) and Mel Gibson's *The Passion of the Christ* (2004).

2. Christopher Deacy, *Screening the Afterlife: Theology, Eschatology and Film* (London and New York: Routledge, 2012), viii–ix.

Appendix One

Case Study: The Making of What Dreams May Come

Without a doubt, *What Dreams May Come* is the most ambitious supernatural romance that has been produced (to date) on screen, and so a study of its production is of value. The project began with a novel by Richard Matheson and its production was preliminarily a partnership between Matheson and producer Stephen Simon.

The same men had launched the screen version of Matheson's novel *Bid Time Return* and the result was the 1980 film *Somewhere in Time*. During the production of that film, Simon had been known as Stephen Deutsch but he later changed his last name to Simon: an adopted son, he embraced the name of his birth father later on in life. Simon has bequeathed to historians in cinema studies an unusually rich and detailed account of the production of *What Dreams May Come*, most of it contained in his 2002 book *The Force Is With You*.

Richard Matheson's career as an author began in the 1950s, when he produced several novels and short stories in the overlapping "horror," "fantasy," and "science fiction" traditions. Among his other accomplishments were screenplays for Rod Serling's celebrated television series *The Twilight Zone*.

Matheson got the idea for a time travel novel in 1970, and *Bid Time Return* was published in 1975. Simon, a young Los Angeles attorney, was given a copy of Matheson's book by a sales clerk in a Beverly Hills bookshop. This clerk was familiar with Simon's literary taste.[1] Simon had dreamed of entering the motion picture industry for years, since both his birth father, S. Sylvan Simon, and his adoptive father, Armand Deutsch, had worked in Hollywood.

Simon read the new Matheson book and his ambitions took fire. "I read the book in one sitting and was just mesmerized," he remembered.[2] He had recently decided to give up practicing law and find work as a film producer. He had been cultivating an acquaintance named Ray Stark, who had known S. Sylvan Simon when the latter was head of production at Columbia. In February 1976, Stark hired Simon as his assistant at Rastar Productions (a subsidiary of Columbia), and Simon immediately pounced upon the opportunity to turn the Matheson book into a film project.[3]

He called Matheson's agent, a lunch was arranged, and the men hit it off. "Look, I just got into the movie business," he told Richard Matheson. "This is my favorite book. Give me a couple of years and, if you won't sell this to anyone else, I promise you, I will make this movie."[4]

So Simon and Matheson began the long process of selling the project. Unfortunately for both of them, Stark was not impressed. "I couldn't get *Bid Time Return* out of my mind," recalled Simon, "and that drove Ray nuts. . . . I had talked him into optioning the book rights, but he just didn't see the commercial potential."[5] In the meantime, the friendship of Matheson and Simon had developed to the point where the metaphysical and mystical interests of the former were captivating the latter; Matheson became Simon's "spiritual guide," according to his own account.[6]

In the course of interviewing an up-and-coming director named Jeannot Szwarc, Simon asked him about his own dreams and goals, and Szwarc revealed that he wanted to direct a "romantic fantasy, something like *Portrait of Jennie* back in the forties." Simon saw his chance and started talking up the merits of *Bid Time Return*, to the chagrin of Stark. "I gave Jeannot the novel," wrote Simon, "and he read it overnight, calling me the next morning to say that he was definitely 'in' and that we should develop the script together." Stark reluctantly agreed to help produce the film.[7]

In December 1978, Simon, Matheson, and Szwarc took the project to Universal Studios, conferring with Vice President Thom Mount and Production Head Ned Tanen. Tanen was extremely skeptical, but approval was given by Universal Chairman Lew Wasserman, who owed Szwarc a favor. And so Matheson began to create the screenplay, in consultation with Szwarc.[8]

And at the very same time Richard Matheson was finishing work on the novel *What Dreams May Come*. He presented the galleys to Simon in 1979, just after the production of *Somewhere in Time* had been finished.

Matheson's novel contained core elements that would find their way into the film version of the story, but there were significant differences. The narrator of the book is Robert Nielson, brother of the book's protagonist Chris Nielson. Robert is visited by a psychic, who gives him a written account that was dictated to her by the ghost of Chris: an account of his life after death. Chris is killed in a car crash and finds himself in "Borderland," a transitional location in the hereafter from which he views the world he just left. He sees his wife Ann and attempts to communicate with her, to no avail. After praying for release from this state, he finds himself in a different and entirely more congenial spot in the afterlife: "Summerland."

"Summerland" is a dream-based realm in which every spirit creates the kind of afterlife it envisions. Chris is visited by the spirit of a cousin, Albert, as well as by the spirit of his deceased family dog, Katie. Then he learns that Ann committed suicide, which will relegate her spirit to a lower realm for twenty-four years—the precise span of time that she would have been given to complete her life on earth.

Chris's rescue of Ann corresponds very closely to its presentation in the film, except that in the book (and also in the original conclusion of the film that was vetoed by the executives of the financial backer, Polygram Filmed Entertainment), she chooses reincarnation immediately as a way to heal her spirit, so Chris is left alone back in Summerland. He dictates his narrative account for the medium as a prelude to seeking reincarnation himself, so that he can follow quickly in her footsteps and seek her out again. It turns out that he and Ann have been "soul mates" in a multitude of previous lives. His memories of being Chris Nielson will vanish in his next incarnation.

One of the major differences between the novel and the film is that the children of Chris and Ann do not die in Matheson's version of story.

Matheson was born a Christian Scientist, but he became a heterodox thinker who was influenced by theosophy. One of the characters in *What Dreams May Come* quotes from the eighteenth-century Swedish mystic Emanuel Swedenborg.[9]

When Simon read the galleys for Matheson's new novel, he decided that "one of the main purposes" of his career thenceforth would be "to produce the film and get it out to the world." The moment was auspicious at least in the sense that he and Matheson had enjoyed their collaboration in producing *Somewhere in Time*. Matheson gave Simon the rights to *What Dreams May Come* on a handshake.[10] Little did either one of them know what a frustrating ordeal lay ahead. But the obstacles appeared right away: Simon encountered a range of stock objections to the project as he "shopped it around." His rueful recollection merits quoting at length:

> The industry scoffed at it and me for thinking it was so special and nobody—*nobody*—understood WDMC [*What Dreams May Come*]. At least, most people acknowledged that SIT [*Somewhere in Time*] was a time travel movie and acknowledged the concept as a device that audiences could buy. But WDMC was all set in the afterlife experience of the main character. How were we going to visually execute that? And, the conventional wisdom continued, the story was too depressing. Nobody wants to deal with that much death, I was told. Lastly, the wife in the book commits suicide after her husband dies while she has two young children at home. How do you sympathize with her when she leaves two kids without either parent? Now *that* one I got. Not only did I get it, but I agreed wholeheartedly that we were going to have to figure that one out.[11]

Several years passed. *Somewhere in Time* had been a failure with the critics, and this further diminished Simon's chances of selling the new project. *What Dreams May Come* was rejected by one studio after another—almost sixty rejections in the course of three years after Matheson and Simon struck their deal.

By 1982, Simon had moved on to an exclusive contract with 20th Century Fox. Then Matheson called him with electrifying news: Steven Spielberg was interested.

Spielberg had a taste for supernatural romance, and he would produce his own remake of *A Guy Named Joe*—with the new title *Always*—within a half-dozen years. He found Matheson's book a "brilliant conception," and he wanted to begin working on a script. If all went well, he would be able to produce *What Dreams May Come* right after he completed work on the next Indiana Jones film, *Temple of Doom*. Spielberg at that time was doing business with both Warner Brothers and Universal, and so he asked Simon and Matheson if they had any preference in regard to the studio that they would approach. When Simon mentioned that he had an exclusive contract with 20th Century Fox, Spielberg replied that he would never make a film at Fox.

It turned out that Spielberg was carrying a grudge against a Fox vice chairman named Norman Levy (who had no idea at the time that he had somehow earned Spielberg's enmity). Spielberg refused to work with any studio that employed Levy.

Simon bore the news to Levy, who was surprised and appalled. They both appealed to the studio's owner, Marvin Davis, who in turn asked George Lucas (under contract to Fox at the time for the *Star Wars* series) to intercede with Spielberg. It didn't work, though Lucas reportedly rendered his own verdict on *What Dreams May Come*: it was "a fantastic project."[12] At the same time, the new head of production at Fox, Joe Wizan, read Matheson's book and told Davis that the studio would never have a better chance to produce "a historic movie."[13] Simon was torn between a celebrity director, Spielberg, and a close friend and mentor in Levy who magnanimously told Simon that he would allow him to escape from his exclusive contract at Fox if he wanted to make the film with Spielberg elsewhere.

Simon believed that Spielberg was being unreasonably harsh about Levy and he turned for advice to Richard Matheson, the originator of the project and also the friend who had, by Simon's own repeated proclamations, become his "spiritual mentor." Matheson told Simon to try to "separate Spielberg's talent from what I thought he would do with *this* particular project," and Simon concluded, for intuitive reasons, that "we had to say no to Spielberg." Years later, having watched Spielberg's *Always*, Simon concluded he had been right to say no to Spielberg for two reasons: "*Dreams* might have become a wonderful adventure in the afterlife with Spielberg directing it in 1985, but it would not have had the soul it needed to have."[14] In addition, he remembered years later, he "would not have been able to live with myself if I had turned my back on a friend (Levy) who had always been so wonderful to me."[15]

Fox purchased the rights to the novel in 1984, and then Simon looked around for a director. After Matheson produced a preliminary screenplay, Simon entered into some promising discussions with director Wolfgang Petersen. But then things fell apart. Davis decided to sell the Fox studio in 1985. The new owners proceeded to fire every single executive of Fox in a wholesale purge. This killed many of the productions in the studio's pipeline because the new executives (perhaps understandably under these maniacal circumstances) had no desire to get blamed if the existing projects failed.

What Dreams May Come almost sank to oblivion in the late 1980s: Simon and Matheson were worse off than ever before since they labored under the new odium of having turned down the *Wunderkind*, Spielberg.

By the early 1990s, Simon had gone to work for producer Dino De Laurentiis. This experience turned out badly when Simon took the wrong side in a quarrel: De Laurentiis was raging at the Academy Award–winning (*Rainman*) writer Ronald Bass, and, when Simon came off as being too sympathetic with Bass's point of view, De Laurentiis fired him. Simon and Bass communed together, and one thing led to another, as Simon elaborates: "Ron called again to see how I was doing and said he wanted to try to do something together, so that we could get the bad taste of that experience out of our mouths. He then asked me if I had anything I wanted to do and—clang!—the red light went off in my head. I went to see Richard Matheson."[16]

And this led to another excruciating choice—another test of loyalties. For the Matheson–Simon collaboration had rested from the start upon the presumption that Matheson would be the writer to produce the screenplay for *What Dreams May Come*, as he had done with *Somewhere in Time*. But in the new scenario, Ronald Bass would replace Richard Matheson as writer. Simon recounts the delicate and painful task of laying the new proposition before Matheson:

> I explained to Richard that Ron had become the most sought-after writer in the business and that he was brilliant with writing scripts that studios understood and in which major actors wanted to star. I thought it was our best chance to get going again and, this time, I left it up to Richard. True to form, he understood completely and agreed with my reasoning. It hurt him, and he didn't like it. Neither did I.[17]

This was probably the genesis of Matheson's later alienation from the film version of his novel, though he tried to put the best face on the situation as long as he could.

Bass read the book and was extremely taken with the story. He doubted, however, whether he could convince the head of any studio to pay him the customary million dollars that he routinely commanded for a script at that time. Simon suggested that they talk to Mike Marcus, an old friend of Bass and Simon who had just taken over the MGM studio.

As Simon and Bass prepared for their meeting with Marcus they puzzled over what Simon called "the Achilles heel of the book:" the fact that Ann's suicide would leave her children by themselves as orphans.

Sure enough, Marcus told them right away that "we had to solve the suicide problem or we could not proceed." And then the solution came to Bass in an instant:

> *Oh,* I know how to do that. The kids are going to die before the hus-
> band in a tragic accident. The only reason Annie barely survives the
> trauma is her love for Chris. So when he dies, she really has nothing to
> live for. We'll understand completely. And I can use the kids as charac-
> ters in the afterlife with different identities until Chris is ready to see
> them for who they really are. They can actually be his guides. Simple.

Simon proclaimed it a "brilliant, inspired solution to a problem that I hadn't been even able to address in fourteen years. Mike loved it, said let's do this, and that was that. We had a deal." [18]

In 1994, Simon met producer Barnet Bain, and the two of them de-cided to form a new company, "Metafilmics." Bain shared Simon's inter-est in "spiritual" movies and was, in his own words, interested in creat-ing a film that would "take you to the edge of logic." [19] Meanwhile, Bass produced the first draft of the screenplay, and the script was so good that Richard Matheson called Bass to congratulate him, saying that "the adap-tation was so good that [he] would have changed some things in the book if he had thought of them first." [20]

The decision makers at MGM were pleased, and the project moved forward. Bass's agents made suggestions as to whom they might tap to direct the film, and one of these candidates, Vincent Ward from New Zealand, emerged as the front runner for several reasons, the most im-portant of them being his ability to create the kind of fantasy worlds on screen that could convince sophisticated viewers. Ward at first was skep-tical about the project because he could not figure out a clear way to visualize the afterlife. But then he hit upon a scheme: make Annie an artist, a painter, a museum curator, so that Chris will find himself inhabit-ing one of her paintings when he arrives in heaven. Simon liked the idea, observing that "the afterlife was going to have to look different from anything that had ever been seen before on screen." When he asked Ward if he had any idea as to how he intended to accomplish this goal, Ward grinned and said, "No, but we'll figure it out." [21]

Then the project appeared to be in danger again: MGM backed out because the price tag was getting too big.

Simon called for help on a friend who had read the Matheson book years earlier and liked it: a film executive named Ted Field, who had founded a production company called Interscope. Field, in turn, had a deal with Polygram, and he used his leverage to get them to finance *What Dreams May Come*, with the condition that a major star would be recruited as insurance. The short list came down to Tom Hanks and Robin Williams, actors whose personalities seemed to exude the kind of qualities that Chris Nielson would possess. Williams agreed to play Nielson in May 1996. The project appealed to him at once; it was "mythological, epic, romantic, a great combination," he recalled.[22] Vincent Ward remembered that Williams seemed at the time to be "someone everyone could identify with."[23]

The rest of the casting was accomplished quickly. Simon and his collaborators approached Cuba Gooding, Jr., right after he had won an academy award as best supporting actor in *Jerry Maguire*. Gooding liked the fact that the film would create "an environment that had never been seen on film before."[24] At first Gooding wanted to play the "tracker" (the spirit who guides Chris into hell in his quest to find Annie). But then he decided he was more interested in playing the spirit of Chris's son Ian, which is to say the spirit of Ian disguised in African American form when the spirit of Chris first encounters him in heaven. By the same token Rosalind Chao was cast as the spirit of Chris's daughter. The reason for the transracial metamorphoses (as presented in the film) was to avoid the psychological complexities of parent-child role reversal as the spirits of Chris's son and daughter teach him the ways of the afterlife.

After Max von Sydow was cast as the tracker, Annabella Sciorra was cast as Annie after a screen test with Robin Williams. Simon had an uphill task in convincing the executives at Polygram that Sciorra should play the leading lady, but he succeeded on the strength of having recruited Williams and von Sydow. Simon had nothing but praise years later for Sciorra's accomplishment; she had, in his opinion, "one of the most amazingly difficult parts to play in any movie in many years" and in light of this fact she delivered "a perfect performance. She never missed a beat or a note throughout and she never received the credit that she deserved."[25]

Erica Huggins was executive producer of the film and Simon, together with Barnet Bain, were co-producers. The score was composed and conducted by Michael Kamen. Eduardo Serra did the cinematography; he shot the film mostly on Fuji Velvia film. The digital special effects were created by Special Effects Supervisors Joel Hynek, Nicholas Brooks, Kevin Mack, Joel Hunket, and Stuart Robinson under the guidance of Art Director Joshua Rosen and Production Designer Eugenio Zannetti.

While the casting proceeded, Vincent Ward and Zannetti started getting the film ready for production. Shooting began on June 23, 1997, in Glacier National Park in Montana and continued for four months. It was a grueling process for a number of reasons; Simon proclaimed that it was "hell" and a "four-month nightmare." When the shooting was over, he recalled, "we all felt that we had experienced the journey through the nightmare alongside Chris." And the creation of the digital effects was in itself a "slow and unbelievably expensive process."[26]

Editor David Brenner had a rough cut version of the film ready for review by December. The extended editing of the rough cut proved to be the next ordeal in the making of *What Dreams May Come*. There were many different ways to present the basic story—different sequences of presentation. The first cut had been edited according to the plot line of Bass's screenplay. As it happened, this meant that the first act presented the disorientation of Chris's spirit just after his death. This was the version of the film that was shown to a preview audience in January 1998. The members of this audience were recruited solely on the basis of their interest in the subject matter.

The members of the preview audience loved the rough cut version of the film. But the executives at Polygram were not comfortable. They insisted on recruiting a second preview audience whose members would be more diversified, especially in light of the fact the first audience consisted of people with a strong interest in films of this type. The concerns of the Polygram executives were well-grounded, since the second preview audience panned the film.

They found it confusing.

So the production team had to change everything around in order to present a much simpler and more straightforward plot line. Simon, for one, took the changes in stride, though he regretted the loss of sophisticated artistic effects in the interest of creating a broader audience for the film. He wrote that

> we had all loved the first cut, and, in my opinion, it is still the best version of the film. . . . [But] not for a broad, mainstream audience and therein lay the dilemma. To get the film made, a lot of money was spent. The sets and effects were extremely expensive, as was the cast; therefore, Polygram had a huge investment, and they needed to have the film appeal to the widest possible audience. . . . They were absolutely right . . . but making it a more mainstream film took some of the power of the experience away from those who were deeply interested in the subject matter.[27]

In the DVD version of the film is an alternative ending that was nixed by Polygram. It was closer by far to the plotline of Matheson's novel. In this version of the story, Chris and Annie are reunited with the spirits of their children *as they looked when they were alive*, but then the children quickly change into the forms that they possessed when Chris first encountered them in heaven. In other words, the son now appears to be African American (as played by Cuba Gooding) and the daughter is Asian (Rosalind Chao). But Annie reassures them (and Chris) that their changed appearance doesn't bother her.

The souls of the children explain to Chris that Annie must experience purgation before she and Chris can be united in eternity: Annie has to be born again through reincarnation to atone for her suicide. After she is born, she will live out the very same number of years on earth that her suicide prevented her from living the last time around. After this, she will die very young and rejoin Chris in heaven.

But Chris insists upon accompanying her, and so provision is made for this to happen. The tracker (von Sydow) admonishes Chris that after Annie dies, he will still be required to live out the remainder of his life on earth all alone before returning to heaven to be reunited with Annie.

This ending was rejected by Polygram as much too confusing.

After the revisions demanded by Polygram, the film was previewed a total of seventeen times. The audience reactions were not reassuring to Polygram (or to anyone else), since the viewers were deeply divided. Those with the intellectual sensibilities to seek out subject matter of this type found the film enthralling. Those who were attracted by the star power of the actors and the expectation of familiar cinematic experiences were turned off.

Simon recollects that "there was a lot of 'buzz' about *Dreams* in Hollywood, as we moved closer to our October 1998 release date. Academy Award buzz. Huge commercial hit buzz. And it was all wrong. There was no way that this intensely challenging and metaphysical movie was ever going to be a critical or box office bonanza."[28]

And it was certainly not a bonanza: it lost money. It cost $115 million to make ($85 million plus $30 million for marketing in the United States) and brought in only $100 million worldwide. The film did get two Academy Award nominations—for design and for visual effects. It won an Oscar in the latter category. It also won an Art Directors Guild award for excellence in production design.

But critical reactions to the film were more negative than positive. Roger Ebert of the *Chicago Sun-Times* praised *What Dreams May Come* for its boldness and lauded the performances of Williams and Sciorra.[29] But Stephen Holden of the *New York Times*—though praising the film for its "magical, hallucinatory" qualities—was snide in his dismissal of the film's alleged "psychobabble" and he also dismissed the characters of Chris and Annie as "idealized greeting-card parents."[30]

It is possible to agree with Holden's point to a limited extent: a few lines in the screenplay, especially as delivered on screen in some of the early heavenly conversations performed by Robin Williams and Cuba Gooding, have a goody-goody quality that might grate upon worldly sensibilities. But such passages are relatively few and far between in this film, and Holden's scorn is accordingly overreaching: it lacks discernment.

Such reviews represented an ironic reversal of the negative audience reactions in the previews. Many members of the preview audiences found the film too confusing and too avant garde. The Polygram executives shared this concern, and so the film was accordingly tamed, as we have seen. But then reviewers like Holden condemned the film as banal.

One wonders whether the rough cut of *What Dreams May Come* would have passed the lofty threshold of sophistication demanded by the journalistic intelligentsia who had the privilege of reviewing films in the 1990s.

In Simon's view, the film was "absolutely excoriated by most of the critics. They hated it and took great glee in listing all their reasons: corny, not believable, overwrought. And those were some of the nicer words. One magazine actually called it 'metaphysical crap.'"[31] It is tempting to engage in speculation as to whether this reviewer found the film too sophisticated or not sophisticated enough.

One cultural issue that pertains to the climates of opinion in the 1990s may be relevant not only to the critical responses to *What Dreams May Come* but to other supernatural romances such as the contemporaneous *Meet Joe Black*. For a multitude of reasons—some commonplace in the *fin-de-siècle* situation and others highly specific to the state of American culture at this particular time—there was a widespread tendency of raucous derision in America, all the way from the literati to the level of the lowest vulgarians. Cynicism, for many, was the order of the day, and a crucial prerequisite for being seen as a highbrow.[32]

In 1995 (on New Year's Day), Martha Sherrill of the *Washington Post* proclaimed that "we're a little hungry for . . . devourings, for crudity and unsweet sex. For snot and vomit and blown-up bits of skull. We want our world un-socialized. We want our establishments eroding. We want our characters unmannered."[33] Small wonder in an atmosphere like this that any hipsters who wanted to remain in good standing with their peers would regard any optimistic ("uplifting") speculation in theological matters as trite. Holden's complaint that eternity in *What Dreams May Come* is too "soothingly" presented typifies this jaundiced state of mind—heaven as a place where you "close your eyes, snap your fingers, and fly, just like Peter Pan." But surely as he dashed off this review, Holden seemed to be forgetting how (a few paragraphs earlier) he marveled at the nightmarish effectiveness of the hell sequences.

Regardless, the film was too "soothing" overall to pass muster with Holden.

In the very same year, critic Janet Maslin's response to *Meet Joe Black* was equally contemptuous—and equally trendy: "Oh, to die in a sugar-coated Hollywood movie while the spiritual schmaltz craze is under way! You look your best. You say wise things. Your loved ones cherish them. Perhaps there'll be a party with a dance band and fireworks in your honor."[34]

The "spiritual schmaltz craze."

Critical reactions are based in the sensibilities of individuals. There is surely no absolute and universal "right and wrong" when it comes to taste. Yet the case can be made that reactions to a great many supernatural romances on screen in the 1990s by the critics partook of a formulaic dismissiveness compounding pretensions to sophistication with ignorance of cultural and literary history. If Chris Nielson's rescue of Annie may be said to constitute "schamltz," then so does the rescue of Alcestis in Euripides's classical drama.

Simon has observed that *What Dreams May Come* is an "emotional Rorschach test," and that the "striking thing about people's responses" to the film is that there is usually "no middle ground: people love it or loathe it." He relays an anecdote about a Santa Barbara party he attended just a few weeks after its release.[35]

In the course of a welcoming speech, the host observed that his friend Stephen Simon was one of the producers of this new film, and he invited any guests who had seen it to share their reactions with Simon. The first guest to approach him was exquisitely polite, and yet Simon was informed that he was nothing less than "an inhuman monster" since the film seemed to preach that all suicides go to hell. The second person who spoke to him turned out to be the director of a suicide-prevention hotline who said, "Bless you. This movie will be saving some lives." The third person complained that only Judeo-Christian imagery was used in the film. The next person complained that there was *not enough* Judeo-Christian imagery for his satisfaction.

Surely the travails and the ironies involved in the production of *What Dreams May Come* reveal the challenge of presenting metaphysical issues to a mass audience. But this is what the legacy of supernatural romance on screen is all about.

Notwithstanding the financial and journalistic let-down suffered by the makers of *What Dreams May Come* in the year or so after its release—so comparable, in the case of Stephen Simon, with the let-down attending the release of *Somewhere in Time*—the 1998 film would make significant profits in the *commercial* "afterlife" of videos and DVDs.

NOTES

1. Bill Shepard, *The Somewhere In Time Story: Behind the Scenes in the Making of a Cult Romantic Fantasy Motion Picture* (LaGrange, IL: Somewhere In Time Gallery, 2004), 21.

2. Stephen Simon, *The Force Is With You: Mystical Movie Messages That Inspire Our Lives* (Newburyport, MA: Hampton Roads, 2002), 187.

3. Simon, *The Force Is With You*, 194–95.

4. Shepard, *The Somewhere In Time Story*, 21.

5. Simon, *The Force Is With You*, 197.

6. Simon, *The Force Is With You*, 196.

7. Simon, *The Force Is With You*, 198.

8. Simon, *The Force Is With You*, 198–99; Shepard, *The Somewhere In Time Story*, 23, 27.

9. For accounts of Matheson's theological sources and inspirations, see Stanley Wiater, Matthew Bradley, and Paul Struve, *The Twilight and Other Zones: The Dark Worlds of Richard Matheson* (New York: Citadel Press, 2009), 24–25.

10. Simon, *The Force Is With You*, 218–19.

11. Simon, *The Force Is With You*, 220.

12. Simon, *The Force Is With You*, 222–23.

13. Simon, *The Force Is With You*, 222–23.

14. Simon, *The Force Is With You*, 225.

15. Stephen Simon to Richard Striner, September 13, 2014.

16. Simon, *The Force Is With You*, 230.

17. Simon, *The Force Is With You*, 231.

18. Simon, *The Force Is With You*, 232.

19. Barnet Bain, quoted in "Featurette," supplement to *What Dreams May Come*, Polygram Video, Special DVD edition, 2002.

20. Simon, *The Force Is With You*, 233.

21. Simon, *The Force Is With You*, 233–34.

22. Robin Williams, quoted in "Featurette."

23. Vincent Ward, quoted in "Featurette."

24. Cuba Gooding, Jr., quoted in "Featurette."

25. Simon, *The Force Is With You*, 236.

26. Ibid., 236.

27. Simon, *The Force Is With You*, 236–37.

28. Simon, *The Force Is With You*, 237–38.

29. Roger Ebert, "*What Dreams May Come*," *Chicago Sun-Times*, October 2, 1998.

30. Stephen Holden, "Film Review: Apparently, The Afterlife Is Anything But Dead," *New York Times*, October 2, 1998, accessible via http://www.nytimes.com/movie/review?res=9E00E1DA1438F931A35753C1A96E958260.

31. Simon, *The Force Is With You*, 238.

32. The comparable reaction of the critics to *Somewhere in Time* has prompted some defenders of that film to trace the trendy cynicism of the 1990s to earlier patterns. Jeffrey Wells, writing in *Films in Review*, wrote that "most critics savaged the film to such a degree that obviously they weren't complaining about its errors as a movie, but its wide-eyed, syrupy sentiment. On this note, they made no attempt to conceal their loathing. Why? It's hard to say, but I think it has something to do with the clash between the '40s' romanticism of *Somewhere in Time*, the sort typified by films such as *Portrait of Jennie* and *Stairway To Heaven* [i.e., *A Matter of Life and Death*], and the '80s' didacticism of most working critics, who would not last very long at what they do if they were known to harbor a sentimental streak." Quoted in Shepard, *The Somewhere In Time Story*, 106.

33. Martha Sherrill, "Learning to Love Vulgarity," *Washington Post*, January 1, 1995, G-1, G-4.

34. Janet Maslin, "Film Review: When Death Comes to Call, Serve Peanut Butter," *New York Times*, November 13, 1998, accessible via http://www.nytimes.com/movie/review?res=9B0CE7DB1431F930A25752C1A96E958260.

35. Stephen Simon, telephone interview with Richard Striner, September 11, 2014.

Appendix Two

Other Patterns in Film that Justify Additional Study

"Genre" or not, "supernatural romance" is indisputably a pattern—a pattern consisting of the love-death-afterlife trinity—and the importance of the pattern is (I trust) sufficiently evident. There are other patterns in film that seem to me worthy of additional study and I offer a few of them here for whatever they might be worth to others.

In "romantic comedy" and also in what some have called "screwball comedy"—the latter term construed by historians and film critics in different ways—one often (but not always) encounters a romance between unlikely lovers who converge at least in part because each of their personalities makes up for some deficiency in the other. The process of falling in love enables them to achieve more individual fulfillment (through maturation) as they also become a good couple through a reconciliation of styles and preferences. In many respects, these lovers empower one another. There is also a frequent use in these films of the *deus ex machina* device: things go wrong, but then everything is put right at the end through an intervention or catharsis. The audience leaves the theater in a state of near-euphoria.[1]

So many movies could be cited to illustrate this particular pattern: *Love Me Tonight* (1932); Frank Capra classics such as *It Happened One Night* (1934), *Mr. Deeds Goes to Town* (1936), *Mr. Smith Goes to Washington* (1939); Ernst Lubitsch classics such as *Ninotchka* (1939) and *Shop Around the Corner* (1940); musicals such as *Harvey Girls* (1945) and *The Music Man* (1962); fin-de-siècle productions such as *French Kiss* (1995); and films from the past decade such as the Disney masterpiece *Enchanted* (2007).[2]

Should these tales be viewed as the quintessence of screwball comedy? Maybe not, since many films that are regarded as screwball comedies do not use the theme of converging unlikely lovers. Maybe not, since some historians believe that screwball comedy was purely a creation of the 1930s, while the list of films above extends from the 1930s all the way to the present.

So how do we label them?

Before leaving this example, we may note that some of these movies overlap with supernatural romances: what better example of unlikely lovers than in films like *The Ghost and Mrs. Muir*, where one of the lovers is alive and the other one is dead?

To give another example, many westerns (though by no means all) contain a love triangle as one of the plot elements. Many examples could be given, and the reasons for this pattern are an interesting topic for conjecture. Perhaps the literary tradition of the knight errant is linked so profoundly to the theme of the "loner" on the range that certain formulae in medieval tales of "courtly love" were transmitted—via the chivalry theme—to movie westerns. Courtly marriages were typically arranged in the Middle Ages for dynastic reasons. So allowance was made for the satisfaction of amorous impulses in extracurricular activity (royal mistresses sometimes had formal standing at court). But marriage vows had sufficient standing for religious reasons at any given time that the theme of adulterous romance could be rendered in tragic terms as in the tales of Tristan and Isolde, and Lancelot and Guinevere. The love of "Shane" for the wife of the homesteading farmer in the classic 1952 film of the same name is repressed, but the result is a different sort of tragedy. The theme of the love triangle (though not necessarily adulterous) could also be used for comic value, as in *Butch Cassidy and the Sundance Kid* (1969) and *Maverick* (1994).

Is the love triangle the quintessence of western movie plots? Surely not, but consider how many of them were created. So what do we call them?

Many British comedies from the 1950s and 1960s are based upon the theme of—how to put it exactly?—a "nobody" trying to be a "somebody." So many examples could be given: the two Alec Guinness classics from 1951 (*The Man in the White Suit* and *The Lavender Hill Mob*), *School for Scoundrels* (1960), *Bedazzled* (1967). What does it all mean? Is it a commentary, perhaps, on the changing patterns of social mobility in mid-twentieth-century Britain?

Is it a genre? Perhaps not, since many other British comedies used different sorts of devices.

So what is it?

NOTES

1. In the 1970s, historian Andrew Bergman wrote that the screwball comedies of Frank Capra had a generalized purpose of promoting themes of reconciliation, even to the point of "reconciling the irreconcilable. They created an America of perfect unity: all classes as one, the rural-urban divide breached, love and decency and neighborliness ascendant. . . . The comic technique of these comedies became a means of unifying what had been splintered and divided. . . . It worked to pull things together." Andrew Bergman, *We're In The Money: Depression America and Its Films* (New York: New York University Press, 1971), Harper Colophon edition, 1972, 133–34. Surely the reconciliations of screwball comedy correlate closely with the reconciliations of supernatural romance, at least in its most optimistic versions: whereas the rapprochements of screwball comedy were social, those of supernatural romance were existential.

2. There is of course ample provenance for the theme of ironic lovers in classics such as Shakespeare's *Much Ado About Nothing,* in several Jane Austen novels, and in many other sources.

Appendix Three

Production Data for Supernatural Romances and Related Films

Forever *(1921)*

Directed by:	George Fitzmaurice
Written by:	George du Maurier (novel), Ouda Bergere (scenario)
Cinematography:	Arthur C. Miller
Production Company:	Famous Players-Lasky
Distributed by:	Paramount
Release date:	October 16, 1921
Running time:	60 minutes
Country:	USA
Language:	English

Cast

Wallace Reid	Peter Ibbetson
Elsie Ferguson	Mimsi
Montagu Love	Colonel Ibbetson
George Fawcett	Duquesnois
Dolores Cassinelli	Dolores
Paul McQAllister	Seraskier
Elliott Dexter	Pasquier
Charles Eaton	Gogo
Jerome Patrick	Duke of Towers

Smilin' Through *(1922)*

Directed by:	Sidney Franklin
Produced by:	Norma Talmadge, Joseph M. Schenk
Written by:	Jane Murfin and Jane Cowl (play), James Ashmore Creelman and Sidney Franklin (screenplay)
Cinematography:	J. Roy Hunt, Charles Rosher
Distributed by:	First National
Release date:	February 13, 1922
Running time:	96 minutes
Country:	USA
Language:	English

Cast

Norma Talmadge	Kathleen and Moonyeen
Harrison Ford	Kenneth and Jeremy Wayne
Wyndham Standing	John Carteret
Alec B. Francis	Dr. Owen
Glenn Hunter	Willie Ainsley

Outward Bound *(1930)*

Directed by:	Robert Milton
Produced by:	Jack L. Warner
Written by:	Sutton Vane (play), J. Grubb Alexander (screenplay)
Cinematography:	Hal Mohr
Distributed by:	Warner Brothers/Vitaphone
Release date:	November 29, 1930
Running time:	83 minutes
Country:	USA
Language:	English

Cast

Leslie Howard	Tom Prior

Douglas Fairbanks, Jr.	Henry
Helen Chandler	Ann
Alec B. Francis	Scrubby
Montagu Love	Mr. Lingley
Lyonel Watts	Rev. William Duke
Alison Skipworth	Mr. Cliveden-Banks

Smilin' Through *(1932)*

Directed by:	Sidney Franklin
Produced by:	Albert Lewin
Written by:	Donald Ogden Stewart, Ernest Vajda (screenplay)
Cinematography:	Lee Garmes
Music:	William Axt, Arthur A. Penn
Distributed by:	MGM
Release date:	September 24, 1932
Running time:	98 minutes
Country:	USA
Language:	English

Cast

Norma Shearer	Kathleen and Moonyeen
Leslie Howard	Sir John Carteret
Fredric March	Kenneth and Jeremy Wayne
O.P. Heggie	Dr. Owen
Ralph Forbes	Willie Ainley
Beryl Mercer	Mrs. Crouch
Margaret Seddon	Ellen

The Mummy *(1932)*

Directed by:	Karl Freund
Produced by:	Carl Laemmle, Jr.
Written by:	John L. Balderston

Distributed by:	Universal
Release date:	December 22, 1932
Running time:	73 minutes
Country:	USA
Language:	English

Cast

Boris Karloff	Imhotep/Ardath Bey
Zita Johann	Helen Grosvenor
David Manners	Frank Whemple
Arthur Byron	Sir Joseph Whemple
Edward Van Sloan	Dr. Müller
Noble Johnson	The Nubian

Berkeley Square *(1933)*

Directed by:	Frank Lloyd
Produced by:	Jesse Lasky
Written by:	John L. Balderston (play)
	Sonya Levien and John L. Balderston (screenplay)
Cinematography:	Ernest Palmer
Music by:	Louis De Francesco
Distributed by:	Fox Film Corporation
Release date:	September 15, 1933
Running time	85 minutes
Country:	USA
Language:	English

Cast

Leslie Howard	Peter Standish
Heather Angel	Helen Pettigrew
Valerie Taylor	Kate Pettigrew
Irene Browne	Lady Ann Pettigrew
Beryl Mercer	Mrs. Barwick

Colin Keith-Johnson	Tom Pettigrew
Alan Mowbray	Major Clinton
Juliette Compton	Duchess of Devonshire
Ferdinand Gottschalk	Mr. Throstle
Olaf Hytten	Sir Joshua Reynolds
David Torrence	Lord Stanley

Death Takes a Holiday *(1934)*

Directed by:	Mitchell Leisen
Produced by:	E. Lloyd Sheldon and Emanuel Cohen
Written by:	Maxwell Anderson and Gladys Lehman
Distributed by:	Paramount
Release date:	March 30, 1934
Running time:	79 minutes
Country:	USA
Language:	English

Cast

Fredric March	Prince Sirki/Death
Evelyn Venable	Grazia
Sir Guy Standing	Duke Lambert
Katharine Alexander	Alda
Gail Patrick	Rhoda
Helen Westley	Stephanie
Kathleen Howard	Princess Maria
Kent Taylor	Corrado
Henry Travers	Baron Cesarea
Otto Hoffman	Fedele

Peter Ibbetson *(1935)*

Directed by:	Henry Hathaway
Produced by:	Louis D. Lighton

Written by:	George du Maurier (novel), John Meehan, Edwin Justus Mayer, Waldemar Young, Constance Collier, Vincent Lawrence (screenplay)
Cinematography:	Charles Lang
Music by:	Ernst Toch
Distributed by:	Paramount
Release date:	October 31, 1935
Running time:	88 minutes
Country:	USA
Language:	English

Cast

Gary Cooper	Peter Ibbetson
Ann Harding	Mary, Duchess of Towers
John Halliday	The Duke of Towers
Ida Lupino	Agnes
Douglass Dumbrille	Col. Forsythe
Virginia Weider	Mimsey (Mary, age 6)
Dickie Moore	Gogo (Peter, age 8)
Doris Lloyd	Mrs. Dorian
Gilbert Emery	Wilkins
Donald Meek	Mr. Slade
Christian Rub	Major Duquesnois
Elsa Buchanan	Madame Pasquier

Topper *(1937)*

Directed by:	Norman Z. McLeod
Produced by:	Hal Roach
Written by:	Thorne Smith (novel), Jack Jevne, Eric Hatch, Eddie Moran (screenplay)
Cinematography:	Norbert Brodine
Music by:	Marvin Hatly
Distributed by:	MGM

Release date:	July 16, 1937
Running time:	97 minutes
Country:	USA
Language:	English

Cast

Cary Grant	George Kerby
Constance Bennett	Marion Kerby
Roland Young	Cosmo Topper
Billie Burke	Clara Topper
Alan Mowbray	Wilkins
Eugene Pallette	Casey
Hedda Hopper	Mrs. Grace Stuyvesant

On Borrowed Time (1939)

Directed by:	Harold S. Bucquet
Produced by:	Sidney Franklin
Written by:	Lawrence Edward Watkin (novel), Paul Osborn (play), Alice D. G. Miller, Frank O'Neill
Cinematography:	Joseph Ruttenberg
Music by:	Franz Waxman
Distributed by:	MGM
Release date:	July 6, 1939
Running time:	99 minutes
Country:	USA
Language:	English

Cast

Lionel Barrymore	Julian Northrup
Sir Cedric Hardwicke	Mr. Brink
Beulah Bondi	Nellie Northrup
Una Merkel	Marcie Giles
Bobs Watson	Pud Northrup
Henry Travers	Dr. James Evans

Grant Mitchell	Ben Pilbeam
Eily Malyon	Demetria Riffle
Nat Pendleton	Mr. Grimes

Our Town *(1940)*

Directed by:	Sam Wood
Produced by:	Sol Lesser
Written by:	Thornton Wilder (play), Harry Chandlee, Frank Craven (screenplay)
Cinematography:	Bert Glellon
Music by:	Aaron Copland
Production Company:	Principal Artists Productions
Distributed by:	United Artists
Release date:	May 24, 1940
Running time:	90 minutes
Country:	USA
Language:	English

Cast

William Holden	George Gibbs
Martha Scott	Emily Webb
Frank Craven	Stage Manager
Fay Bainter	Mrs. Julia Gibbs
Beulah Bondi	Mrs. Myrtle Webb
Thomas Mitchell	Dr. Frank Gibbs
Guy Kibbee	Charles Webb

Here Comes Mr. Jordan *(1941)*

Directed by:	Alexander Hall
Produced by:	Everett Riskin
Written by:	Harry Segall (play), Sidney Buchman, Seton I. Miller
Cinematography:	Joseph Walker
Music by:	Friedrich Hollaender

Distributed by: Columbia
Release date: August 7, 1941
Running time: 94 minutes
Country: USA
Language: English

Cast

Robert Montgomery	Joe Pendleton
Evelyn Keyes	Bette Logan
Claude Rains	Mr. Jordan
Edward Everett Horton	Messenger 7013
James Gleason	Max Corkle
John Emery	Tony Abbott
Rita Johnson	Julia Farnsworth
Donald MacBride	Inspector Williams
Don Costello	Lefty

Smilin' Through *(1941)*

Directed by: Frank Borzage
Produced by: Frank Borzage, Victor Saville
Written by: Donald Ogden Stewart, John L. Balderston
Cinematography: Leonard Smith
Music by: Herbert Stothart
Distributed by: MGM
Release date: October 1941
Running time: 100 minutes
Country: USA
Language: English

Cast

Jeanette MacDonald	Kathleen and Moonyeen
Brian Aherne	Sir John Carteret
Gene Raymond	Kenneth and Jeremy Wayne

Ian Hunter Reverend Owen Harding

Cabin in the Sky (1943)

Directed by:	Vincente Minnelli
Produced by:	Arthur Freed, Albert Lewis
Written by:	Lynn Root (play), Marc Connelly, Joseph Schrank (screenplay)
Cinematography:	Sidney Wagner
Music by:	Harold Arlen, Vernon Duke, George Bassman, Roger Edens
Distributed by:	MGM
Release date:	April 9, 1943
Running time:	98 minutes
Country:	USA
Language:	English

Cast

Ethel Waters	Petunia Jackson
Eddie "Rochester" Anderson	Little Joe Jackson
Lena Horne	Georgia Brown
John William Sublett	Domino Johnson
Kenneth Spencer	Reverend Green/the General
Louis Armstrong	the Trumpeter
Rex Ingram	Lucius/Lucifer, Junior
Butterfly McQueen	Lily

A Guy Named Joe (1943)

Directed by:	Victor Fleming
Produced by:	Everett Riskin
Written by:	Chandler Sprague David Boehm (story), Dalton Trumbo (screenplay), Frederick Hazlitt Brennan (adaptation)
Cinematography:	George L. Folsey, Karl Freund

Music by:	Herbert Stothart, Alberto Colombo
Distributed by:	MGM
Release date:	December 23, 1943
Running time:	122 minutes
Country:	USA
Language:	English

Cast

Spencer Tracy	Pete Sandidge
Irene Dunne	Dorinda Durston
Van Johnson	Ted Randall
Ward Bond	Al Yackey
James Gleason	"Nails" Kilpatrick
Lionel Barrymore	The General
Barry Nelson	Dick Rumney
Esther Williams	Ellen Bright

Heaven Can Wait *(1943)*

Directed by:	Ernst Lubitsch
Produced by:	Ernst Lubitsch
Written by:	Leslie Bush-Fekete, Samson Raphaelson (screenplay)
Cinematography:	Edward Cronjager
Music by:	Alfred Newman
Distributed by:	20th Century Fox
Release date:	August 11, 1943
Running time:	112 minutes
Country:	USA
Language:	English

Cast

Gene Tierney	Martha
Don Ameche	Henry Van Cleve
Charles Coburn	Hugo Van Cleve

Marjory Main	Mrs. Strable
Laird Cregar	His Excellency
Spring Byington	Bertha Van Cleve
Allyn Joslyn	Albert Van Cleve
Eugene Pallette	E. F. Strable
Signe Hasso	Mademoiselle
Louis Calhern	Randolph Van Cleve
Helene Reynolds	Peggy Nash
Aubrey Mather	James
Tod Andrews	Jack Van Cleve
Scotty Beckett	Henry Van Cleve, age 9
Dickie Moore	Albert Van Cleve, age 15

Between Two Worlds *(1944)*

Directed by:	Edward A. Blatt
Produced by:	Mark Hellinger, Jack L. Warner
Written by:	Sutton Vane (play), Daniel Fuchs (screenplay)
Cinematography:	Carl E. Guthrie
Music by:	Erich Wolfgang Korngold
Distributed by:	Warner Brothers
Release date:	May 20, 1944
Running time:	112 minutes
Country:	USA
Language:	English

Cast

Paul Henreid	Henry
Eleanor Parker	Ann
Edmund Gwenn	Scrubby
John Garfield	Tom Prior
Sara Allgood	Mrs. Midget
George Coulouris	Mr. Lingley

Dennis King	Reverend William Duke
George Tobias	Pete Musick
Sydney Greenstreet	Reverend Tim Thompson

Blithe Spirit *(1945)*

Directed by:	David Lean
Produced by:	Nöel Coward
Written by:	Nöel Coward (play), David Lean, Ronald Neame, Anthony Havelock-Allen (screenplay)
Cinematography:	Ronald Neame
Music by:	Richard Addinsell
Distributed by:	Arthur Rank/Two Cities Films
Release date:	May 14, 1945
Running time:	96 minutes
Country:	UK
Language:	English

Cast

Rex Harrison	Charles Condomine
Constance Cummings	Ruth Condomine
Kay Hammond	Elvira Condomine
Margaret Rutherford	Madame Arcati
Hugh Wakefield	Dr. George Bradman
Joyce Carey	Violet Bradman
Jacqueline Clarke	Edith

A Matter of Life and Death/Stairway To Heaven *(1946)*

Directed by:	Michael Powell and Emeric Pressburger
Produced by:	Michael Powell and Emeric Pressburger
Written by:	Michael Powell and Emeric Pressburger
Cinematography:	Jack Cardiff
Music by:	Allan Gray
Production Company:	The Archers

Distributed by:	J. Arthur Rank/Eagle-Lion Films
Release date:	November 1, 1946
Running time:	104 minutes
Country:	UK
Language:	English

Cast

David Niven	Peter Carter
Kim Hunter	June
Roger Livesey	Dr. Frank Reeves
Robert Coote	Bob Trubshawe
Kathleen Byron	An angel
Joan Maude	Chief Recorder
Marius Goring	Conductor 71
Raymond Massey	Abraham Farlan

It's A Wonderful Life *(1946)*

Directed by:	Frank Capra
Produced by:	Frank Capra
Written by:	Philip Van Doren Stern (story), Frances Goodrich, Albert Hackett (screenplay)
Cinematography:	Joseph Walker
Music by:	Dimitri Tiomkin
Production Company:	Liberty Films
Distributed by:	RKO Radio Pictures
Release date:	December 20, 1946
Running time:	130 minutes
Country:	USA
Language:	English

Cast

James Stewart	George Bailey
Donna Reed	Mary Hatch Bailey
Henry Travers	Clarence Oddbody

Lionel Barrymore	Henry F. Potter
Thomas Mitchell	Uncle Billy Bailey
Samuel S. Hinds	Peter Bailey
Beulah Bondi	Ma Bailey
Frank Faylen	Ernie Bishop
Ward Bond	Bert the Cop
Gloria Grahame	Violet Bick
H.B. Warner	Mr. Gower
Todd Karns	Harry Bailey
Frank Albertson	Sam Wainwright
William Edmunds	Giuseppe Martini

Down To Earth *(1947)*

Directed by:	Alexander Hall
Produced by:	Don Hartman
Written by:	Harry Segall, Edwin Blum
Cinematography:	Rudolph Mate
Music by:	George Duning, Heinz Roemheld
Distributed by:	Columbia
Release date:	August 21, 1947
Running time:	101 minutes
Country:	USA
Language:	English

Cast

Larry Parks	Danny Miller
Roland Culver	Mr. Jordan
Rita Hayworth	Terpsichore
James Gleason	Max Corkle
Edward Everett Horton	Messenger 7013
Adele Jergens	Georgia Evans and New Terpsichore
James Burke	Detective Kelly
Marc Platt	Eddie

The Ghost and Mrs. Muir *(1947)*

Directed by:	Joseph L. Mankiewicz
Produced by:	Fred Kohlmar
Written by:	Josephine Aimee Campbell Leslie/"R. A. Dick" (novel), Philip Dunne (screenplay)
Cinematography:	Charles Lang
Music by:	Bernard Herrmann
Distributed by:	20th Century Fox
Release date:	June 26, 1947
Running time:	104 minutes
Country:	USA
Language:	English

Cast

Gene Tierney	Lucy Muir
Rex Harrsion	Daniel Gregg
George Sanders	Miles Fairley
Edna Best	Martha Huggins
Natalie Wood	Anna Muir
Robert Coote	Mr. Coombe
Victoria Horne	Eva Muir
Whitford Kane	Mr. Sproull

Heaven Only Knows *(1947)*

Directed by:	Albert S. Rogell
Produced by:	Seymour Nebenzall
Written by:	Aubrey Wisberg, Rowland Leigh
Cinematography:	Karl Struss
Music by:	Heinz Roemheld
Production Company:	Nero Films
Distributed by:	United Artists
Release date:	September 12, 1947
Running time:	100 minutes

Country: USA

Language: English

Cast

Robert Cummings   Mike

Brian Donlevy   Adam "Duke" Byron

Marjory Reynolds   Ginger

Jorja Curtright   Drusilla Wainwright

Bill Goodwin   Bill Plumber

John Litel   Reverend Wainwright

Stuart Erwin   Sheriff Matt Bodine

Gerald Mohr   Treason

Edgar Kennedy   Judd

Lurene Tuttle   Mrs. O'Donnell

Peter Miles   Speck O'Donnell

Will Orleans   Kansas City Kid

The Red Shoes *(1948)*

Directed by: Michael Powell and Emeric Pressburger

Produced by: Michael Powell and Emeric Pressburger

Written by: Michael Powell and Emeric Pressburger

Cinematography: Jack Cardiff

Music by: Brian Easdale

Distributed by: Arthur Rank/ Eagle-Lion

Release date: September 6, 1948

Running time: 133 minutes

Country: UK

Language: English and French

Cast

Moira Shearer   Victoria Page

Marius Goring   Julian Craster

Anton Walbrook   Boris Lermontov

Léonide Massine	Grischa Ljubov
Robert Helpmann	Ivan Boleslawski
Albert Bassermann	Sergei Ratov
Ludmila Tchérina	Irina Boronskaja
Austin Trevor	Professor Palmer

Portrait of Jennie *(1948)*

Directed by:	William Dieterle
Produced by:	David O. Selznick, David Hempstead
Written by:	Robert Nathan (novel), Paul Osborn, Peter Berneis, Leonardo Bercovici (screenplay)
Cinematography:	Joseph H. August
Music by:	Dimitri Tiomkin, Bernard Herrmann
Distributed by:	Selznick International
Release date:	December 25, 1948
Running time:	86 minutes
Country:	USA
Language:	English

Cast

Joseph Cotten	Eben Adams
Jennifer Jones	Jennie Appleton
Ethel Barrymore	Miss Spinney
Lillian Gish	Mother Mary of Mercy
Cecil Kellaway	Matthews
David Wayne	Gus O'Toole
Albert Sharpe	Moore

Pandora and the Flying Dutchman *(1951)*

Directed by:	Albert Lewin
Produced by:	Joe Kaufmann, Albert Lewin
Written by:	Albert Lewin
Cinematography:	Jack Cardiff

Music by:	Alan Rawsthorne
Production Company:	Romulus Films
Distributed by:	MGM
Release date:	February 1951
Running time:	122 minutes
Country:	UK
Language:	English

Cast

James Mason	Hendrik van der Zee
Ava Gardner	Pandora Reynolds
Nigel Patrick	Stephen Cameron
Sheila Sim	Janet
Harold Warrender	Geoffrey Fielding
Mario Cabré	Juan Montalvo
Marius Goring	Reggie Demarest
John Laurie	Angus
Pamela Mason	Jennie
Patricia Raine	Peggy
Margarita D'Alverez	Senora Montalvo

The House on the Square/I'll Never Forget You *(1951)*

Directed by:	Roy Ward Baker
Produced by:	Sol C. Siegel
Written by:	John L. Balderston (play), Ranald MacDougall
Distributed by:	20th Century Fox
Release date:	December 7, 1951
Running time:	90 minutes
Country:	UK
Language:	English

Cast

Tyrone Power	Peter Standish

Ann Blyth	Helen Pettigrew
Michael Rennie	Roger Forsyth
Dennis Price	Tom Pettigrew
Beatrice Campbell	Kate Pettigrew
Kathleen Byron	Duchess of Devonshire
Raymond Huntley	Mr. Throstle
Irene Browne	Lady Anne Pettigrew

Brigadoon *(1954)*

Directed by:	Vincente Minelli
Produced by:	Arthur Freed
Written by:	Alan Jay Lerner
Music by:	Frederick Lowe
Cinematography:	Joseph Ruttenberg
Distributed by:	MGM
Release date:	September 8, 1954
Running time:	108 minutes
Country:	USA
Language:	English

Cast

Gene Kelly	Tommy Albright
Van Johnson	Jeff Douglas
Cyd Charisse	Fiona Campbell
Elaine Stewart	Jane Ashton
Barry Jones	Mr. Lundie
Hugh Laing	Harry Beaton
Virginia Bosler	Jean Campbell
Jimmy Thompson	Charlie Dalrymple
Dodie Heath	Meg Brockie

Vertigo *(1958)*

| Directed by: | Alfred Hitchcock |

Produced by:	Alfred Hitchcock
Written by:	Pierre Boileau, Thomas Nacejak (novel), Maxwell Anderson, Alec Coppel, Samuel Taylor (screenplay)
Cinematography:	Robert Burke
Music by:	Bernard Herrmann
Distributed by:	Paramount
Release date:	May 9, 1958
Running time:	128 minutes
Country:	USA
Language:	English

Cast

James Stewart	John "Scotty" Ferguson
Kim Novak	Judy Barton ("Madeleine Elster")
Barbara Bel Geddes	Midge Wood
Tom Helmore	Gavin Elster
Konstantin Shayne	Pop Liebel

On a Clear Day You Can See Forever *(1970)*

Directed by:	Vincente Minnelli
Produced by:	Howard F. Koch
Written by:	Alan Jay Lerner
Music by:	Burton Lane
Cinematography:	Harry Stradling, Sr.
Distributed by:	Paramount
Release date:	June 17, 1970
Running time:	149 minutes
Country:	USA
Language:	English

Cast

Barbra Streisand	Daisy Gamble
Yves Montand	Marc Chabot

Larry Blyden	Warren Pratt
Bob Newhart	Dr. Mason Hume
Simon Oakland	Dr. Conrad Fuller
John Richardson	Robert Tentrees
Jack Nicholson	Tad Pringle
Roy Kinnear	Prince Regent

Solaris *(1972)*

Directed by:	Andrei Tarkovsky
Produced by:	Viacheslav Tarasov
Written by:	Stanislaw Lem (novel), Fridrikh Gorenstein
Cinematography:	Yadim Yusov
Music by:	Eduard Artemyev
Release date:	May 13, 1972
Running time:	165 minutes
Country:	USSR
Language:	Russian

Cast

Donatis Banionis	Kris Kelvin
Natalya Bondarchuk	Hari
Jüri Järvet	Dr. Snaut
Anatoly Solonitsyn	Dr. Sartorius
Nikolai Grinko	Kelvin's father
Olga Barnet	Kelvin's mother

Heaven Can Wait *(1978)*

Directed by:	Warren Beatty, Buck Henry
Produced by:	Warren Beatty
Written by:	Harry Segall (play), Elaine May, Robert Towne, Buck Henry (screenplay)
Cinematography:	William A. Fraker
Music by:	Dave Grusin

Distributed by:	Paramount
Release date:	June 28, 1978
Running time:	101 minutes
Country:	USA
Language:	English

Cast

Warren Beatty	Joe Pendleton
Julie Christie	Betty Logan
James Mason	Mr. Jordan
Jack Warden	Max Corkle
Charles Grodin	Tony Abbott
Dyan Cannon	Julia Farnsworth
Buck Henry	The Escort
Vincent Gardenia	Detective Krim
Joseph Maher	Sisk

Xanadu *(1980)*

Directed by:	Robert Greenwald
Produced by:	Lawrence Gordon, Joel Silver
Written by:	Richard Christian Danus, Marc Reid Rubel
Cinematography:	Victor J. Kemper
Music by:	Barry De Vorzon
Distributed by:	Universal
Release date:	August 8, 1980
Running time:	96 minutes
Country:	USA
Language:	English

Cast

Olivia Newton-John	Kira/Terpsichore
Michael Beck	Sonny Malone
Gene Kelly	Danny McGuire

James Sloyan	Simpson
Dimitra Arliss	Helen
Katie Hanley	Sandra
Fred McCarren	Richie
Ren Woods	Jo
Melvin Jones	Big Al
Ira Newborn	Band Leader
Jo Anne Harris	Singer

Somewhere in Time *(1980)*

Directed by:	Jeannot Szwarc
Produced by	Stephen Deutsch, Ray Stark
Written by:	Richard Matheson
Cinematography:	Isadore Mankofsky
Music by:	John Barry
Production Company:	Rastar
Distributed by:	Universal
Release date:	October 3, 1980
Running time:	103 minutes
Country:	USA
Language:	English

Cast

Christopher Reeve	Richard Collier
Jane Seymour	Elise McKenna
Christopher Plummer	William Fawcett Robinson
Teresa Wright	Laura Roberts
Bill Erwin	Arthur
George Voskovec	Prof. Finney

Kiss Me Goodbye *(1982)*

| Directed by: | Robert Mulligan |
| Produced by: | Keith Barrish |

Written by:	Bruno Barreto (novel), Charlie Peters (screenplay)
Cinematography:	Donald Peterman
Music by:	Ralph Burns
Distributed by:	20th Century Fox
Release date:	December 22, 1982
Running time:	101 minutes
Country:	USA
Language	English

Cast

Sally Field	Kay
James Caan	Jolly
Jeff Bridges	Rupert
Claire Trevor	Charlotte
Paul Dooley	Kendall
Stephen Elliott	Edgar
Michael Ensign	Billy
Mildred Netwick	Mrs. Reilly
Dorothy Fielding	Emily
Maryedith Burrell	Mrs. Newman
Alan Haufrect	Mr. Newman

Made in Heaven *(1987)*

Directed by:	Alan Rudolph
Produced by:	David Blocker, Bruce A. Evans, Raynold Gideon
Written by:	Bruce A. Evans, Raynold Gideon
Cinematography:	Jan Kiesser
Music by:	Mark Isham
Distributed by:	Lorimar Productions
Release date:	November 6, 1987
Running time:	102 minutes
Country:	USA

Language:　　　　　English

Cast

Timothy Hutton	Mike Shea/Elmo Barnett
Kelly McGillis	Annie Packert/Ally Chandler
Maureen Stapleton	Aunt Lisa
Ann Wedgeworth	Annette Shea
James Gammon	Steve Shea
Mare Winningham	Brenda Carlucci
Don Murray	Ben Chandler
Timothy Daly	Tom Donnelly
David Rasche	Donald Summer
Amanda Plummer	Wiley Fox
Marj Dusay	Mrs. Packert
Debra Winger	Emmett Humbird

Wings of Desire *(1987)*

Directed by:	Wim Wenders
Produced by:	Wim Wenders, Anatole Dauman
Written by:	Wim Wenders, Peter Handke, Richard Reitinger
Cinematography:	Henri Alekan
Music by:	Jürgen Knieper
Production Company:	Road Movies Filmproduktion, Westdeutscher Rundfunk, Basis-Film Verleihe GmbH, Argos Films
Distributed by:	Orion Classics, Axiom Films
Release dates:	September 23, 1987 (France), October 27, 1987 (West Germany), May 6, 1988 (United States)
Running time:	127 minutes
Country:	West Germany and France
Language:	German, English, French, Turkish, Hebrew, Spanish

Cast

Bruno Ganz	Damiel
Solveig Dommartin	Marion
Otto Sander	Cassiel
Curt Bois	Homer
Peter Falk	Himself
Nick Cave and the Bad Seeds	Themselves
Crime and theCity Solution	Themselves

Rouge *(1988)*

Directed by:	Stanley Kwan
Produced by:	Jackie Chan, Leonard Ho
Written by:	Lilian Lee (novel), Yau Tai Ping On
Cinematography:	Bill Wong
Music by:	Michael Lai, Tang Siu Lam
Production Company:	Golden Harvest/Golden Way Films
Release date:	January 7, 1988
Running time:	96 minutes
Country:	Hong Kong
Language:	Cantonese

Cast

Anita Mui	Fleur
Leslie Cheung	Chan Chen-Pang
Alex Man	Yuen
Irene Wan	Shu-Hsien
Emily Chu	Ah Chor
Kara Hui	Ghost

Beetlejuice *(1988)*

| Directed by: | Tim Burton |

Produced by:	Larry Wilson, Michael Bender, Richard Hashimoto
Written by:	Michael McDowell and Larry Wilson (story), Michael McDowell and Warren Skaaren (screenplay)
Cinematography:	Thomas E. Ackerman
Music by:	Danny Elfman
Production Company:	Geffen Films
Distributed by:	Warner Brothers
Release date:	March 30, 1988
Running time:	92 minutes
Country:	USA
Language:	English

Cast

Michael Keaton	Beetlejuice
Alec Baldwin	Adam Maitland
Geena Davis	Barbara Maitland
Winona Ryder	Lydia Deetz
Catherine O'Hara	Delia Deetz
Jeffrey Jones	Charles Deetz
Glenn Shadix	Otho
Sylvia Sidney	Juno
Robert Goulet	Maxie Dean
Dick Cavett	Bernard
Annie McEnroe	Jane
Tony Cox	Preacher

Always *(1989)*

Directed by:	Steven Spielberg
Produced by:	Kathleen Kennedy, Frank Marshall
Written by:	Jerry Belson, Diane Thomas
Cinematography:	Mikael Salomon
Music by:	John Williams

Production Company:	Amblin Entertainment
Distributed by:	Universal, United Artists
Release date:	December 22, 1989
Running time:	122 minutes
Country:	USA
Language:	English

Cast

Richard Dreyfuss	Pete Sandich
Holly Hunter	Dorinda Durston
John Goodman	Al Yackey
Brad Johnson	Ted Baker
Audrey Hepburn	Hap
Roberts Blossom	Dave
Keith David	Powerhouse
Ed Van Nuys	Nails
Marg Helgenberger	Rachel
Dale Dye	Don
Brian Haley	Alex
James Lashly	Charlie
Michael Steve Jones	Grey

Ghost *(1990)*

Directed by:	Jerry Zucker
Produced by:	Lisa Weinstein
Written by:	Bruce Joel Rubin
Cinematography:	Adam Greenberg
Music by:	Maurice Jarre
Distributed by:	Paramount
Release date:	July 13, 1990
Running time:	126 minutes
Country:	USA
Language:	English

Cast

Patrick Swayze	Sam Wheat
Demi Moore	Molly Jensen
Whoopi Goldberg	Oda Mae Brown
Tony Goldwyn	Carl Bruner
Rick Aviles	Willie Lopez
Vincent Schiavelli	Subway Ghost

Truly, Madly, Deeply (1990)

Directed by:	Anthony Minghella
Produced by:	Robert Cooper
Written by:	Anthony Minghella
Cinematography:	Remi Adefarasin
Music by:	Barrington Pheloung
Production Company:	BBC Films/Lionhart Winston
Distributed by:	Samuel Goldwyn Company
Release date:	November 10, 1990
Running time:	106 minutes
Country:	UK
Language:	English

Cast

Juliet Stevenson	Nina
Alan Rickman	Jamie
Jenny Howe	Burge
Carolyn Choa	Translator
Bill Paterson	Sandy
Christopher Rozycki	Titus
Keith Bartlett	Plumber
David Ryall	George
Stella Maris	Maura
Ian Hawkes	Harry
Deborah Findlay	Claire
Arturo Venegas	Roberto

Richard Syms   Symonds

Michael Maloney   Mark

Defending Your Life *(1991)*

Directed by:	Albert Brooks
Produced by:	Robert Grand, Michael Grillo, Herb Nanas
Written by:	Albert Brooks
Cinematography:	Allen Daviau
Music by:	Erroll Garner, Michael Gore
Production Company:	Geffen Pictures
Distributed by:	Warner Brothers
Release date:	March 22, 1991
Running time:	112 minutes
Country:	USA
Language:	English

Cast

Albert Brooks	Daniel Miller
Michael Durrell	Agency Head
Rip Torn	Bob Diamond
Meryl Streep	Julia
Lee Grant	Lena Foster
George D. Wallace	Daniel's Judge
Rachel Bard	Julia's Judge
S. Scott Bullock	Daniel's Father
Carol Bivens	Daniel's Mother
Buck Henry	Dick Stanley

Dead Again *(1991)*

Directed by:	Kenneth Branagh
Produced by:	Lindsay Doran
Written by:	Scott Frank
Music by:	Patrick Doyle

Distributed by:	Paramount
Release date:	August 23, 1991
Running time:	107 minutes
Country:	USA
Language:	English

Cast

Kenneth Branagh	Mike Church and Roman Strauss
Emma Thompson	Amanda Sharpe/"Grace" and Margaret Strauss
Andy Garcia	Gray Baker
Derek Jacobi	Franklyn Madson
Wayne Knight	Pete Dugan
Robin Williams	Cozy Carlisle
Hanna Schygulla	Inga
Richard Easton	Father Timothy
Gregor Hesse	Frankie

Sleepless in Seattle (1993)

Directed by:	Nora Ephron
Produced by:	Gary Foster
Written by:	Nora Ephron, David S. Ward, Jeff Arch
Cinematography:	Sven Nykvist
Music by:	Marc Shaiman
Distributed by:	Tristar Pictures
Release date:	June 25, 1993
Running time:	106 minutes
Country:	USA
Language:	English

Cast

Tom Hanks	Sam Baldwin
Meg Ryan	Annie Reed

Bill Pullman	Walter
Ross Malinger	Jonah Baldwin
Rosie O'Donnell	Becky
Gaby Hoffmann	Jessica
Victor Garber	Greg
Rita Wilson	Suzy
Barbara Garrick	Victoria
Cary Lowell	Maggie Baldwin
Dana Ivey	Claire
Rob Reiner	Jay

To Gillian on Her 37th Birthday *(1996)*

Directed by:	Michael Pressman
Produced by:	Marykay Powell, David E. Kelley
Written by:	Michael Brady (play), David E. Kelley (screenplay)
Cinematography:	Tim Suhrstedt
Music by:	James Horner
Production Company:	Rastar
Distributed by:	Triumph Films
Release date:	October 18, 1996
Running time:	93 minutes
Country:	USA
Language:	English

Cast

Peter Gallagher	David Lewis
Michelle Pfeiffer	Gillian Lewis
Claire Danes	Rachel Lewis
Laurie Fortier	Cindy Bayles
Wendy Crewson	Kevin Dollof
Bruce Altman	Paul Wheeler
Kathy Baker	Esther Wheeler

Freddie Prinze, Jr.	Joey Bost
Rachel Seidman-Lockamy	Megan Weeks
Seth Green	Danny

City of Angels *(1998)*

Directed by:	Brad Silberling
Produced by:	Charles Roven, Dawn Steel
Written by:	Dana Stevens
Cinematography:	John Seale
Music by:	Gabriel Yared
Production Company:	Regency Enterprises, Atlas Entertainment
Distributed by:	Warner Brothers
Release date:	April 10, 1998
Running time:	114 minutes
Country:	USA
Language:	English

Cast

Nicholas Cage	Seth
Meg Ryan	Dr. Maggie Rice
Andre Braugher	Cassiel
Colm Feore	Jordan Ferris
Dennis Franz	Nathaniel Messinger
Robin Bartlett	Anne
Joanna Merlin	Teresa Messinger
Sarah Dampf	Susan

Sliding Doors *(1998)*

Directed by:	Peter Howitt
Produced by:	Sydney Pollack, Philippa Braithwaite
Written by:	Peter Howitt
Cinematography:	Remi Adefarasin

Music by: David Hirschfelder

Production Company: Intermedia, Mirage Enterprises

Distributed by: Miramax Films, Paramount

Release date: April 24, 1998

Running time: 99 minutes

Country: UK

Language: English

Cast

Gwynneth Paltrow   Helen Quilley

John Hannah   James Hammerton

John Lynch   Gerry

Jeanne Tripplehorn   Lydia

Zara Turner   Anna

Douglas McFerran   Russell

What Dreams May Come *(1998)*

Directed by: Vincent Ward

Produced by: Stephen Simon, Barnet Bain

Written by: Richard Matheson (novel), Ronald Bass (screenplay)

Cinematography: Eduardo Serra

Music by: Michael Kamen

Production Company: Interscope Communications

Distributed by: Polygram Filmed Entertainment, Universal

Release date: October 2, 1998

Running time: 113 minutes

Country: USA

Language: English

Cast

Robin Williams   Christopher Nielsen

Annabella Sciorra   Annie Nielsen

Cuba Gooding, Jr.	Albert Lewis/Ian
Max Von Sydow	The Tracker/Albert Lewis
Jessica Brooks Grant	Marie Nielsen
Josh Paddock	Ian Nielsen
Rosalind Chao	Leona

Meet Joe Black *(1998)*

Directed by:	Martin Brest
Produced by:	Martin Brest
Written by:	Bo Goldman, Kevin Wade, Ron Osborn, Jeff Reno
Cinematography:	Emmanuel Lubezki
Music by:	Thomas Newman
Production Company:	City Light Films
Distributed by:	Universal
Release date:	November 13, 1998
Running time:	181 minutes
Country:	USA
Language:	English

Cast

Brad Pitt	Joe Black (Death)/Young Man in Coffee Shop
Anthony Hopkins	Bill Parrish
Claire Forlani	Susan Parrish
Jake Weber	Drew
Marcia Gay Harden	Allison Parrish
Jeffrey Tambor	Quince

Down to Earth *(2001)*

Directed by:	Chris Weitz, Paul Weitz
Produced by:	Sean Daniel, James Jacks, Michael Rotenberg
Written by:	Chris Rock, Lance Crowther
Cinematography:	Richard Crudo

Music by:	Jamshied Sharifi
Production Company:	Village Roadshow Pictures
Distributed by:	Paramount
Release date:	February 12, 2001
Running time:	87 minutes
Country:	USA
Language:	English

Cast

Chris Rock	Lance Barton
Regina King	Sontee Jenkins
Mark Addy	Cisco
Eugene Levy	Keyes
Frankie Faison	Whitney Daniels
Greg Germann	Sklar
Jennifer Coolidge	Mrs. Wellington
Chazz Palminteri	King
Wanda Sykes	Wanda
John Cho	Phil Quon

Dragonfly *(2002)*

Directed by:	Tom Shadyac
Produced by:	Gary Barber, Roger Birnbaum, Mark Johnson
Written by:	Brandon Camp, Mike Thompson (story), Brandon Camp, Mike Thompson, David Seltzer (screenplay)
Cinematography:	Dean Semler
Music by:	John Debney
Production Company:	Spyglass Entertainment, Shady Acres Entertainment, Gran Via, Kalima Productions, NDE Productions

Distributed by:	Universal Pictures and Buena Vista International
Release date:	February 22, 2002
Running time:	104 minutes
Country:	USA
Language:	English

Cast

Kevin Costner	Dr. Joe Darrow
Susannah Thompson	Dr. Emily Darrow
Joe Morton	Hugh Campbell
Ron Rifkin	Charlie Dickinson
Kathy Bates	Miriam Belmont
Linda Hunt	Sister Madeline
Jacob Vargas	Victor
Robert Bailey, Jr.	Jeffrey Reardon

Solaris *(2002)*

Directed by:	Steven Soderbergh
Produced by:	James Cameron, Jon Landau, Rae Sanchini
Written by:	Stanislaw Lem (novel), Steven Soderbergh (screenplay)
Cinematography:	Peter Andrews
Music by:	Cliff Martinez
Production Company:	Lightstorm Entertainment
Distributed by:	20th Century Fox
Release date:	November 29, 2002
Running time:	99 minutes
Country:	USA
Language:	English

Cast

George Clooney	Chris Kelvin
Natascha McElhone	Rheya
Viola Davis	Dr. Gordon
Jeremy Davies	Snow
Ulrich Tukur	Gubarian

The Haunted Mansion *(2003)*

Directed by:	Rob Minkoff
Produced by:	Andrew Gunn, Don Hahn
Written by:	David Berenbaum
Cinematography:	Remi Adefarasin
Music by:	Mark Mancina
Production Company:	Walt Disney Pictures
Distributed by:	Buena Vista Pictures
Release date:	November 26, 2003
Running time:	88 minutes
Country:	USA
Language:	English

Cast

Eddie Murphy	Jim Evers
Marsha Thomason	Sara Evers
Terence Stamp	Ramsley
Nathaniel Parker	Master Edward Gracey
Jennifer Tilly	Madame Leota
Dina Waters	Emma
Marc John Jefferies	Michael Evers
Aree Davis	Megan Evers

De-Lovely *(2004)*

Directed by:	Irwin Winkler
Produced by:	Simon Channing Williams

Written by:	Jay Cocks
Cinematography:	Tony Pierce-Roberts
Music by:	Cole Porter
Production Company:	Winkler Films
Distributed by:	MGM
Release date:	July 2, 2004
Running time:	125 minutes
Country:	USA
Language:	English

Cast

Kevin Kline	Cole Porter
Ashley Judd	Linda Lee Thomas Porter
Jonathan Price	Gabriel
Kevin McNally	Gerald Murphy
Sandra Nelson	Sara Murphy
Allan Corduner	Monty Woolley
Peter Polycarpou	Louis B. Mayer
Keith Allen	Irving Berlin
James Wilby	Edward Thomas
Kevin McKidd	Bobby Reed
Richard Dillane	Bill Wrather
John Barrowman	Jack
Peter Jessop	Diaghilev
Edward Baker-Duly	Boris Kochno
Jeff Harding	Cody
Caroline O'Connor	Ethel Merman

Birth *(2004)*

Directed by:	Jonathan Glazer
Produced by:	Lizie Gower, Nick Morris, Jean-Louis Piel
Written by:	Jean-Claude Carrière, Milo Addica, Jonathan Glazer

Cinematography:	Harris Savides
Music by:	Alexandre Desplat
Distributed by:	New Line Cinema
Release date:	November 8, 2004
Running time:	96 minutes
Country:	USA
Language:	English

Cast

Nicole Kidman	Anna
Cameron Bright	Young Sean
Danny Huston	Joseph
Lauren Bacall	Eleanor
Arliss Howard	Bob
Michael Desautels	Sean
Anne Heche	Clara
Peter Stormare	Clifford
Ted Levine	Mr. Conte
Cara Seymour	Mrs. Conte

Corpse Bride *(2005)*

Directed by:	Tim Burton, Mike Johnson
Produced by:	Tim Burton, Allison Abbate
Written by:	John August, Caroline Thompson, Pamela Pettler
Cinematography:	Pete Kozachik
Music by:	Danny Elfman
Production Company:	Laika Entertainment, Tim Burton Productions
Distributed by:	Warner Brothers
Release date:	September 7, 2005
Running time:	77 minutes
Country:	UK, USA
Language:	English

Cast

Johnny Depp	Victor Van Dort
Helena Bonham Carter	Emily
Emily Watson	Victoria Everglot
Tracey Ullman	Nell Van Dort
Paul Whitehouse	William Van Dort
Joanna Lumley	Lady Maudeline Everglot
Albert Finney	Lord Finnis Everglot
Richard E. Grant	Lord Barkis Bittern
Christopher Lee	Pastor Gallswells
Michael Gough	Elder Gutknecht
Jane Horrocks	The Black Widow
Enn Reitel	Maggot
Deep Roy	General Bonesapart
Danny Elfman	Bonejangles

Just Like Heaven *(2005)*

Directed by:	Mark Waters
Produced by:	Walter F. Parkes, Laurie MacDonald
Written by:	Marc Levy (novel), Peter Tolan, Leslie Dixon (screenplay)
Music by:	Rolfe Kent
Distributed by:	Dreamworks Pictures
Release date:	September 16, 2005
Running time:	95 minutes
Country:	USA
Language:	English

Cast

Reese Witherspoon	Dr. Elizabeth Masterson
Mark Ruffalo	David Abbott
Jon Heder	Darryl
Donal Logue	Jack

Dina Waters	Abby Brody
Ivana Milicêvić	Katrina
Rosalind Chao	Dr. Fran Lo
Ben Shenkman	Dr. Brett Rushton

Wristcutters *(2006)*

Directed by:	Goran Dukić
Produced by:	Chris Coen, Tatiana Kelly, Mikal P. Lazarev, Adam Sherman
Written by:	Etgar Keret, Goran Dukić
Cinematography:	Vanja Cernjul
Music by:	Bobby Johnson, Gogol Bordello
Production Company:	No Matter Pictures, Crispy Films, Halcyon Pictures
Distributed by:	Autonomous Films
Release date:	January 24, 2006
Running time:	88 minutes
Country:	USA
Language:	English

Cast

Patrick Fugit	Zia
Shannyn Sossamon	Mikal
Shea Whigham	Eugene
Leslie Bibb	Desiree Randolph
Tom Waits	Kneller
Mark Boone, Jr.	Mike
Clayne Crawford	Jim
Will Arnett	Messiah King
Mary Pat Gleason	Eugene's mother
Anatol Rezmeritza	Eugene's father
Cameron Bowen	Kostya
Abraham Benrubi	Erik
John Hawkes	Yan

Anthony Azizi	Hassan
Sarah Roemer	Rachel
Azura Skye	Tania
Mikal P. Lazarev	Nanuk
Amy Seimetz	Nina

Hereafter (2010)

Directed by:	Clint Eastwood
Produced by:	Clint Eastwood, Kathleen Kennedy, Robert Lorenz, Steven Spielberg
Written by:	Peter Morgan
Cinematography:	Tom Stern
Music by:	Clint Eastwood
Production Company:	Kennedy/Marshall, Malpaso Productions, Amblin Entertainment
Distributed by:	Warner Brothers
Release date:	September 12, 2010
Running time:	129 minutes
Country:	USA
Language:	English

Cast

Matt Damon	George Lonegan
Cécile de France	Marie Lelay
Frankie and George McLaren	Marcus and Jason
Lyndsey Marshall	Jackie
Thierry Neuvic	Didier
Jay Mohr	Billy Lonegan
Bryce Dallas Howard	Melanie

Select Bibliography

Auiler, Dan. *Vertigo: The Making of a Hitchcock Classic* (New York: St. Martin's Press, 1998).

Christie, Ian. *Arrows of Desire: The Films of Michael Powell and Emeric Pressburger* (London: Faber & Faber, 1994).

Christie, Ian and Moor, Andrew, eds. *The Cinema of Michael Powell: International Perspectives on an English Film-Maker* (London: British Film Institute, 2005).

Crowl, Samuel. *The Films of Kenneth Branagh* (Westport, CT: Praeger, 2006).

Deacy, Christopher. *Screening the Afterlife: Theology, Eschatology and Film* (London and New York: Routledge, 2012).

Deacy, Christopher and Ortiz, Gaye, *Theology and Film: Challenging the Sacred/Secular Divide* (Malden, MA: Blackwell, 2008).

Dunne, Nathan. *Tarkovsky* (London: Black Dog, 2008).

Fagg, Lawrence. *The Becoming of Time: Integrating Physical and Religious Time* (Atlanta: Scholars Press, 1995).

Genelli, Lyn and Tom Davis. *Death at the Movies: Hollywood's Guide to the Hereafter* (Wheaton, IL: Quest Books, 2013).

Gott, J. Richard. *Time Travel in Einstein's Universe* (Boston: Houghton Mifflin, 2001).

Grafe, Frieda. *The Ghost and Mrs. Muir* (London: British Film Institute, 1995).

Grant, Barry Keith, ed. *Film Genre Reader* (Austin: University of Texas Press, 1986).

Greene, Brian. *The Elegant Universe: Superstrings, Hidden Dimensions, and the Quest for the Ultimate Theory* (New York: Random House, 1999).

Hoare, Philip. *Noël Coward: A Biography* (New York: Simon & Schuster, 1995).

Johnson, Vida T. and Petrie, Graham. *The Films of Andrei Tarkovsky: A Visual Fugue* (Bloomington, IN: Indiana University Press, 1994).

Kovacs, Lee. *The Haunted Screen: Ghosts in Literature and Film* (Jefferson, NC: McFarland, 1999).

Maltby, Richard. *Hollywood Cinema* (Malden, MA: Blackwell Publishing, 1995).

Marsh, Clive. *Theology Goes to the Movies: An Introduction to Critical Christian Thinking* (London and New York: Routledge, 2007).

Neale, Steven. *Genre* (London: British Film Institute, 1980).

————. *Genre and Hollywood* (London: Routledge, 2000).

Nelson, Victoria. *Gothicka: Vampire Heroes, Human Gods, and the New Supernatural* (Cambridge, MA: Harvard University Press, 2012).

Parry, Sally E. *We'll Always Have The Movies: American Cinema During World War II* (Lexington: University Press of Kentucky, 2006).

Ruffles, Tom. *Ghost Images: Cinema of the Afterlife* (Jefferson, NC: McFarland, 2004).

Salwolke, Scott. *The Films of Michael Powell and the Archers* (Lanham, MD: Scarecrow Press, 1997).

Schatz, Thomas. *Hollywood Genres: Formulas, Filmmaking, and the Studio System* (New York: Random House, 1981).

Shepard, Bill. *The Somewhere In Time Story: Behind the Scenes in the Making of a Cult Romantic Fantasy Motion Picture* (LaGrange, IL: Somewhere In Time Gallery, 2004).

Simon, Stephen. *The Force Is With You: Mystical Movie Messages That Inspire Our Lives* (Newburyport, MA: Hampton Roads, 2002).

Vieira, Mark A. *Hollywood Horror: From Gothic to Cosmic* (New York: Harry N. Abrams, 2003).

Wilder, Robin G. and Bryer, Jackson R., eds. *The Selected Letters of Thornton Wilder* (New York: HarperCollins, 2008).

Worley, Alec. *Empires of the Imagination: A Critical Survey of Fantasy Cinema from Georges Méliès to* The Lord of the Rings (Jefferson, NC: McFarland, 2005).

Index

About the Author

Richard Striner is professor of history at Washington College in Chestertown, Maryland. An intellectual historian, he is the author of over ten books, including studies on presidential leadership, economics, architecture, film, historic preservation, and literature. He has contributed to the online *New York Times* "Disunion" series about the Civil War, and he has written for the *Washington Post*, History News Network, and *The American Scholar*. His most recent book is *How America Can Spend Its Way Back to Greatness*.